D1599563

Rigging
Sail

Other TAB books by the author:

No. 894   *Do-It-Yourselfer's Guide to Furniture Repair & Refinishing*
No. 937   *Modern Sailmaking*
No. 1044   *The Woodturner's Bible*
No. 1179   *The Practical Handbook of Blacksmithing & Metalworking*
No. 1188   *66 Children's Furniture Projects*
No. 1237   *Practical Knots & Ropework*
No. 1247   *The Master Handbook of Fine Woodworking Techniques and Projects*
No. 1257   *The Master Handbook of Sheetmetalwork . . . with projects*
No. 1312   *The GIANT Book of Wooden Toys*
No. 1365   *The Complete Handbook of Drafting*
No. 1424   *Constructing Tables and Chairs . . . with 55 Projects*
No. 1454   *Constructing Outdoor Furniture, with 99 Projects*
No. 1504   *53 Space-Saving, Built-In Furniture Projects*
No. 1574   *The Illustrated Handbook of Woodworking Joints*

Rigging Sail

By Percy W. Blandford

TAB BOOKS Inc.
BLUE RIDGE SUMMIT, PA. 17214

FIRST EDITION

FIRST PRINTING

Copyright © 1983 by TAB BOOKS Inc.
Printed in the United States of America

Library of Congress Cataloging in Publication Data

Blandford, Percy W.
Rigging sail.

Includes index.
1. Masts and rigging. I. Title.
GV811.45.B57 1983   797.1'24   83-4884
ISBN 0-8306-1634-9 (pbk.)

Contents

Introduction

THAT REMARK BY WATER RAT IN *THE WIND IN the Willows* about the joy of messing about in boats can be taken a step further. Your enjoyment is increased if you have done much of the work on the boat yourself. Many people make their own sails (*Modern Sailmaking*, TAB book No. 937); there is not so much mystery about the activity as you might think. With sails, you are faced with a multiplicity of fiber and wire ropes that make up the rigging of even the simplest sailing boat. All of this you can make yourself.

Dealing with ropes and the associated equipment can be fascinating. If you keep your rigging in order and deal with repairs; if you learn to handle the rigging and set it up efficiently; if you can moor and anchor like an expert and coil ropes smartly; if you can call the parts by their proper names and respond correctly when an expert uses technical rigging terms; if you can rig your boat so it sails efficiently; and if you can look aloft to see that everything is shipshape and Bristol fashion—you will experience one of the rare pleasures of modern

days, and you can call yourself a rigger. That is what this book is about.

Sailing craft have always had rigging. As sailing craft sizes increased, rigging complexity increased, but the basics of rigging reached a stage where there was little real advance for many centuries. Not much more than 100 years ago came efficient fore and aft rigs, as man better understood how to use the wind to sail in directions other than downwind. This has been followed in more recent years with the coming of synthetic fiber ropes, metal masts, and stainless steel fittings and ropes. These along with synthetic fiber sails have revolutionized sailing craft.

There might still be uses for some of the older materials, but techniques have changed with the new materials. The present-day sailing boat is efficient as well as beautiful.

This is obvious in the great popularity of sailing. Sailing is within the reach of far more people than it used to be. The days of only wealthy owners and paid crews are gone. Instead, most of us not only enjoy getting afloat, but we also increase our enjoyment by doing all we can for the boat. If it is possible to do work yourself, there is much more satisfaction as well as economy.

There is really nothing about the rigging of a boat that a reasonably practical man cannot do himself. He no longer needs to master some of the skills that were part of the trade secrets of the old-time rigger. He could choose to learn some of them, but modern equipment can take the place of such things as a wire splice. By all means learn to wire splice—this book explains how—but you can rig your boat equally efficiently with other wire rope terminals that are easy to fit.

Some readers might want to restore or rebuild a traditional sailing boat in the original manner. Such work can be very satisfying, but using modern methods and the latest equipment can be equally satisfying when you see your boat go a little faster or point a little higher towards the wind—because of your skill in rigging.

Rigging has been described as "marlinespike seamanship," but that only refers to dealing with ropes. There is quite a lot of ropework in rigging, but there is a lot of other equipment as well, as you will discover when reading this book.

I was fortunate to have been born in Bristol, England; where the term "shipshape and Bristol fashion" came from. I learned my boating and rigging skills there. This has left me with the desire to see that every rope is whipped, every bit of rigging is correctly tensioned, and the whole craft is seamanlike. The title of *rigger* is a proud one. I hope you will not only sail better, but will treasure the name rigger for yourself.

Good rigging and therefore good sailing!

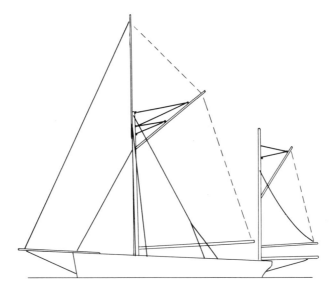

Chapter 1

Rigging Fundamentals

W HEN THAT PRIMITIVE ANCESTOR OF OURS discovered that the wind would help him along on his log raft if he held up a skin, he had started man on the use of wind as a motive power afloat. Until the recent development of steam and other sources of power, sailing rigs have been the only means of taking craft across the oceans. The only alternative for shorter hauls was the strenuous use of manpowered oars. Of course, sailing still continues to be a great source of pleasure and recreation. With the advent of oil shortages, the return of commercial sailing is more than an idle dream.

That primitive man with a skin must have soon discovered that he could get it into a more effective position if he suspended it from a horizontal pole lashed across a vertical one. This makes what we now call a *square sail*. That sail would take him downwind or a few degrees either side of it. If he wanted to go in another direction, he lowered it all and settled down to paddling. The idea of only sailing downwind persisted until recent times.

Ocean voyages were planned to make use of the *trade winds*, those winds that could usually be depended on to blow in a particular direction. A sailing ship might be held up by contrary winds for long periods, often almost within sight of their destination. More scientific sails that would move a hull in almost any direction in relation to the wind are very recent inventions when considered in relation to the whole history of sailing.

With his improvised square sail on a raft, that early sailor had to discover how to hold the mast up and how to control the sail. If he held up the pole mast himself, he might have gripped the bottom with his feet and used his hands to grasp higher up. He would have soon discovered an easier way to resist the pull by reaching high. If he fitted the base into the hole, the resistance to pulling over would have depended on the depth of the hole (Fig. 1-1A), plus any inherent stiffness in the pole.

The next step would have been a rope aft, possibly from partway up (Fig. 1-1B). A rope from the top of the mast would be even better able to do

1

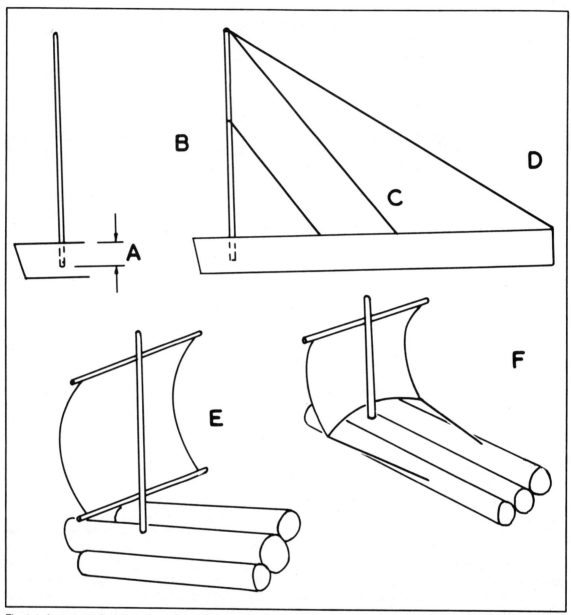

Fig. 1-1. A mast may be held up by its base (A) or by stays that benefit by being at wide angles (B through D). Early raft sailors learned the use of a boom (E) and sheets (F).

the job without any increase in the load on the rope itself (Fig. 1-1C). In any supporting situation, the widest spacing and the most direct pull will give the best results. Taking the supporting rope as far aft as possible makes better use of its strength and pro-

vides better support than attaching it nearer to the mast (Fig. 1-1D).

Besides holding the mast so it resisted being pulled over, the man on the raft had to control his sail. He might have put another pole across the bottom (Fig. 1-1E), but he would probably have found it was possible to make better use of the wind, particularly when it was not directly aft, if he held the bottom corners of the skin and manipulated them so the sail was formed and angled to the positions that would make the raft go faster. Holding the corners with his hands was obviously rather awkward, so he soon added ropes, which we now call *sheets*, and was able to sit in comfort to control the sail (Fig. 1-1F).

With the coming of weaving and the making of cloth, better sails could be made. At the same time boat hulls were developing. Where at first man might have sat astride a log, later men hollowed the logs to sit inside. Others developed the construction of boats and ships built of a large number of boards and other wooden parts.

FORE AND AFT SAILS

A square sail was and still is a good driver for downwind use. Ocean voyagers may still include a square sail and its rigging for use in suitable circumstances. For most sailing they and other users of sails have what are collectively called *fore and aft* sails. The users of primitive square sails must have discovered that by pulling the sail around it was possible to move at increasing angles to the direction of the wind.

When a sail is pulled around so the wind is no longer coming straight over the stern, the stress on the mast tries to bend it sideways as well as forward. With a simple pole mast in a secure support at the bottom, the loads might be resisted, but otherwise there has to be another supporting rope, which we now call a *shroud* (Fig. 1-2A). The obvious snag is the fact that the rope would foul the sail if it had to be brought to the other side of the mast, so a pair of shrouds had to be provided, but only one set could be used at a time. If the crew were not quick enough in releasing one rope and setting up the other, the whole rig might be blown overboard.

LUGSAILS

Somewhere along the way man discovered that, on a deep hull or one fitted with a keel to resist blowing sideways through the water, it was possible to pull the square sail around so that it was quite close to the way the hull was pointing. The effect was to sail across or even slightly towards the wind (Fig. 1-2B). Very soon it was discovered that tilting the upper pole (the *yard*) made the boat sail better to windward (Fig. 1-2C). There was no need to control the forward lower corner of the sail and that was held down inside the bow of the boat. This sail, known as a *dipping lug* persisted almost to the present day, particularly as a small boat rig, in the navies of the world.

In the days of massive, square-rigged fighting ships, a dipping lug was the rig of the smaller craft that served them while in harbor. Despite this knowledge of sail setting to get at least slightly to windward, larger craft still only had sails to drive downwind. The name dipping lug indicates the method of changing tack, or moving the sail from one side of the mast to the other. The yard was partially lowered and dipped around the mast to the other side before hoisting again.

There had to be another piece of rigging to raise and lower the yard—a rope over a wheel near the top of the mast to suspend the yard, possibly with a hook into an eye (Fig. 1-2D). The rope became known as the "haul yard" and the name continues today with the spelling *halyard* or *halliard*.

The foot of the sail in the dipping lug was free, but if most sailing is to windward, the cloth can be stretched to a more effective shape by having a spar across the bottom as well as one across the top. With the *boom* added to a dipping lugsail, it was better to haul its forward end back to the mast with a short *tack line*, to produce what is usually called a *balance lugsail* (Fig. 1-3A). The word "lug" implies a four-sided sail. "Balance," in this case, means part of the sail is forward of the mast.

STAYS

At this stage the idea of arranging the sail square across the boat for making use of the wind aft was abandoned. For running before the wind, the sail was allowed to swing out to either side almost square with the boat. Having the sail arranged in this way meant that there could not be a *backstay*, or

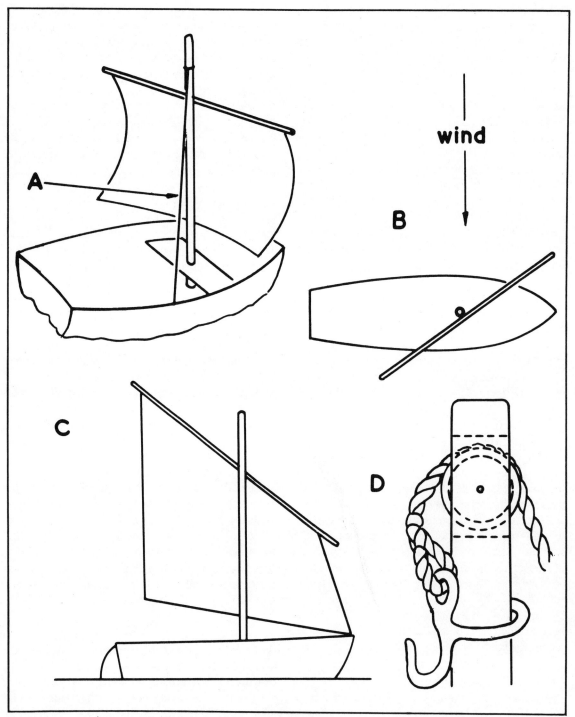

Fig. 1-2. A stay resisted wind pressure (A) as early sailors discovered how to use a square sail across the wind (B). This developed into the dipping lug (C), hoisted by a mast traveler (D).

supporting rope leading aft, because that would interfere with the sail swinging across.

For smaller craft it was possible to support a stiff mast through decking or a *thwart* at gunwale level. This provided a good spread of supports (Fig. 1-3B) to resist bending stresses in all directions. Providing the mast was strong enough not to break, there was no need to provide any rope supports. However, in most craft with masts of reasonable dimensions there have to be supporting ropes, collectively called *stays*. A simple arrangement for a small open boat has a *forestay* to the stem head and a pair of *shrouds* leading to the gunwales aft of a line square across the boat through the mast. By keeping these shrouds aft, they serve some of the functions of the missing backstay in resisting the forward pull of the mast (Fig. 1-3C). They may be supplemented by *running backstays* that are like shrouds taken further aft along the gunwales. Only the one on the windward side is set up. This means quick work when "going about" as the sail changes sides, so the new backstay is taking the load when the sail fills on the other *tack*, or direction.

Balanced lugsails can still be found on general-purpose small boats. The rig is simple and does not require many fittings. Experimenters discovered that windward capability was improved by sloping the yard higher, to make the sail *high peaked*. It was better to have the boom entirely aft of the mast, where it was pivoted on a universal joint called a *gooseneck*. The balanced lug had then become a *standing lug* (Fig. 1-3D).

FORESAILS

Experimenters also found an advantage in having a triangular sail forward of the mast. To rig it, there had to be another halyard and two sheets, so it could be controlled from either side of the mast, depending on which side of the boat was to windward. Rather than hold the sheets directly by hand, they were given a better pull for setting the sail by leading them through eyes on the gunwales (Fig. 1-3E). Only the sheet on the leeward side was used, while the other was left loose. This is the general arrangement still in use.

If two sails are used, there is no reason for having part of the mainsail forward of the mast, so the next step was to bring it entirely aft. That meant more arrangements of ropes to support the top spar, which is more correctly called a *gaff*. (It is only a yard if it crosses the mast.) Such a sail is more often called *graf-headed* today than a lugsail. With a mainsail and a foresail the whole rig is a *gaff-headed sloop* (Fig. 1-3F).

With the knowledge that a high-peaked sail is better to windward, there came the urge to get the gaff even higher until it continued the line of the mast. Such an arrangement produces a *gunter* sail (Fig. 1-4A). There are mechanical problems in arranging the gaff to overlap the mast and the gaff often falls away in varying degrees from the ideal straight up-and-down arrangement. There is also a problem of weight carried high, which makes a gunter sail unsuitable for larger craft. For small craft the attraction is in having all spars shorter than the boat for storage or transport.

The next step was to combine the gaff and the mast into one upright pole. Although the idea was a good one, it was some time before man was able to devise a mast that was slender and strong, and the rigging that would hold it up. As we know, the problems have been overcome and we have the almost universally used *Bermudan* sail (Fig. 1-4B). With one foresail the complete rig is described as a *Bermudan sloop*. The name comes from what is believed to be the first use of such triangular sails in Bermuda, although they were not of the height we accept as normal today.

Less commonly we may call this mainsail a *jib-headed sail* or a *Marconi sail*. It has been called a *leg of mutton sail*. Aerodynamic research into the shapes of airplane wings has shown also that tall narrow sails are more effective than low, wide ones. These are described as "high aspect ratio sails," but that is not the name of the sail.

If there is more than one sail forward of a single mast, the rig is a *cutter* instead of a sloop. It could be a *gaff-headed cutter* or a *Bermudan cutter*. Some authorities spell the word "Bermudian," but putting the "i" in the word does not flow as easily and "Bermudan" is used in this book.

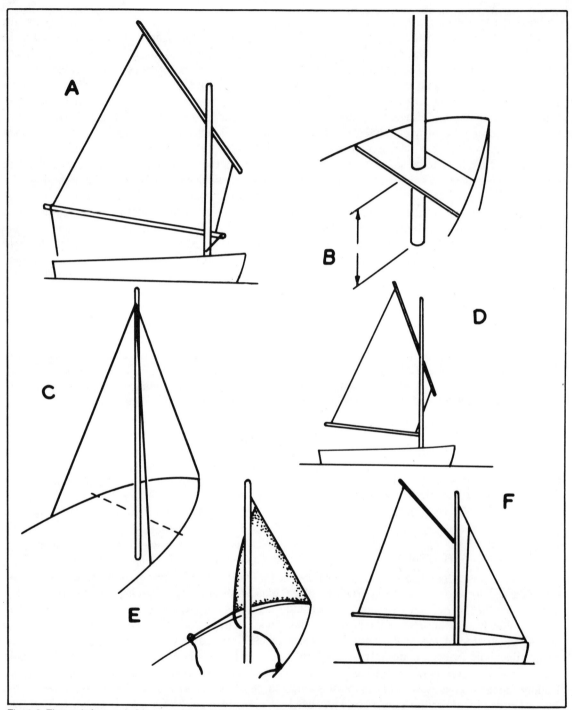

Fig. 1-3. The early fore and aft balanced lugsail (A) had a mast without stays (B), then these were added (C) and the boom was brought back to make a standing lugsail (D), to which was added a jib (E), and the mainsail brought completely aft of the mast (F).

6

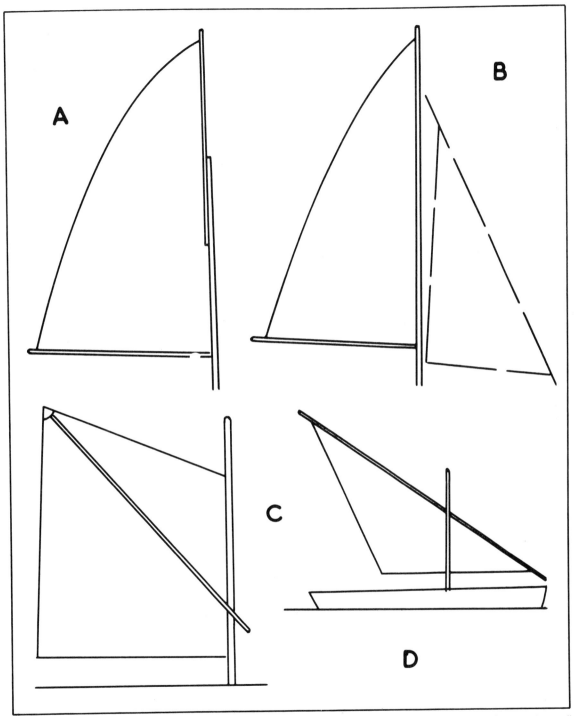

Fig. 1-4. A gunter sail has the gaff upright (A), a jib-headed Bermudan sail has a one-piece mast, a sprit supports a sail diagonally (C), and a lateen sail has a very long yard (D).

OTHER RIGS

Other sail forms have developed and some are still in use. A *spritsail* has four sides and a spar called a *sprit* diagonally across it to support the far corner (Fig. 1-4C). This is found in the popular "Optimist" junior dinghy, but it was also used in the massive mainsail of the British Thames barge, many of which are still sailing. In the days of its commercial use, it was claimed to be the largest sailing rig that could be handled by a crew consisting of a man and a boy. The sail and sprit were hauled into the mast by *brails* and never lowered.

Another single sail is the *lateen* (Fig. 1-4D). This has a short mast and a very long yard. It is particularly good in a *beam wind*, but not so satisfactory on other angles of sailing. With a beam wind it also has a more lifting effect than other rigs, so it has less tendency to push the bow down. It is popular where beam winds are normal, as in sailing up and down the Nile. It is also found in use between some Pacific islands.

In one arrangement of the lateen rig the boat is double-ended, with the mast in the middle. To change direction the high part of the yard is hauled down to the deck and the rudder taken to the other end of the boat, so the hull now goes through the water the other way.

The Chinese had a different approach to sail design and we tend to call all their sails *junk rig* (Fig. 1-5A). There are four sides to the sail and a number of light spars across. The mast is unstayed and all or part of the sail can be set anywhere around the mast.

Modern scientific investigation has shown that the most effective way of using a given sail area is to put it all in one sail, but there are practical difficulties in rigging and handling, more so in the past. Sails are better in sizes that can be handled by the available crew, and larger craft have been given more than one mast so a variety of sails could be set.

TWO-MAST RIGS

If there are two masts and the forward one is higher than the other, which is stepped forward of the rudder head, the rig is a *ketch* (Fig. 1-5B). The sails may be gaff-headed or Bermudan and there could be one or several sails forward of the forward mast. It is still a ketch.

If there are two masts and the smaller, rear mast is aft of the rudder head, the rig is a *yawl*. It is the position of the rear mast that settles the name (Fig. 1-5C). Usually the aft (*mizzen*) sail is much smaller than in a ketch. In the Thames barge the tiny mizzen sail is sheeted to the rudder as an aid in steering.

If the aft mast is higher and its sail larger than the other one, the rig is a *schooner*. As with the other two-masted rigs, the name applies whatever the type of sails. The schooner rig is a good performer in beam winds, as are often found along the American coast. Although ketch and yawl really only apply to two-masted rigs, a schooner may have more masts and some schooners have had six or more. The only advantage to all these masts is in bringing the sail sizes down to those that can be managed by a small crew. The arrangement is not only of historical interest, for multi-masted sail plans have been used in single-handed trans-Atlantic races.

ADDITIONAL SAILS

At the turn of this century, when yachting was in the hands of wealthy owners with paid crews, "improvements" in sailing were to have plenty of sail in many pieces and complicated rigging. The value of simple sail plans and tall rigs was yet to be realized, but there was a belief that something was to be gained by getting sail higher, so sails were set above gaff-headed mainsails (Fig. 1-6A) and the crew were constantly changing the sails forward of the mast. Sail plans were spread, with a *bowsprit* going a long way forward and possibly a *bumpkin* doing the same thing aft (Fig. 1-6B).

Occasionally, modern craft were rigged in this way. Such an arrangement is nostalgic and may arouse interest, but better and much more efficient sailing rigs are available.

Some modern craft have more than one sail forward of the mast. Some are designed with one large foresail of greater area than the mainsail (Fig. 1-7A). Even when its not larger, it may go to the

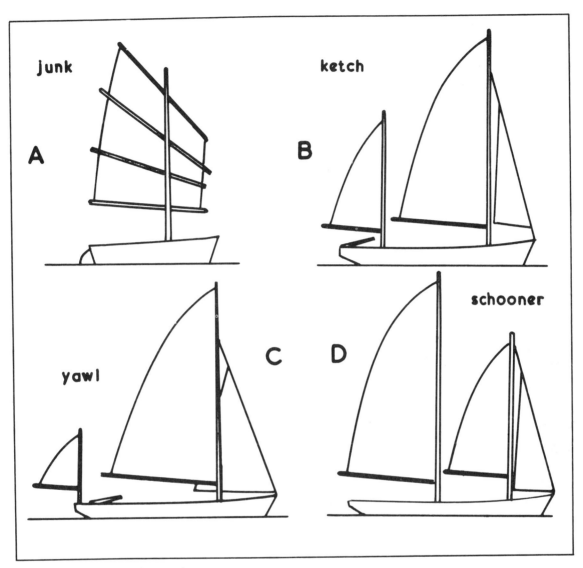

junk

ketch

A

B

yawl

C   D

schooner

Fig. 1-5. Some other rigs that may be seen.

mast top and the rig is a *masthead sloop* (Fig. 1-7B). There have been many arguments about what to call a sail forward of the mast. A single one is usually called a *jib*, which is a convenient, simple word. Purists argue that it should be a *staysail*, but jib has come to stay, although an alternative is foresail.

If there are three sails forward of the mast in a cutter or yawl, the one attached to the stem head is a staysail, the one to the end of the bowsprit is the jib, and one above it is a *jib topsail* (Fig. 1-7C).

NAUTICAL TERMS

The language of the sea developed into a large range of terms that reached its peak in the days of commercial sail and fighting ships—just before the coming of steam. With complex rigs, it was essential that every item of equipment had a distinct name, and that these names were understood by members of the crew so there was no mistake in an emergency. Modern sailing craft are much simpler and most of those earlier words are no longer

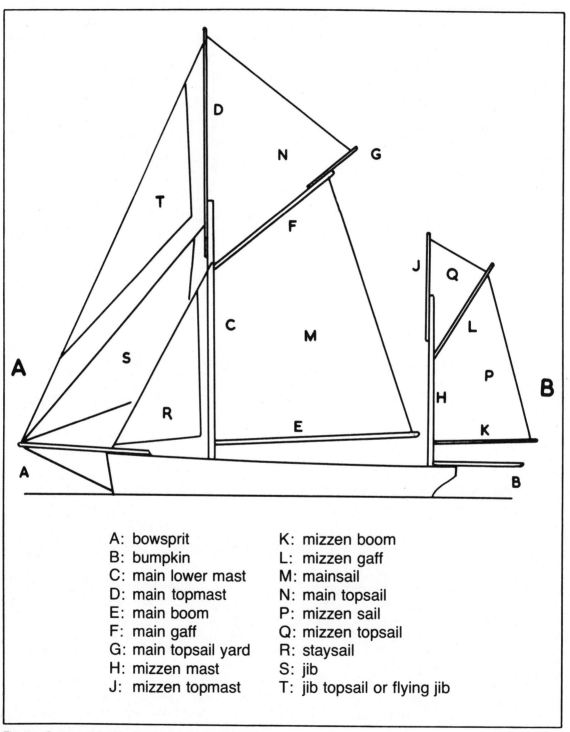

Fig. 1-6. Spars and sprits.

A: bowsprit
B: bumpkin
C: main lower mast
D: main topmast
E: main boom
F: main gaff
G: main topsail yard
H: mizzen mast
J: mizzen topmast
K: mizzen boom
L: mizzen gaff
M: mainsail
N: main topsail
P: mizzen sail
Q: mizzen topsail
R: staysail
S: jib
T: jib topsail or flying jib

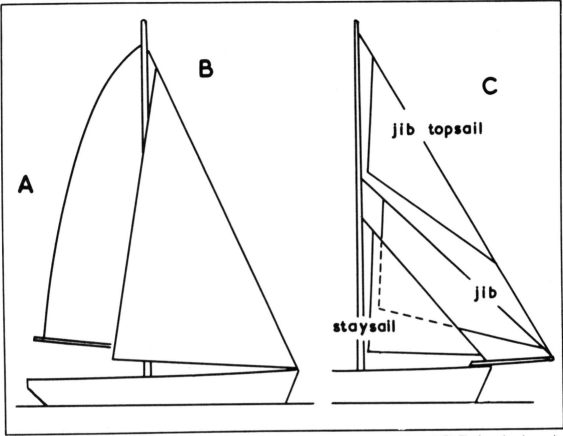

Fig. 1-7. The mast may be brought back so there is a small mainsail (A) and more area in a foresail (B). The fore triangle may be divided into several sails (C).

needed. It is too easy for some people to drop into a jargon based on reading about earlier sailing and to use words incorrectly. This can only lead to confusion and shows the ignorance that goes with only partial knowledge of a subject.

Anyone concerned with the rigging of a boat should make himself familiar with some general nautical terms in use today, as well as with those particularly applicable to rigging. Plain language can be used when the correct term is not known, but the right name is normally simpler and more positive. For instance, "that rope by the bottom cleat" is not as simple and direct as "the jib sheet," if that is what you mean.

The forward part of a boat is the *bow*. The actual pointed part is the *stem*. The direction you

are looking over the bow is *ahead*. At the other end is the *stern*. If it is cut straight across, that part is the *transom*. The direction you are looking over the stern is *astern* (Fig. 1-8A). The width of the boat is its *beam* and anything outside the boat to one side is *abeam*. Within the boat, the direction towards the bow is *forward* and the direction towards the stern is *aft*. Upwards is *aloft* and downwards inside the boat is *below* (Fig. 1-8B).

There is a problem in naming general directions in relation to the sides of the boat. If you are standing in a boat and facing forward, what is on your left side may be described as on the left of the boat and similarly with the right side. If you turn to face the stern, your own right and left sides have changed in relation to the boat. Which are now the

11

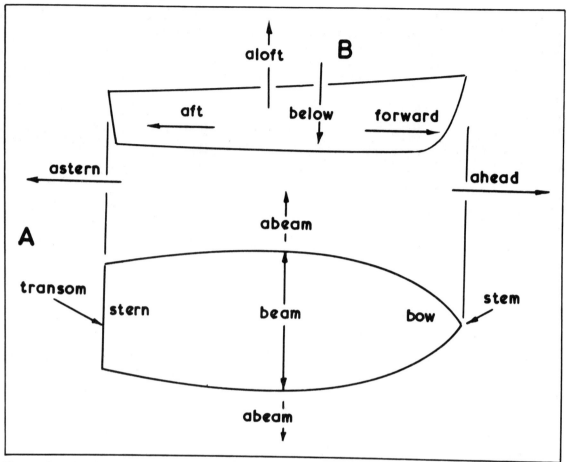

Fig. 1-8. Directions in and about a boat.

right and left sides of the boat? Providing you adopt the names of directions used when you are facing forward, there should be no mistakes. Today it is common to talk of left and right sides of a boat, but it has not always been so and most of the seafaring nations of the world still do not do so.

HISTORICAL TERMS

In nautical terms, the left side as seen when facing forward is the *port* side. The right side is the *starboard* side. As an aid to remembering which is which, left is a shorter word than right, port is a shorter word than starboard. The short words go together.

The history of these words may make their choice clearer. Before the advent of rudders, boats

were steered by a large oar or sweep pivoted at one side of the stern. This was called the *steer board*. As most people were right-handed, the steer board was arranged to the right of the helmsman when he was standing facing forward, so that side of the boat became known as the "steerboard side." The name was corrupted easily to "starboard." As the man who controlled the steer board controlled the ship, that side was considered the superior side and the captain slept near the steer board. It is still customary in many ships for the captain's cabin to be to starboard.

The steer board was usually secured in place fairly permanently, so it might be damaged if knocked against a dock or other obstruction. This meant that the other side of the boat was brought alongside a dock or bank for loading and unloading cargo or passengers. That side was known as the *loading board*. This became corrupted in use to *larboard*. Until comparatively recent times, the left side of a boat was known as the "larboard side" and the right side was the "starboard side." If not spoken clearly or amid noises, as when directing a man up the rigging in a howling gale, confusion was possible and could have serious consequences. An international convention agreed on the use of the word "port" in place of "larboard" as being a word with an entirely different sound from "starboard." (Fig. 1-9A).

There are other terms used for a sailing boat in relation to the wind. The side the wind is coming from is *windward*. That direction may be spoken of as *upwind*. The direction away from the wind is *downwind*. That side of the boat is the *lee side* and that direction is also *leeward*. Although it is not

wrong to pronounce it as written, a seaman pronounces it "looard" (Fig. 1-9B).

These directions apply whether the wind is abeam or anywhere between that and almost dead ahead or astern. If the boat is running with the wind dead aft, the mainsail will be out to one side and that may be considered leeward. This applies to any angle of sail setting, the side the main boom is on is leeward and the other side windward.

SAILING DIRECTIONS

A rigger should understand the names given to the main directions of sailing a fore-and-aft rigged boat. No boat can sail directly into the wind and most modern sailing craft can be expected to come within about 45° of that. When a boat is sailing at that angle, its sails are hauled in by their sheets quite tightly and the direction is described as sailing *close-hauled* (Fig. 1-10A). Sailing across the wind is

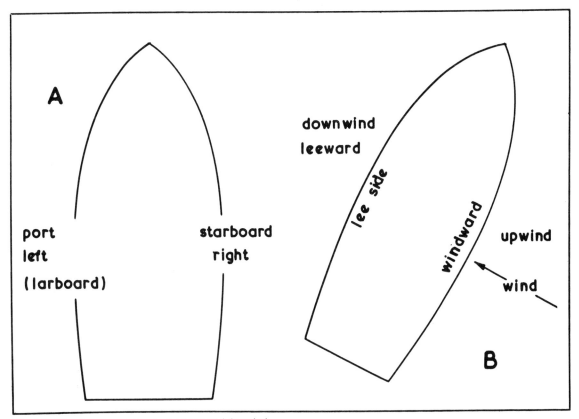

Fig. 1-9. Directions in relation to the boat and the wind.

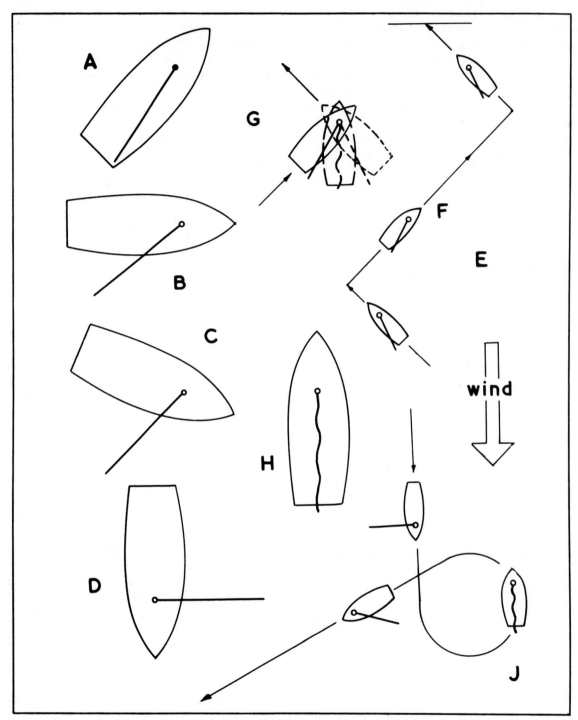

Fig. 1-10. Sailing directions according to the angle of the boat to the wind. Close-hauled (A), reaching (B), on a broad reach (C), running (D), tacking (E), on the port tack (F), going about (G), in irons (H), and wearing (J).

one of the easiest directions in which to handle a sailing boat. The sail angle is eased and the direction is called *reaching* (Fig. 1-10B). Seamen may describe a beam wind as a "soldier's wind," meaning that even a soldier could sail in that direction.

Sailing at any angle between a reach and about 45° away from the wind is a *broad reach* (Fig. 1-10C). Sailing further downwind is *running* (Fig. 1-10D). Sailing directly downwind carries the risk of a *gybe* (gibe), when the wind catches the sail *aback* and causes it to swing quickly to the other side. There is the danger of the boom doing damage on the way over or of capsizing a small boat if the crew is unprepared. It is more usual, if conditions permit, to sail slightly to one side of downwind.

If the destination is to windward, sailing close-hauled has to be in alternate directions on a zig-zag course if you are to get there. This is called *tacking* (Fig. 1-10E). Each direction is a *board,* and if you are sailing with the wind coming on the starboard side you are on a *starboard tack* (Fig. 1-10F) or, alternatively, it could be a *port tack.* At the end of each board you *go about* (Fig. 1-10G).

If the boat is turned directly into the wind so the sails flap like flags, it is *in irons* (Fig. 1-10H). This happens when you go about and the rudder is used to turn the boat on to the other tack. The only way to stop a boat is turn it into the wind. When sailing anywhere between a reach and close-hauled, turning into the wind to stop is easy, but when

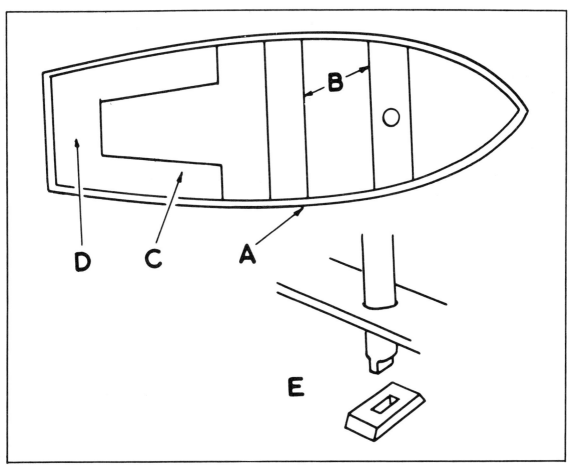

Fig. 1-11. Main parts of an open boat: gunwale (A), thwarts (B), side benches (C), stern sheets (D), and mast step and thwart (E).

sailing "off the wind" there has to be room to turn the boat upwind. This can be a particular problem when the boat is running.

With the boom to one side, the boat may be turned towards the other side to get it into the wind, but suppose you are following a winding channel that goes the other way. Using the rudder to direct the boat that way will cause the sail to gybe. If you are prepared for it and the wind is not too strong, a calculated gybe may be acceptable. However, there is another way of getting the boom to the other side more quietly and this is known as *wearing*. You turn

a complete circle so the boom crosses when the boat is in irons and the sail is empty (Fig. 1-10J).

BOAT PARTS

Many other parts of a boat may not be directly the concern of a rigger and he may learn them as he progresses. The top edge of the boat, to which the shrouds and other rigging will connect is the *gunwale* (Fig. 1-11A), which may be pronounced "gunnel" and is sometimes spelled that way or incorrectly "gunwhale." It is the last surviving use of an obsolete word. "Wale" is an old term for

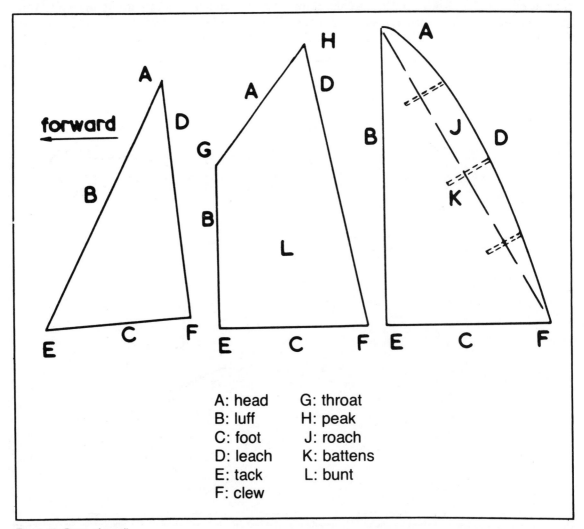

A: head   G: throat
B: luff   H: peak
C: foot   J: roach
D: leach   K: battens
E: tack   L: bunt
F: clew

Fig. 1-12. Parts of a sail.

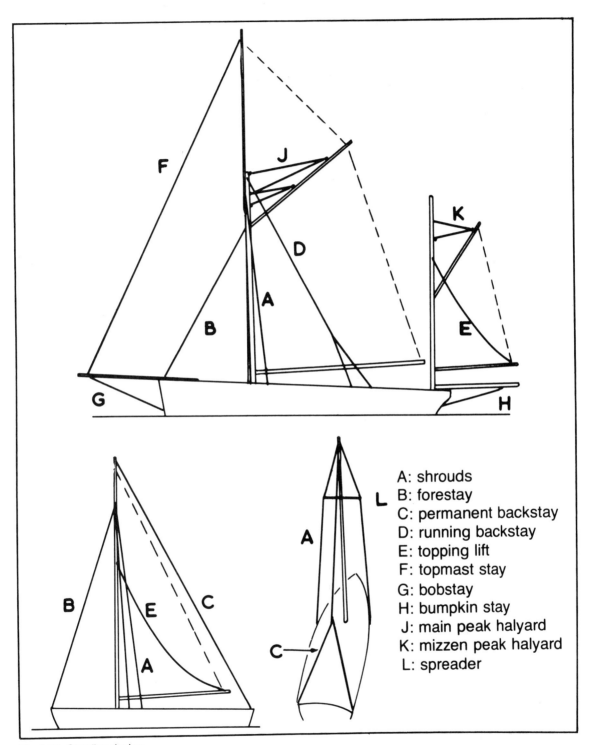

A: shrouds
B: forestay
C: permanent backstay
D: running backstay
E: topping lift
F: topmast stay
G: bobstay
H: bumpkin stay
J: main peak halyard
K: mizzen peak halyard
L: spreader

Fig. 1-13. Standing rigging.

"plank" or "strake," meaning the lengthwise pieces of wood forming the skin of a hull. The gunwale of a fighting sailing ship was the top part of the edge of the hull through which the gun ports were cut.

A direction across a boat is *athwart* or *athwartships*. A piece of wood across the boat is a *thwart*. It may be for sitting on or it could be at gunwale level to support the mast (Fig. 1-11B). Seats going lengthwise, as they do in a small, open boat are *benches* or *side benches* (Fig. 1-11C), but the seats around the stern are traditionally *stern sheets* (Fig. 1-11D).

If a mast goes through to the bottom of the boat, it fits on to a *mast step* (Fig. 1-11E). There is some controversy over the name of what that rests on in a boat of modern construction. Externally, the lengthwise piece is the *keel*, but inside, in traditional wood construction, there was a *keelson* and a *hog*. It is probably more accurate to call any lengthwise modern internal part by the last name, although it is common to talk of a mast "stepped on the keel." Fiberglass construction has meant that many terms that applied to hulls built of parts can no longer be used. It is wise to avoid trying to transpose these older terms into modern usage.

Many of the terms that apply to details of sails and rigging will be dealt with as they occur in the following chapters. It is wise to learn the common terms, such as the parts of a sail and the usual names for parts of the rigging (Figs. 1-12 and 1-13). The boating world is only now settling to new terminology to deal with the almost universal use of modern materials such as fiberglass for hulls, aluminum alloy for spars and fitting, synthetic materials for sails, and stainless steel for wire ropes and fittings. All of these things, which have developed since the end of World War II, have made new methods of construction and techniques possible. Some have revolutionized the construction of sailing craft and their equipment, with new thinking about the way such boats can be used. One result has been the modification of some terms and the coining of new ones. The terms used in this book are believed to be those most generally used and accepted in the English-speaking world.

Chapter 2

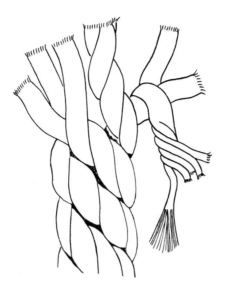

Cordage

THE ROPES THAT MAKE UP THE RIGGING OF A sailing boat are broadly grouped into *standing rigging* and *running rigging*. The standing rigging holds the mast and other fairly rigid things in position. The running rigging consists of the various ropes used to hoist and control sails. The material of the standing rigging is not subject to much movement, but the running rigging has to be flexible.

Traditional seamen seemed to avoid the word *rope* to a large extent. Ropes were named after their function and rarely did the word "rope" come into the name. The collective word for all the ropelike materials from the smallest to the largest was, and still is, *cordage*.

Many forms of rope has been used by man from the earliest times. Some of the earliest examples must have been natural creepers, fronds, and climbing plants found in the jungle. The technique of twisting fibers to make ropes is believed to go back to 3000 B.C. and the ancient Egyptians. Their fibers came from papyrus leaves, hemp, flax, and date palms. From then until very recent times all ropes have been made from natural fibers. The materials of 5000 years of ropemaking have now been superseded by synthetic materials. Most of this change has taken place since the end of World War II. Man-made filaments, instead of natural fibers, are now the mainstay of the ropemaker's art. Natural fibers are still used and a rigger should be aware of them and their characteristics, although most of his work will be with synthetic cordage.

Fiber rope is the obvious choice for running rigging, while most standing rigging today is made of wire rope. Some wire rope is sufficiently flexible for use as halyards. Information on wire rope is given later in the chapter.

NATURAL FIBERS

Some of the natural fibers that are still used for making cordage are hemp, cotton, sisal, and coir. In general, they are not as strong as comparable synthetics and they will absorb water more readily, with a tendency to rot if left wet. Synthetics will not rot and most have negligible tendency to water absorption.

Of the many hemps, Italian hemp has been considered strongest and smoothest and easiest to use. Until the coming of synthetics, hemp rope was the first choice for heavily loaded and frequently handled sailing craft ropes. *Manila* is the name given to a fiber that comes from plantain leaves. It has sometimes been classed with hemp, as it looks the same and has similar characteristics.

Cotton does not make as strong a rope as hemp, but it can be very flexible. It has been a choice for small boat sheets, where flexibility and its ease on the hands made it attractive. When new it is white, but it absorbs dirt and is darkened by it. Grit in any rope will abrade the fibers, but this seems a particular problem with cotton.

Sisal is a fiber obtained from aloe leaves. It came into popularity because it is inexpensive compared with the other natural fibers. It is a light brown color and has a rather rough feel and appearance. It is still used where economy is attractive and where appearance and feel are not so important. Strength is slightly less than hemp. There are not many places where sisal would be used in the rigging of a boat, but it has advantages in general ropework, such as temporary lashings or emergency rigging.

Coir is probably the least likely natural fiber rope still to be found. It is made from the fibers of coconuts and some users called it "grass" rope. Coir ropes are only about one-quarter of the strength of the same size hemp rope, but coir will float almost indefinitely where all other natural fiber ropes would sink. It is also much more elastic than any of the others. Because of its ability to float, coir was used for mooring lines, making it easy to pull across instead of through the water. Because of its elasticity, it was also used for towing lines. In both cases it had to be of quite large section to provide enough strength. Today there are synthetics with the qualities of coir and considerably more strength, so new coir rope is not made.

SYNTHETIC FIBERS

The development of synthetic fibers and their application to ropemaking is still an ongoing process. Where natural fiber ropes followed an unchanging pattern over centuries, synthetic ropes are still changing and improving. This chapter describes the usual materials and constructions, but a current catalog from a ropemaker may have something different. Synthetic materials allow ropes to be made to closely suit particular requirements in a way that was not possible with natural fibers.

All synthetic ropes have a chemical base and some have extremely ponderous chemical names. Because of this, it is common to know a rope by a trade name. This is satisfactory, except that it may not be immediately obvious that two very different trade names indicate the same ropemaking materials by different manufacturers. The technical literature of the makers will usually give the chemical names.

One of the best known synthetics is nylon, which is not a trade name. Chemically it is described as a polyamide polymer. As one of the earliest of the synthetics, some people have used the name as a loose term for all synthetics. This can be misleading and should be avoided. Of the synthetic rope materials this one is the most elastic. It should not be used for any application where the rope has to pull tight. Where some stretch is desirable it is the best choice. Compared with the other synthetics, nylon is very absorbent, but compared with the natural fiber ropes, its absorption of water is slight.

The general-purpose boating rope material that has taken over from hemp and manila is polyethylene terephthalate, commonly called polyester. It is at least twice as strong as hemp and manila ropes of the same size. Two trade names are Dacron and Terylene.

A lighter and generally cheaper rope is made from polypropylene. It is not as strong as polyester ropes but is stronger than any natural fiber ropes. As it will float, it is now used where coir would have been the choice. One snag is its comparatively low melting point of 250-350° F. Such temperatures are unlikely, but possible, due to friction, so this is not really the rope for serious rigging. It is convenient afloat for all of the many nonrigging needs for rope.

All natural fibers are short. This means that a rope of any size is made up of a large number of short pieces and their ends stick out, giving rope its characteristic hairy feeling. Synthetic ropes are made up of continuous filaments. In many cases they are much finer and, therefore, in larger numbers in a given size rope. The filaments may go through the full length of the rope, resulting in a smooth rope surface except for an occasional broken filament. The traditional hairy rope surface has some advantage in providing a grip, so it is possible to get some synthetic ropes made with this sort of exterior.

Unlike natural fibers, synthetics react badly to sunlight. This is called photochemical deterioration. The effect is less on nylon than on the polyesters. It is possible to include additives in the material to counteract the effect of sunlight. Darker rope is less affected than light-colored rope. The makers may indicate if there are additives or pigments to act as ultraviolet inhibitors. If there are not, the rope will have a longer life if it is kept out of the sunlight whenever possible.

All of the synthetics have a better resistance to abrasion than their natural fiber counterparts. Their greater strength and resistance to water absorption make them much better for use afloat. In particular, they can be stored wet without risk of rot. Various methods of proofing were, and are, used on natural fiber ropes, but they delayed, rather than prevented, rot. Springing open the strands of a natural fiber rope may show darkness inside, indicating the onset of rot. A wet natural fiber rope is not as strong as a dry one, but moisture does not affect the strength of a synthetic fiber rope, except for nylon, which is not quite as strong when wet. Where weight is a consideration, a saturated natural fiber rope is considerably heavier, but a wet synthetic rope is little different in weight from a dry one.

Many synthetic fibers used for rope are also woven into sailcloth. Like developments in rope-making, synthetics have almost completely superseded natural fiber cloths for sails.

ROPE LAY

Most traditional ropes were made three-stranded.

This is still a common configuration, although modern manufacturing methods have made several other constructions usual for boat ropes. In a section containing three round strands, each strand touches the other two and the total section cannot go out of shape (Fig. 2-1A). With a greater number of round strands, this condition does not apply again until seven strands are used (Fig. 2-1B). The six outer strands rest against their neighbors and the central heart strand. This arrangement is used in wire ropes, but only rarely in fiber ropes, although some French rope has been made in this way. There have been four-stranded ropes, but to keep the rope in shape there has to be a thin, straight central strand (Fig. 2-1C). Some makers and users of four-strand rope claimed it was more flexible than three-strand rope.

Nearly all traditional three-strand rope is laid up right-handed and may be called *hawser-laid*. If you look along this rope, the strands twist away from you clockwise, towards the right (Fig. 2-1D). Stranded rope may be laid up left-handed for special purposes. Slings for lifting loads may have opposite ropes twisted in opposite ways. This lessens the risk of ropes twisting around each other at the crane hook.

Shroud-laid is a term used in some older books to indicate four-strand rope laid up right-handed, but this formation is rare today.

For very large ropes there is a limit to what can conveniently be made with three strands. *Cable-laid* ropes were made with three three-strand ropes laid up right-handed and twisted together left-handed (Fig. 2-1E). This allowed a large cross section, but still retained the formation of three circles within the three ropes, and again in the cable made of the three ropes (although in total there were nine strands). The arrangement is unusual today except for cables much larger than would be used on a present-day sailing boat.

In a rope, the fibers or filaments are twisted together to form yarns (Fig. 2-1F). The yarns are twisted together to form strands (Fig. 2-1G). The strands are twisted together to form the rope. The twist at each stage is the opposite way to the previous one so each twist in any attempt to unwind

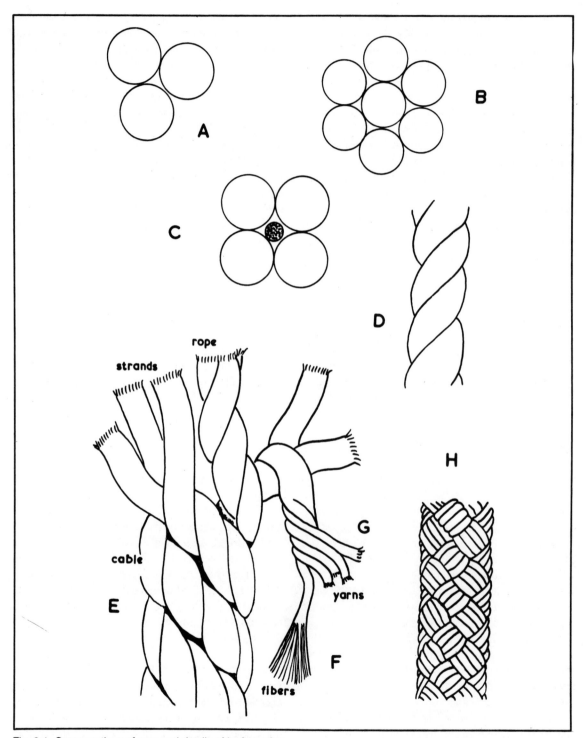

Fig. 2-1. Cross sections of rope and details of its formation.

tightens the previous one. In this way the rope retains its construction. Ropes of some materials, when cut, will keep their formation, but most synthetics will rapidly unlay if left to their own devices. Whipping or other preventive methods have to be used.

Traditionally, rope was made by hand in a rope walk, where lengths of rope were kept straight during construction by a man walking backwards and feeding in fibers to a simple mechanism. Now mechanized, this basic method is still used in forming three-stranded rope.

However, mechanization and the use of synthetics has resulted in other rope formations. In particular, for sailing boat work there are braided or plaited ropes. The outer casing has groups of yarns woven across each other diagonally, so there is a pattern of yarns going around in a helical manner in each direction (Fig. 2-1H). This makes a smooth flexible rope that is comfortable to handle and easy to use around wheels or through other solid equipment. The interior of the rope varies. The heart may be made up of a large number of straight yarns laid lengthwise. The heart may be a three-strand rope with the casing fitted around it. It may contain two braided tubular casings, both fairly loosely laid around a three-strand or straight yarn heart. Flexibility varies according to how tightly the rope is made up.

ROPE SIZES

In the past, the size of rope was determined by its circumference. Anyone regularly using rope might recognize rope size in this way, but the casual user would have to visualize a thickness, or diameter, from the quoted circumference. The diameter is slightly less than one-third of the circumference, so a 1½-inch circumference rope is slightly less than ½-inch thick.

Some makers have always described their ropes by diameter, but it may be necessary to check the method used when ordering rope. With a move towards metrication there has been a tendency to favor using diameter size only. Fortunately, there is a convenient relationship between circumference in fractions of an inch and diameter in millimeters. If circumference is expressed in one-eighths of an inch, that is the same number as the diameter in millimeters. For instance, a 2-inch circumference is 16 × ⅛ inches, so the diameter is then 16 millimeters. Or a 1⅛-inch circumference is 9 × ⅛ inches, so the diameter is 9 millimeters.

The nautical way of measuring the length of a rope uses a *fathom* (6 feet), but it is better to use feet or meters. Some other measurements for longer pieces were based on the length that could be made in a rope walk or the size that could be conveniently coiled. These are not necessarily the same everywhere. They might be historically interesting, but for practical purposes they are obsolete.

Strength tables provided by ropemakers refer to the straight rope. In boat rigging, most flexible ropes will have their direction altered, usually by going around wheels (sheaves or pulleys). Some strength is then lost. The larger the wheel the less will be the loss of strength, but very large wheels are often impractical in a boat's rig. Another loss of strength comes in knots and splices. There is no way that ropes can be joined that does not reduce strength. Some knots have easier curves than others and therefore less tendency to reduce strength. A splice should weaken less than a knot. Although a knot is weaker than the body of the rope, when a knotted rope is tested to destruction, the break usually comes where the rope enters the knot.

With modern ropes, be careful to choose a knot to suit the smoothness of the materials. This is dealt with in more detail later, but it must be remembered that some knots regularly and safely used in the past with natural fiber ropes may not be suitable for synthetics. Because of this, it is unwise to accept statements made in some older knotting books. Make sure any knotting or splicing instruction is appropriate to your materials.

WIRE ROPE

By its nature, wire rope is much more rigid than fiber rope. Early standing rigging was made of fiber rope because there was no suitable wire rope. The square-rigged fighting ships had fiber rope rigging, and many a battle was lost because fiber rope parted under fire and the masts went over the side. Many might have survived with wire rope. They would have sailed better because wire rope offers much less wind resistance, because a much smaller diameter can provide the same strength as a thick fiber rope. Because it can be set up tighter, wire rope allows a mast to be supported much more rigidly. The amount of stretch is negligible compared with even the least elastic fiber rope.

As with synthetic fiber ropes, there have been many developments that have altered the characteristics of wire ropes. There are new metals and new ways of laying up the wires to form ropes. It would be unwise to rely on old manuals concerning wire rope, as their information could be out of date.

At one time, iron rope (probably mild steel) was used for situations where the rope would not have to flex much. Once it was in position it remained under tension. It was used in standing rigging to support masts that did not have to be lowered. Rod rigging also has been tried. Instead of a rope made of several strands, each piece of standing rigging is a single wire or rod. This provides maximum strength, but there are problems with removing and storing the rigging.

When iron rope was used for standing rigging, steel was used for running rigging. Steel rope could be used where there had to be flexibility, as when the wire rope had to be wound around a drum of a windlass. It could not be taken around wheels of small diameter as this would soon cause wires to break. Of course, iron and steel will rust if unprotected, so they were galvanized with zinc. Rust will eventually break through galvanizing, so such wire had to be further protected with grease, varnish, and covering.

Although stainless steel has been known for a long time, the grades available were unsuitable for making wire ropes. Since World War II there have been salt-water resistant stainless steels produced with considerable strength. Nearly all standing rigging of pleasure craft is stainless steel. The standard alloy is called 302/304 stainless steel. There is not much iron rope used and galvanized steel, although still available, has given way to stainless steel in most applications.

There are a few other metals made into wire ropes, but these are mostly for special purposes, such as engine controls, and are not intended for rigging.

Wire ropes are mostly made with six strands around a heart (Fig. 2-1A). In some ropes the heart is fiber (Fig. 2-2A). The fiber does not provide strength, but it is the same diameter as the other strands and is there to keep the rope in shape. Stainless steel is more likely to have a wire heart strand. This wire can be recognized, when the rope is opened; it is not wavy like the other strands. It is then a strength member in the rope. Each strand of a wire rope is made up of a number of individual wires. A large number of fine wires in a given size will make a more flexible rope than a smaller number of thicker wires in the same size rope.

A rope of 19 strands will also have all circles meeting to keep the rope in shape (Fig. 2-2B). This configuration is used for many stainless steel ropes. Seven-strand rope is suitable where there is little need for the rope to flex much, but where the rope is taken around sheaves or has to be fairly tightly curved in other ways, 19-strand is the modern choice. In practice many boats have standing and running rigging made of the same nineteen-strand stainless steel wire rope.

To make large or more flexible wire ropes, strands can be arranged in a similar build-up to the fiber rope cable, by taking seven-strand ropes and twisting them together the opposite ways to their lays. This has also been done with seven 19-strand ropes. In a catalog the ordinary seven-strand rope would be described as 1 × 7, the others are 7 × 7 and 19 × 7. In boat rigging the last two types are rarely seen.

Wire rope sizes have always been quoted by diameter. Variations can be quite small and only an approximation can be obtained by putting a rule across. It is better to use sliding calipers, preferably with broad jaws that will pass over two or three wires each side.

Kinks must be avoided in handling wire rope. It usually comes rolled on a drum or reel. It is better to keep it that way. If a piece is cut off, roll it on to

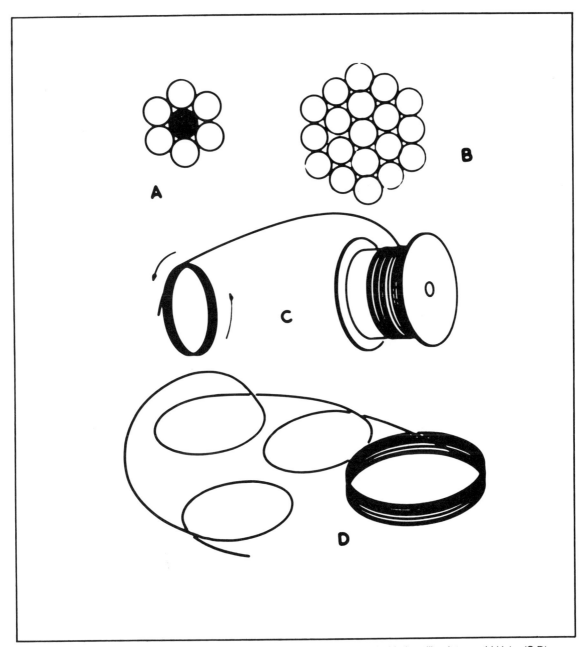

Fig. 2-2. Wire rope may have seven (A) or nineteen strands (B). Care is needed in handling it to avoid kinks (C,D).

another reel. Don't coil it as you would fiber rope, as that could lead to kinking when the wire is opened out. A bad kink cannot be removed and will weaken the rope.

If wire rope has to be taken from a drum or large coil, arrange it to unwind, then wind as you take it up (Fig. 2-2C), even if you are not putting it around another drum. Do not take it from a stationary supply by drawing off loops (Fig. 2-2D). This encourages the formation of kinks.

Chapter 3

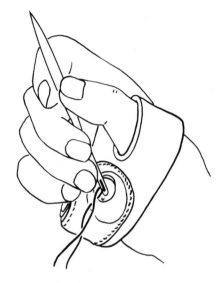

Fiber Rope Ends and Knots

I T IS IMPORTANT THAT THE END OF ANY ROPE should be prevented from unlaying or the strands and yarns coming adrift. Plaited or braided rope is less likely to open up and separate, but some three-strand rope will spring apart and unwind for a considerable distance if left unrestrained. This is particularly so with most man-made fibers. Once a length of rope has unlaid, it is almost impossible to put it back together satisfactorily, so you may be left with a rather expensive, wasted piece to cut off. The old-time seaman called this state of affairs a *mare's tail.*

It is possible to seal the end of a synthetic fiber rope with heat. The ends of the filaments can be melted and run together. If you try to do this with natural fiber ropes, you will char or ignite the ends. They will certainly not show any signs of melting. If you have any doubts about whether a piece of rope is natural or synthetic fiber, putting a flame to the end with a match or cigarette lighter will soon show what it is; synthetic fiber will start melting as soon as it gets hot, while natural fiber will turn black.

Heat is used to cut synthetic fiber ropes. A warm knife will go through the rope and melt the cut ends at the same time, so there is no risk of them separating as the rope is parted. There are electrically heated cutting devices that raise the knife to the right temperature. It is unwise to try to do this with a knife that you wish to keep for other purposes, as heat will destroy its temper, leaving it too soft for general use. For occasional cutting it may be better to use a cold knife, but restrain the rope with temporary whippings or stoppings each side of the intended cut.

Even with heat-sealed ends it is advisable to apply whippings as well. A sealed end may give way in use and part of the rope starts to unlay. A whipping provides a backup and prevents any stray filaments running loose further back along the rope. Whipping of natural as well as synthetic ropes is best done with synthetic twine, as there is no risk of it rotting and coming away. Synthetic sail twine is about the right thickness for use on the usual boat ropes. One beginner's mistake is to use whipping twine, which is too thick in relation to the rope. Thin is better than thick. Sail twine can be bought waxed and this helps the turns stay put as they are pulled tight.

When rope is to be cut put a few turns of twine fairly close to where the cut is to come (Fig. 3-1A). You could use electrician's or other adhesive tape, but this is of no use for a permanent whipping. After cutting, seal both ends with heat. You can do this with a match or other flame, but there is less discoloring due to carbon if you use a gas cigarette lighter. Twirl the end in the flame so you melt it fairly equally all around (Fig. 3-1B). Remove the flame. Wet your finger and thumb and squeeze the end into shape. Wetting is important or you will burn yourself and the semimolten plastic will cling to your skin. You must squeeze the end so it is no bigger than the rest of the rope (Fig. 3-1C). A cut with a hot knife or an unsqueezed end will usually finish larger than the rope, making it difficult to push through a block or fairlead. If the rope you buy has been cut with a hot knife machine, you will have to reheat the end and squeeze it to size. Remove any temporary whipping after the ends are sealed.

WHIPPING

Any comprehensive book on knotting contains a very large range of whippings. To a certain extent you can choose the method that appeals to you. It is important to make the binding stay put under any circumstances, and some whippings are firmer than others. It may help in practice work to use thicker twine so you can see what you are doing, but for working whippings use fine sail twine and put on all the turns as tightly as you can. So long as the finished whipping is squeezing the rope tightly and will not separate or start to unwind, you have done the job properly, whatever the method employed.

A whipping should not usually be longer than the diameter of the rope (Fig. 3-1D). It is really the number of turns that matter and these have to be found by experience with various materials. For thick ropes there is no need to make the whipping as long as the diameter. Above about a ⅝-inch diameter the length can be less—about 20 turns are enough. How far to have the whipping from the end

is a matter of experience. With the usual heat-sealed end, somewhere between ¼-inch and ½-inch will do (Fig. 3-1E). With natural fiber ropes, the distance can be about the same on smaller ropes, but may have to be rather more on thick ones. The loose fibers will spread a little, but that may not matter. If it does, the whipping may be made nearer the end, but going too close on natural fibers may sometimes result in whipping turns eventually slipping off the end and the whipping coming apart. If a rope is expected to get very rough treatment, as when reef points flail about in the wind, it may be a sort of insurance to put a second whipping on a short distance behind the first (Fig. 3-1F).

Old-time knotting instructions always say that whipping turns should be put on against the lay (Fig. 3-1G). This follows the reasoning in the design of rope, where fibers, strands, and yarns are twisted opposite ways, so any tendency of one to loosen tightens the next in sequence. There is some point in this reasoning, but in practice it does not seem to matter which way the turns are made, providing they are tight. It is actually easier to get a whipping tight by putting it on with the lay (Fig. 3-1H). With braided rope or other rope that does not have a lay, the whipping can go on either way. Tightness is the vital thing; a whipping that is loose is a waste of time, and probably of rope.

Common Whipping

The best-known method of whipping goes under many different names, but here we are calling it a *common whipping*. Although it is the most widely known it is not the best method. There are a few variations, but the results are similar. The common whipping should be understood, but when the other whippings are learned, one of them will probably be preferred.

To make the common whipping, lay the starting end along the rope towards the end and then put tight turns over it (Fig. 3-2A). After going more than half the length the whipping is to be, turn back the first end to leave a loop projecting (Fig. 3-2B). Put on more turns over this. After three or four turns, put the working end through the loop (Fig. 3-2C). Pull the first end that is projecting through

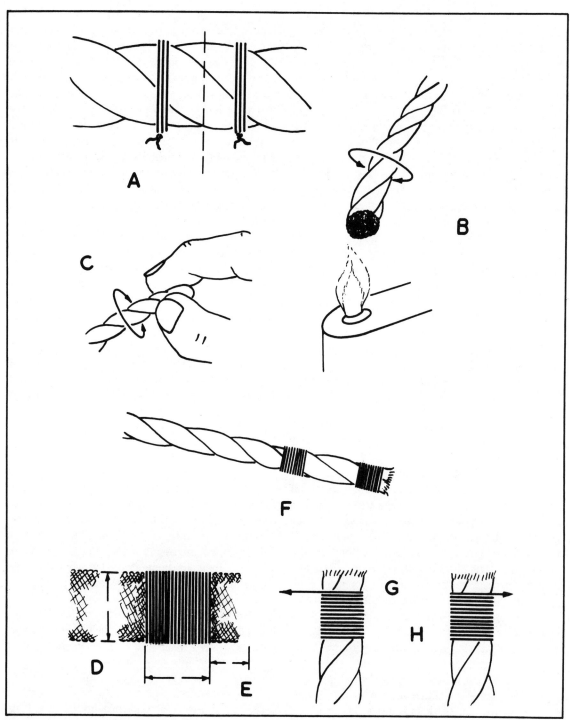

Fig. 3-1. Cut rope between seizings (A). Seal ends of synthetic rope (B,C). Whip an end once or twice (D,E,F) and the turns may be either way (G,H).

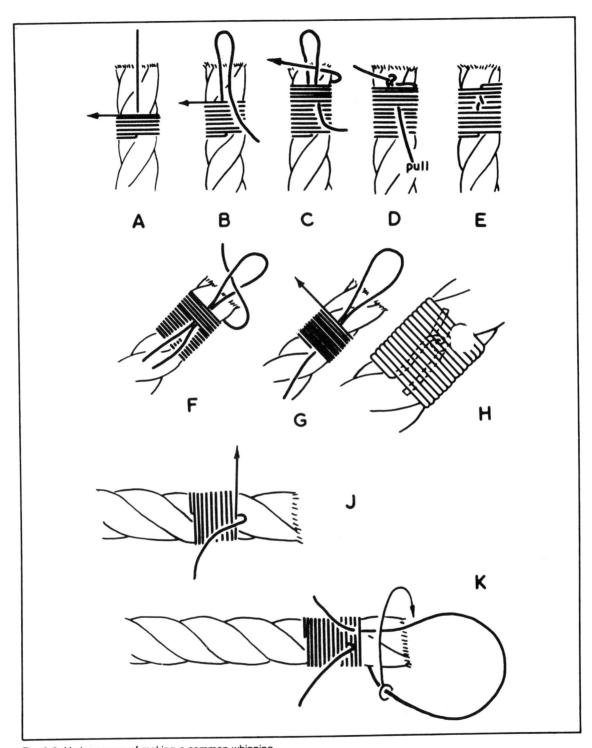

Fig. 3-2. Various ways of making a common whipping.

the turns further back (Fig. 3-2D). This will draw the working end back under the turns, so both ends project and can be cut off to complete the whipping (Fig. 3-2E).

Another way of getting the same result is to use a separate piece to make the loop. Do not insert it until the turns have reached the stage where the end would be turned back in the first example (Fig. 3-2F). When the working end has been pulled back, the pieces that made the loop is discarded.

A possibly tighter way of locking the two ends is to double back the first part before putting on the turns (Fig. 3-2G), then pass the working end through the loop after all the turns have been applied. Pull back on the first end until the linked loops are halfway (Fig. 3-2H). Cut the ends off. It is important to get the linked part near the center of the whipping, otherwise one end of the whipping may loosen.

Another variation gets a similar result without using a loop. This is the method most used by regular seafarers. Put on turns over the first end until about half enough turns are on, then let the end project (Fig. 3-2J) while putting on more turns, After a few more turns, lay the working end back along the rope and continue to put on more turns with the resulting loop (Fig. 3-2K). When sufficient turns have been put on, pull on the working end to draw back what is left of the loop. Pull both projecting ends tight and cut them off. If both projecting ends are allowed to come out of the same space, they can be joined by knotting before cutting off.

There are two contradictory snags with all of the variations of the common whipping. If the final turns are slack enough to allow the end to be pulled back, the completed whipping will not be as tight as it should be. If the whipping is made very tight, it may not be possible to pull the end back without breaking the line. Another problem comes if one turn is cut or worn through. The whole whipping will come away. This does not happen with some of the other whippings. There is also the problem of working tightly. If one turn is put on loosely, the whole whipping will loosen. In some other whippings there is better locking of the turns.

West Country Whipping

The name comes from the southwestern part of England, where so many famous voyages started, including that of the Pilgrim Fathers. The group of countries west of Bristol are collectively called the West Country. This whipping can be applied on any type of rope and is at least as easy to make as the common whipping. Tightness and security are obtained by locking each turn as it is applied. On the drawing, the heavier lines necessary to show construction may make the whipping appear clumsy, but in the actual whipping the crossings of the line are almost invisible.

Cut a suitable length of line and put its middle behind the rope. At the front twist the two parts together in an overhand knot (Fig. 3-3A). Pull this as tight as possible. With waxed twine the knot will not slip. If you have bought unwaxed twine, it helps to rub it first with beeswax or a piece of candle. Take the line to the back of the rope and do the same there (Fig. 3-3B). Come to the front and do it again, close to the first knot. Continue in this way, knotting back and front tightly, until a sufficient length of whipping has been made. Form all knots the same way so they fit neatly against each other. Keep all turns as close together as possible. Make the final knot into a reef knot by making another twist the opposite way (Fig. 3-3C), then cut off the ends.

West Country and common whippings may sometimes be used away from the end of a rope. This allows them to indicate a position along a rope. It also makes them suitable for backup whippings a short distance behind end whippings.

Palm and Needle Whipping

The greatest strength in a whipping comes if some of the twine goes through the rope as well as around it. There are two ways of getting this result. The first requires a needle and a palm to push it, so giving the whipping its name. The other method is suitable for three-strand rope ends and may also be called a *sailmaker's whipping*.

The best needle to use for this type of whipping is a sail needle, which is triangular behind the point (Fig. 3-4A). Sail needles are known by their

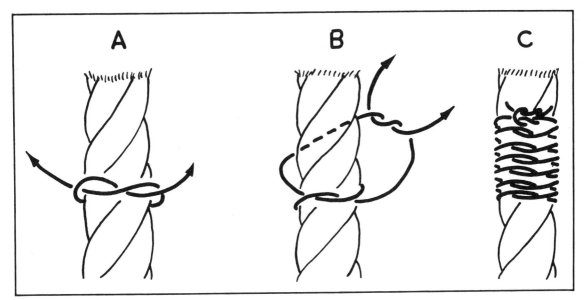

Fig. 3-3. Steps in making a West Country whipping.

gauge size. For this sort of whipping a needle about gauge 16 should be suitable. However, if a rigger is expecting to deal with many jobs on a boat he should accumulate a collection of needles of many sizes, ranging from about gauge 8 to gauge 22. The smaller gauge number is the thicker needle.

The *palm* used with a sail needle is a device to fit over the hand so the needle can be given a thrust from the whole hand, it is leather, with a hole for the thumb and a metal plate cased in leather over the palm of the hand so that you can push against the eye end of the needle (Fig. 3-4B). Palms are primarily sailmakers' tools and are made in several types, but unless the rigger intends to do much sailmaking, a general-purpose one should serve all his needs. Any type of palm can be used for pushing a needle through rope when whipping.

Have the needle on the twine. Do not knot it, but turn back just enough to keep the twine through the eye of the needle. Start the whipping by pushing the needle through a strand or a part of braided rope, probably twice, so the starting end of the twine is sewn in. The projecting end can be covered by the whipping turns. Put on sufficient tight turns, then take the needle through a strand.

The round turns of the whipping are covered by *worming turns*, which go over the whipping outside the spaces between strands of a laid rope or straight along a braided rope. How this is done depends on the tightness of the construction of the rope. If it is possible to take the needle diagonally through the rope for the length of the whipping, take it from the top to the bottom, so it emerges from a space, then up the outside (Fig. 3-5A) following a space between strands if it is a laid rope, and down through the center to another space. In this way a worming turn follows over each space between strands. If you wish, these worming turns can be followed again, so there is a double line at each position. Then the needle is thrust through once more and the line cut off (Fig. 3-5B).

Much synthetic rope is too tightly laid for a needle to go through in this way. Instead of going through the rope inside the whipping to get from one space to the next, it can be taken through or around a strand at the end of the whipping (Fig. 3-5C).

That method can be used with three-strand or braided rope, but there is a variation, called a *sailmaker's whipping*, which can be used at the end of a

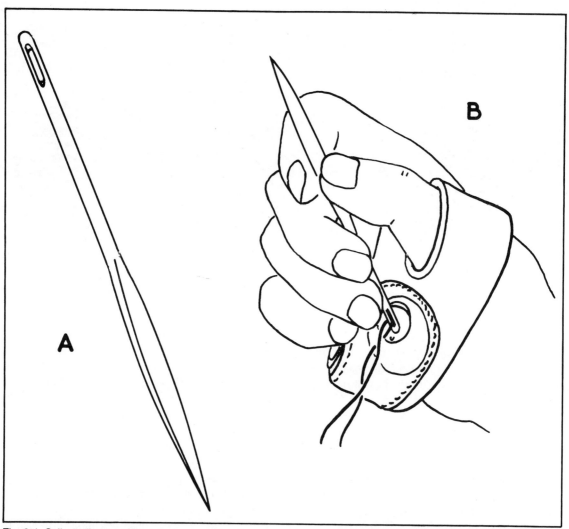

Fig. 3-4. Sail needle and palm.

three-strand rope, without the need of needle and palm. The finished whipping shows single worming turns and should be as secure as a whipping made with a needle.

To prepare the rope, seal the ends of the strands separately, but do not bond them together as a whole rope. After the whipping has been made the ends can then be melted together in the usual way. Be careful that the rope does not unlay unintentionally. A few turns of adhesive tape near what will be at the bottom of the whipping will prevent unlaying. This will be about three times the diameter of the rope from the end. In any case, unlay as far as this, whether the rope needs taping or not.

Turn back the whipping line into a loop with long and short ends. Let the short end be about 6 inches long, so you have enough to grip. The long end has to be enough to put on the turns, with a little to spare. Put this line into the opened rope so the loop loosely encircles one strand and the two ends project from the opposite space (Fig. 3-5D). Lay up the rope strands again. Give each a twist in the way it was made up of yarns as you do this, to get it back

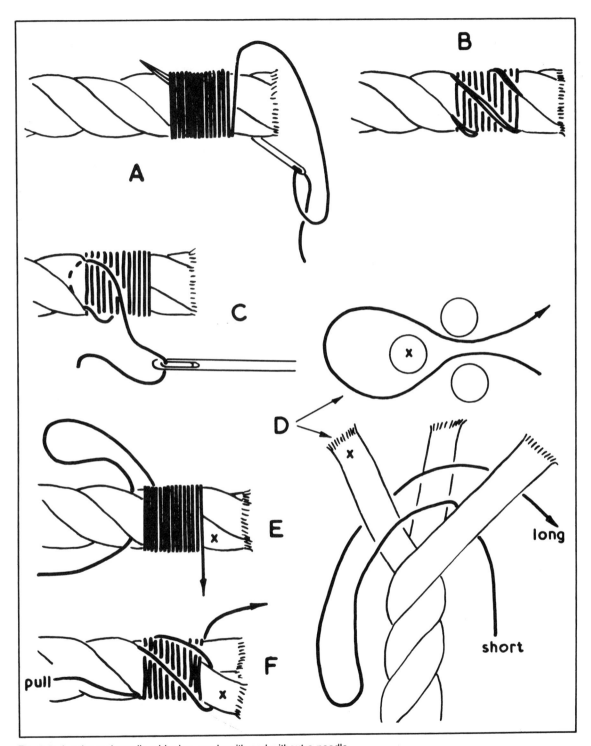

Fig. 3-5. A palm-and-needle whipping, made with and without a needle.

into the form it was. Hold the loop and the short end down the rope out of the way, while turns are put on with the long part (Fig. 3-5E). It helps to keep the rope in shape if the whipping turns are put on in the direction of the lay.

Note which strand the loop is encircling. When sufficient turns have been put on, hold them tight and lift the loop over the top of the strand it is already encircling (Fig. 3-5F). Pull the short end to tighten the sides of the loop that form worming turns. See that the end of the loop beds down into the center of the end of the rope. This leaves you with two worming turns in place and the short end projecting from the space between the strands that do not have a worming turn outside the whipping.

Take the short end over the whipping to form the third worming turn, then into the center of the rope, where it is tied tightly with a reef knot, to the remains of the long end. Cut off the surplus. Roll the end of the rope round. If there is any unevenness, cut the end level, but do not go too close to the whipping. If it is synthetic fiber rope, fuse the ends together with gentle heat. Be careful not to let the flame touch the whipping twine, as that could be melted.

KNOTS

There have been a bewildering number of knots devised, mostly by seamen in the days of large, commercial, square-rigged sailing craft, when the miles of rope on the ship formed a vital part of the means of propulsion, and its correct deployment was important for the safety and performance of the ship. The making of correct knots quickly and accurately, probably in difficult conditions, was one of the essential skills of crew members.

Those days are gone. In our simpler sailing craft, with modern equipment, the number of knots needed are comparatively few. However, what there are should be thoroughly mastered. When a knot is needed, it may have to be formed quickly and accurately. You may not have time to experiment with the way you cross the ends or even to think which knot to use. This means that everyone who goes to sea as a crew member on a sailing boat should know how to make the important knots, how to select the one to use, and be able to form the knot when conditions are far from ideal.

The old-time seaman did not like the word "tie," but it seems the obvious choice today. He *bent* ropes together or used some other rather archaic terms. He also claimed that the word "knot" should only apply to something made in one rope and what he used to join ropes together was a *bend*. If he attached a rope to something solid he used a *hitch*. Unfortunately, he seems to have immediately broken his rules by misnaming many knots. However, anyone using rope should be aware of these distinctions, while realizing that the names are rather loosely applied.

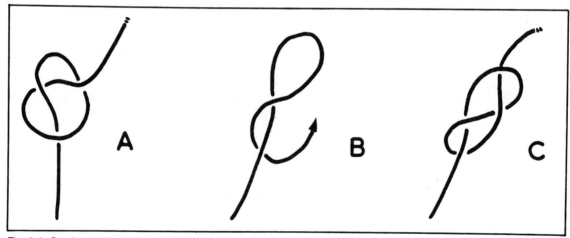

Fig. 3-6. Overhand (A) and figure-eight (B,C) stopper knots.

Anyone rigging a boat will usually do his knotting under leisurely conditions, but he should still be able to form the appropriate knots correctly and reasonably quickly. The knots that follow in this chapter are those that should be learned thoroughly. After learning the knot, try using it in its correct application on a boat. Try forming it in the dark or behind your back. A good way to be certain that you know how to make a knot is to work with a partner, using one hand each. Try using line from twine up to the largest rope on the boat. For learning knots, use rope rather than twine. If you are handling rope of about ½-inch diameter, you can see all the details in the knot.

Stopper Knots

Your first need is a knot near the end of a rope to prevent it running back through a block or hole or of slipping out of your hand. The usual choice is the simple *overhand knot* (Fig. 3-6A). It has many other names. Do not make it too near the end, particularly if it is a smooth rope, as it might work along and come apart. There is no need to form anything more complicated if this will produce enough bulk.

A slightly more bulky knot and one less likely to slide on smooth rope is the *figure-eight knot*. Start as if making an overhand knot, but take the end around to the other side (Fig. 3-6B) and into the loop that way (Fig. 3-6C). The figure-eight knot does not hold that shape once it is loaded, but bunches up to make a bigger stopper than the overhand knot.

Joining Knots

In everyday life many people think that if they master the reef knot, they are equipped to tie anything. In fact, this is not the general joining knot. There are a very large number of joining knots, but a small selection will serve all a rigger's needs.

If the two ropes are to be joined the knot to use is the *common bend*, which some users call a *sheet bend*. This can be used between ropes of the same or different thicknesses. When any ropes have to be joined end-to-end, this is nearly always the bend to use.

To form a common bend, turn back a *bight* (loop) on the end of one rope. Take the end of the other rope up through it (Fig. 3-7A), around the back of it (Fig. 3-7B), then across the front and under itself (Fig. 3-7C). Draw the knot tight by holding the sides of the bight in one hand and pulling the *standing part* (loaded part) of the other in line, with the other hand. There are two ways that the working end could go around the bight. Tests have shown that there is little difference in strength, whichever way is used. It is more usual to have the ends finish on opposite sides of the knot.

If the ropes are of different thicknesses, the thicker rope is the one bent into a bight and the thinner one is worked around it (Fig. 3-7D). If there is a considerable difference in the thickness of the ropes or the ropes are smooth or wet, it is better to use a *double sheet bend* (Fig. 3-8). It is made in the same way as a single sheet bend, but enough length of the thinner rope is left to go around again after completing the single knot (Fig. 3-7E). Sometimes, if diameters are very different, there can be further turns.

The knot is called a sheet bend from its use in attaching the sheet to a *cringle* (rope eye) in the corner of a square sail (Fig. 3-7F). In a similar way, it could be used to join the end of a line to an eye spliced in the end of another rope. This, or any of the normal versions, could be made quick-release by doubling back the working end (Fig. 3-7G). A pull on the end will then release the knot.

The *reef knot* or *square knot* is used for joining ropes of the same thickness, when the knot will be bearing against something. If the joined ropes will have the knot in mid-air, it should be a common bend. The name comes from the use of the knot in joining the ends of reef points on a sail, under the gathered-in canvas when the sail area is reduced by reefing. The knot is then bearing against something. (Another common application is in bandaging, when the knot comes against part of the body.)

To make a reef knot, twist the meeting ends together one way (Fig. 3-9A), then the other way (Fig. 3-9B), and pull tight. When correctly formed, at both sides of the knot the ends come alongside the standing parts. You can say "right over left and left over right" while learning, but it is better to

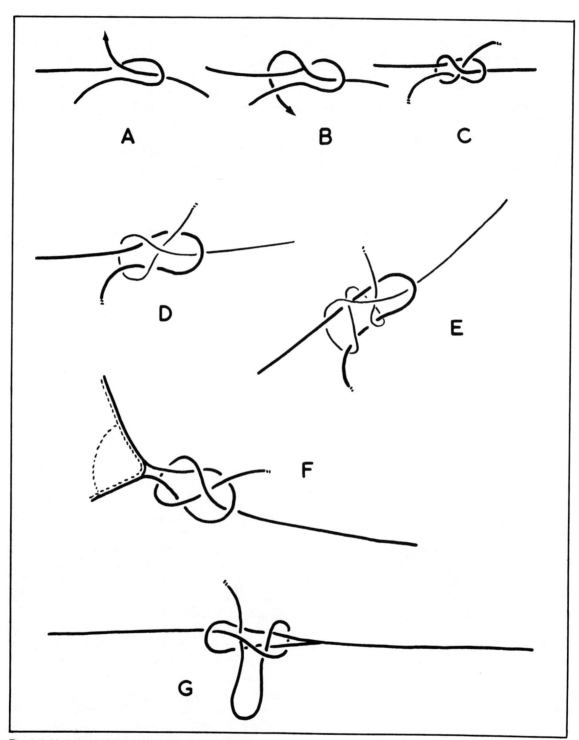

A   B   C

D

E

F

G

Fig. 3-7. Variations of the common or sheet bend.

36

Fig. 3-8. A double sheet bend, used for joining ropes of different thicknesses.

watch the twisting action and go the opposite way the second time.

If both twists are made the same way, the result is a *granny knot*, which tends to slip and has no place in boat ropework. The fault can be seen when you make one twist (Fig. 3-9C) and follow with exactly the same action (Fig. 3-9D). The ends finish pointing across the knot when it is tightened, instead of alongside the standing parts.

You can make a *slip reef* or a *reef bow* by turning back one or both ends to form bights as you make the second part of the knot (Fig. 3-9E). Pulling an end from a bight will release the knot.

Bowline

If there has to be a permanent loop in the end of a rope, an eye splice is used, but if you want to make a loop of any size by knotting, so it can be cast off

(undone) later, the only knot you need to know is the bowline. It helps to learn more than one way of making it. If a bowline is examined, the worked part will be seen to be the same as a common bend (Fig. 3-10).

For a first attempt, take enough of the rope's end to make a loop—a large one is less confusing than a small one. Twist a small eye where the top of the loop is to come (Fig. 3-11A). Arrange this so the part that continues into the loop is on top of the starting part. If twisted the other way, the subsequent actions are reversed. Bring the end up through the eye (Fig. 3-11B), but only pull through enough to form the knot. Hold the crossing of the eye in shape until after the tucking has been completed. Take the end around the standing part (Fig. 3-11C). Note the direction. Pass the end down through the eye so the end comes between the sides of the loop (Fig. 3-11D), not the other way.

Be careful to keep the knot in shape as you tighten it. Pull the standing part one way, while coaxing the sides of the loop and the end between them the other way.

That is how to make a bowline if you have the rope on the deck in front of you. If it is to be formed around your waist or a large solid object, there is a quick method. Make sure you have mastered the basic method before tackling this one. Put the rope around yourself or the object, with the end pointing upwards over the standing part (Fig. 3-11E). Pass the end around the standing part and outwards straight alongside the slack standing part. This will force the eye into the standing part with the end already through it (Fig. 3-11F). Go around the back of the standing part with the end and down through the eye to complete the knot (Fig. 3-11G). With

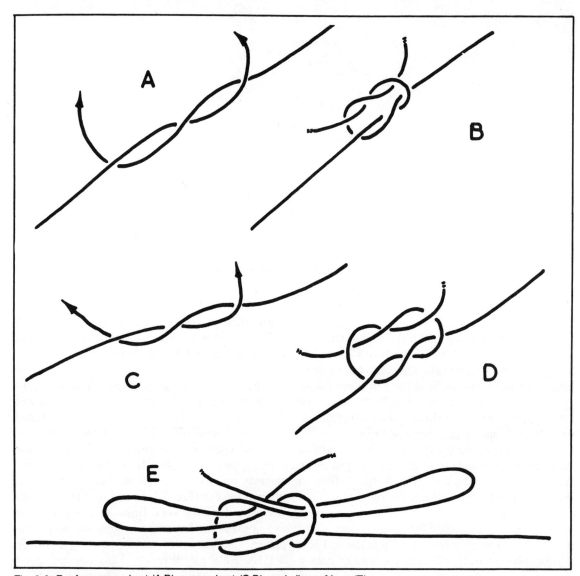

Fig. 3-9. Reef or square knot (A,B), granny knot (C,D), and slip reef bow (E).

Fig. 3-10. A bowline for making a loop in the end of a rope.

large rope, your hand may go around with the first twist of the end to force the eye into the standing part.

HITCHES

If you take a rope around a spar or hook once, that is a *half hitch* (Fig. 3-12A). If you continue around to completely encircle the spar, it is a *round turn* (Fig. 3-12B). In many hitches and knots to solid objects it is the friction of the turns against the hard surface that provides most of the strength of the attachment. If a stout rope is stretched and a lighter rope is to be attached to it, the thick rope may then be treated as a spar, but if there is slackness in the thick rope or there is not much difference in sizes, do not use this method between ropes.

The basic attachment is a *clove hitch* (Fig. 3-13), which is a jamming form of two half hitches. It is made without using the standing part. Put the rope over the spar with enough extending to make the hitch, then go around with the end and over the first turn (Fig. 3-14A). Continue the same way round the spar. When learning, it is easier to see what is happening if you go around some way from the first half hitch. As the end comes around the second time take it under its own standing part (Fig.

3-14B). Draw the hitch tight with the parts close together (Fig. 3-14C).

If the clove hitch is to go over the end of a spar, a bollard, or anything else where the end is accessible, the clove hitch can be made with loops and dropped over. Twist a loop in the standing part so the end comes under it (Fig. 3-14D). Hold this in shape and do the same above it (Fig. 3-14E). These are the two parts of the clove hitch, which can be put over the post or other solid end. If the rope is under strain, you can drop the first half hitch on and hold the load, while forming the second half hitch and pulling tight.

For most purposes it would be wrong to change direction as you make the half hitches, but if you do, go back with the second half hitch (Fig. 3-14F). The result is a *cow hitch* or *lark's head* (Fig. 3-14G). A cow hitch can be used when there will be a load on both ends at the same side of the spar or ring (Fig. 3-14H).

A clove hitch is really only satisfactory when there is a load on both ends towards opposite sides of the knot. It is often used as a temporary fastening for one end of a rope, but except for brief holding, it is better to use a *round turn and two half hitches*, which has never acquired a shorter name.

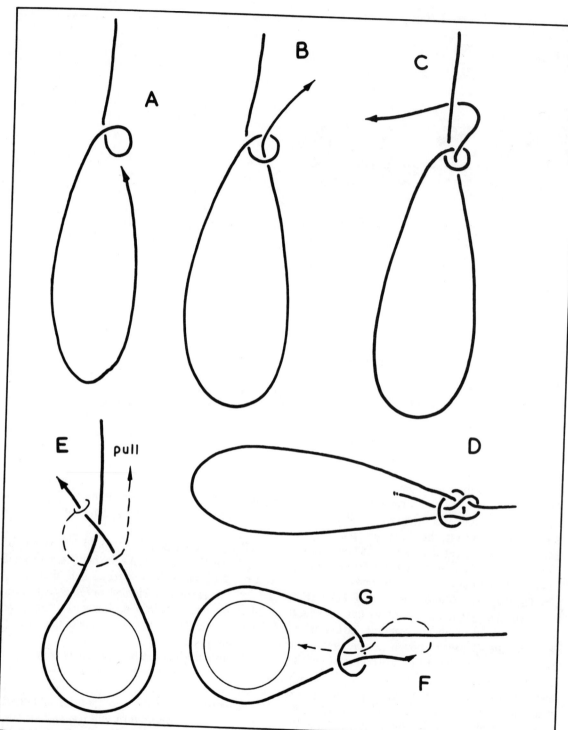

Fig. 3-11. Two ways of making a bowline.

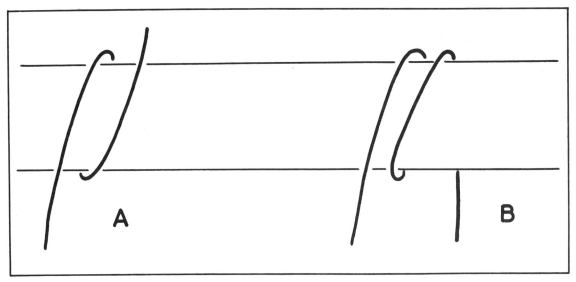

Fig. 3-12. A half hitch (A) and a round turn (B).

Fig. 3-13. A clove hitch for joining a rope to a spar or ring.

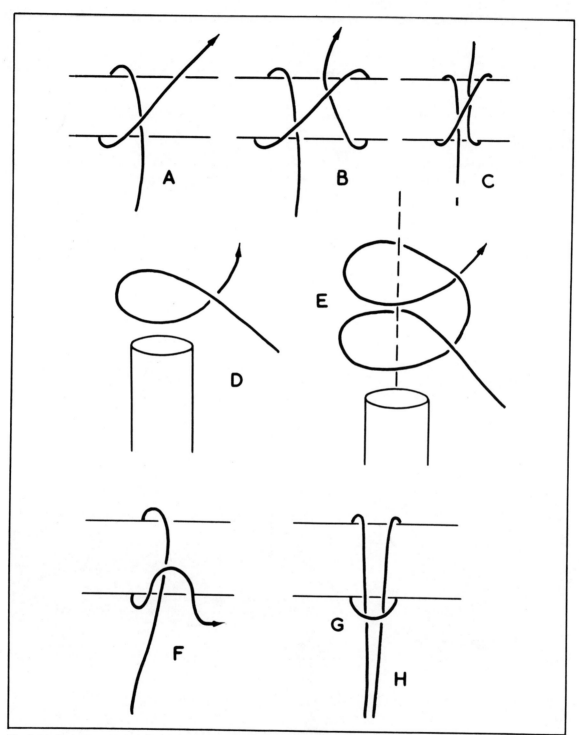

Fig. 3-14. Steps in making a clove hitch (A to E) and a lark's head (F,G,H).

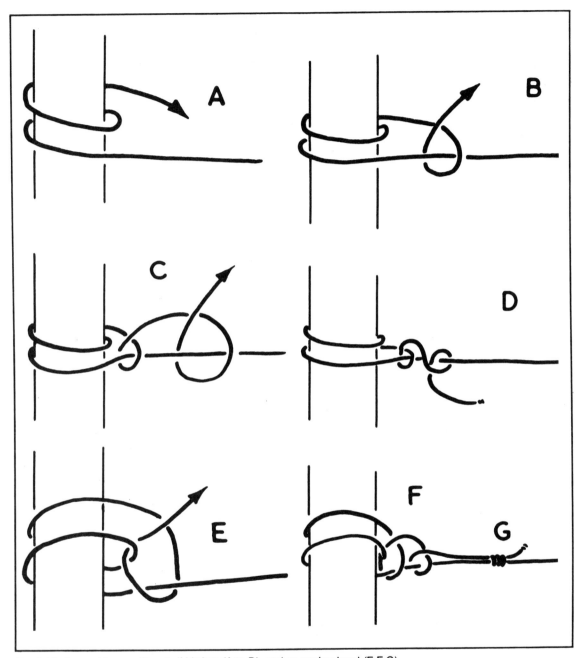

Fig. 3-15. A round turn and two half hitches (A to D), and an anchor bend (E,F,G).

Keep the standing part straight, then put on a round turn (Fig. 3-15A). With the end, put a half hitch around the taut standing part (Fig. 3-15B) and continue around it in the same way to make the second part of a clove hitch (Fig. 3-15C). Let the two half hitches slide along the standing part close to the round turn (Fig. 3-15D).

This is sometimes incorrectly called a *fisher-*

man's bend or an *anchor bend*. These are names of a variation used particularly for attaching a rope to the shackle of an anchor. For greater security in a place that is hidden when in use, the first half hitch is taken under the center of the round turn (Fig. 3-15E). With this part pulled tight, the second half hitch goes on in the usual way (Fig. 3-15F). When everything has been pulled tight, the free end may then be seized with light line, put on like a whipping (Fig. 3-15G).

The clove hitch and the other hitches described hold best when the load comes at about right-angles to the solid object. If the load comes along a spar or almost that way, they tend to slide and increased friction has to be provided. This can be done by making a *rolling hitch*, which is a clove hitch with an extra turn. Start as for a clove hitch, but go twice over the standing part (Fig. 3-16A). Continue around the same way and put on a half hitch (Fig. 3-16B). The loaded part should be the one covered by two turns. Be careful not to assemble the knot the other way.

The complete rolling hitch can be used as it is for a temporary attachment, but if it is to take a load

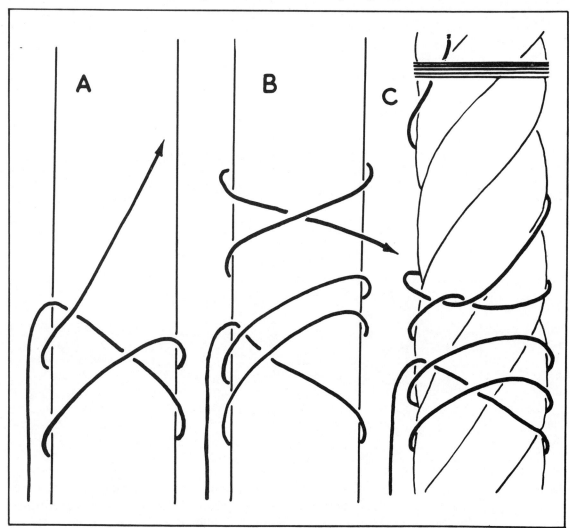

Fig. 3-16. Steps in making a rolling hitch.

for long, it is improved by taking the end further along the spar and seizing it. If a thick rope is used in place of a spar, follow around the lay (Fig. 3-16C).

TIGHTENING KNOTS

There are many occasions when parts have to be pulled together or some extra strain applied. There are many knots that will do this, but the following few should serve all rigging purposes. For a simple slip knot the standing part can be taken through the loop of a bowline to form a *running bowline* (Fig. 3-17A).

A *figure-eight slip knot* may also be called a *packer's knot* and it is well-known to those who have to tie parcels. It is useful in light line on a boat where parts have to be pulled together and held. With the line around the load, make a figure-eight knot around the standing part, in such a direction that the end stands upwards (Fig. 3-17B). Pull the bundle tight with the standing part. When you have got the tension you require, make a half hitch over the standing end of the figure-eight knot (Fig. 3-17C) to lock the knot.

Another simple slip knot is a *timber hitch*. Its name shows that it originated as a means of putting a rope around a log or tree, but it has many other applications. Take the end around the standing part, which is looped around the load (Fig. 3-17D) then twist it back on itself. Three times is usually enough (Fig. 3-17E). You can then pull a bundle of spars together or the hitch can be used for attaching the end of a rope to a post, particularly if it is a rough one with bark on it. If a spar or log is to be lifted or drawn through the water, put on a timber hitch some way from the end, then put a half hitch in the standing part over the spar near the end to keep the pull straight.

There is a development of the timber hitch called a *killick bend*. "Killick" is an old name for an anchor. Its particular use is in attaching a rope cable to a heavy rock, which is being used as a temporary anchor. Make the timber hitch, then put on a half hitch close beside it (Fig. 3-17F).

If you want to provide a handgrip while pulling on twine or other light line, there is the *marline-spike hitch*. It is not intended to be a permanent fastening. With thin flexible line and a pointed tool, twist the line with the point (Fig. 3-18A). Turn this into a loop (Fig. 3-18B) and pull the spike back far enough to allow you to pick up one part (Fig. 3-18C). Push the spike back across so as to trap that part to one side of the loop (Fig. 3-18D). Another way of forming the hitch is to start to make an overhand knot, but do not pull the working part through. Instead, push a spike or piece of wood across to trap it, getting the same result as in the other method.

Arrange the hitch so the pull you put on it comes against the twisted part of the hitch (Fig. 3-18E). If you pull the other way, the hitch will tend to open. The marlinespike hitch can also be used with a lever. It is then called a *lever hitch*. Form the hitch as before, but push a rod or pole through it. Hold the free end of the rope in one hand while levering the pole with the other (Fig. 3-18F).

The *constrictor knot* does not have a square-rigger history, but is supposed to have come from tying mailbags. It will pull tight as a temporary whipping or seizing, or it will hold the neck of a bag or a bundle of canvas close. It is most suitable for light disposable twine as it will usually have to be cut to release it.

The constrictor knot is really a thumb knot with another turn over it. Put a complete round turn loosely around whatever is to be secured. Twist the two ends together, while the outer part of the round turn is pushed aside (Fig. 3-19A). Draw this tight and arrange the outer turn to come over the twist of the knot as you put on the final tightening (Fig. 3-19B).

Much tightening during rigging a boat is done with blocks and tackle, screwed fasteners such as *turnbuckles*, and other mechanical devices. There is one way of getting a temporary purchase that can be arranged without any equipment other than the rope concerned. This is a *waggoner's hitch*. It gets its name from its use in tightening ropes over a load on a waggon or truck. It gives a theoretical advantage of two to one, but because of friction, the result will be rather less than this, depending on the smoothness of the rope.

Double back an S shape in the rope some way

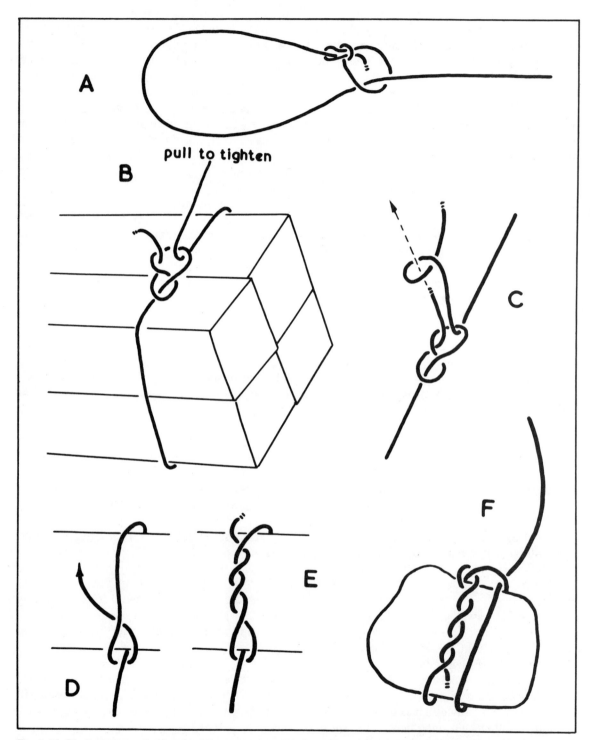

pull to tighten

Fig. 3-17. Slip knots: a running bowline (A), packer's knot (B,C), a timber hitch (D,E), and a killick bend (F).

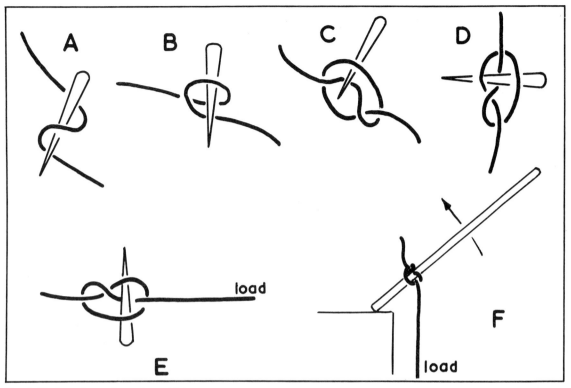

Fig. 3-18. A marline spike or lever hitch.

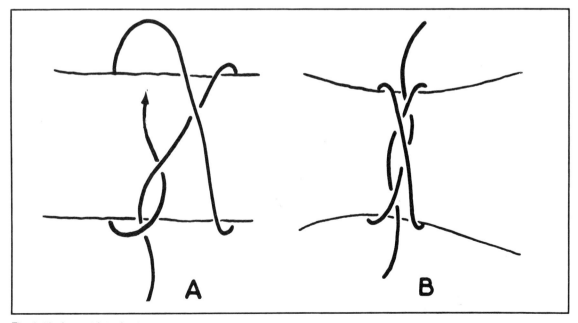

Fig. 3-19. A constrictor knot.

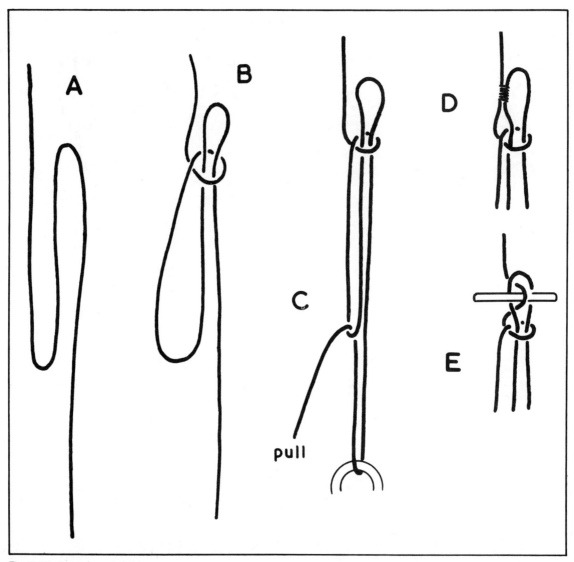

Fig. 3-20. A waggoner's hitch.

from the end (Fig. 3-20A). With the standing part, put a half hitch over the bight (Fig. 3-20B). Bring the end up through the other bight, after going around the hook or other securing point, and pull down on this to tighten (Fig. 3-20C). With very slippery rope, you could seize the upper loop to the standing part (Fig. 3-20D) or, for a temporary arrangement, put a piece of wood across (Fig. 3-20E).

It is worthwhile mastering all the knots de-scribed in this chapter. They are the basic ones with many applications in rigging. Other more spe-cialized knots are described where they apply in later chapters. Some are developments of the ones described here. Anyone who claims to have rigging skills should be adept at all the knots involved in his work. If you want to learn more about knotting, you will find a large number described in the author's *Practical Knots & Ropework* (TAB book No. 1237).

Chapter 4

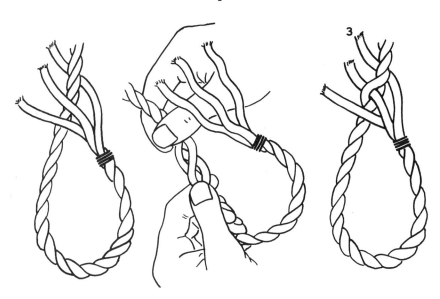

Fiber Rope Splicing

A SPLICE IS MORE PERMANENT THAN A KNOT. IN most cases it cannot be taken apart and even if it can, the rope will be left in an unsatisfactory condition. Splices are neater than knots and generally stronger. If a temporary loop is needed in the end of a three-strand rope, it is correct to use a bowline, which will have a strength about 80 percent of the rope. If the loop is to be permanent, an eye splice is the correct choice and this has a strength about 90 percent of the rope.

A rigger has to make up the parts of rigging in permanent form and many of the ropes used need an eye at one or both ends. Compared with a knotted loop the splice is smoother and has no projecting lumps, so it will pull closer into a sheave or fairlead and is more satisfactory to handle. On many sailing boats the only splice needed is the eye splice. There are a large number of other splices shown in comprehensive knotting books, but many of them are of little use to the rigger of modern boats.

A complication has been the introduction of braided synthetic ropes. Most traditional splic-

ing has been done in three-strand rope. Although braided natural fiber rope was available, its construction did not suit splicing. Some modern braided rope can be spliced, as described later in this chapter. However, most splicing to be done is in three-strand synthetic ropes, laid up right-handed. If an eye splice in this rope is mastered, other splices will be more easily understood and tackled.

Splicing differs from knotting in using the strands of the rope to tuck into each other to provide security and strength. This means the rope has to be opened. How this is done depends on the particular rope. With soft, loosely-laid rope it is possible to hold it in both hands with the part to be opened between them. Twisting your hands in opposite directions will untwist the rope so the strands come apart. Most rope is too tightly laid to do this and a tool has to be used.

The splicing tool is a *spike*. For small ropes it could be any pointed metal object, such as an ice pick. The correct tool is a *marlinespike*, which may be a simple tapered piece of steel, possibly with a hole in the thick end to take a lanyard, or it may be part of a clasp knife. Both are valuable, but a separate marlinespike, with its own section in a knife sheath, is of more use if much rigging has to be done. There are also handled, hollowed spikes, which allow the strand being tucked to slide along the spike. Most riggers use a plain round steel marlinespike (Fig. 4-1).

Larger spikes are called *fids* and are made of hard wood. Wood is easier on the rope fibers and is preferable for larger ropes. For very large ropes it may be necessary to drive the fid through with a hammer or mallet. It is usual to taper the end of a spike or fid to a round point, but some riggers prefer to have a narrow flat end, something like a small screwdriver with rounded corners, so it can be pushed between strands and turned to open the gap a little more. It is possible to use a screwdriver as a spike, but it must not have any sharp corners. The advantage is in being able to get it into tightly laid rope, so it can be turned edgewise to force open a gap, possibly to allow a normal spike to be thrust in.

The only other essential tool is a sharp knife, probably in addition to the general-purpose one used for cutting rope. It is used for scraping away fibers, so it needs a razor-sharp edge. A razor blade in a holder could be used. Very thick rope may be cut with a hatchet or a fine saw, but most boat ropes can be cut with a knife. A pair of pliers may be needed to pull through a stubborn strand. They will be needed for wire rope in any case.

Strands have to be unlaid for tucking. There should be some extra length allowed for handling besides the actual length estimated to go in the tucks. You cannot bring a splice to a satisfactory neat finish if there are no projecting ends to grip. Expect to waste a small amount of rope. Experience will show how much to allow, but as a guide, about 8 inches should be allowed on rope up to ½-inch thick.

Some natural fiber three-strand rope can be unlaid as far as required and it will stay as you want it without restraint, but synthetic rope would con-

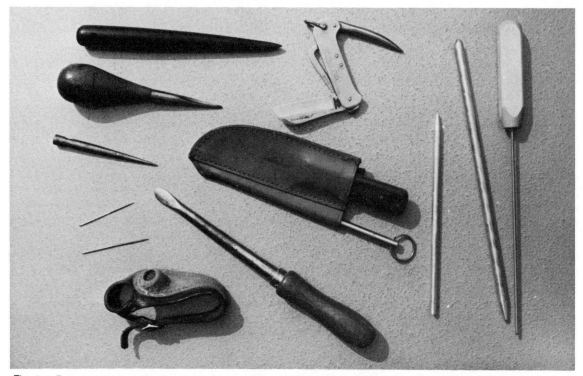

Fig. 4-1. Ropeworking tools: spikes and knives, a leather palm and sail needles, tools for splicing braided rope.

tinue to unlay, both in the fibers making up the strands and the strands making up the rope, if nothing is done to restrain them. If the rope end was sealed by heat when it was cut, measure back from the end as far as you intend to unlay and put on a temporary seizing with twine. It could be a constrictor knot or a few turns of a West Country whipping. This stays in place during tucking, but is cut off when the splice has been finished. The end of each strand must be fused. If you separate the strand ends, you may find they are thick from the first sealing as the rope was cut. If left in this way there could be difficulty in tucking, so reheat each strand end and roll it so a rounded end no thicker than the rest of the strand is produced.

See that the fibers in the strands keep their shape and the rope is not allowed to partly open below the seizing. Synthetics will unwind if allowed the slightest amount of freedom.

EYE SPLICE

This is by far the most used splice in three-strand rope. When completed there is an eye formed in the end of the rope, with the strands of the rope end tucked back neatly into their standing parts below the eye. The eye could be a free loop of any size or it might be closed around a metal or plastic thimble or some other item, such as a toggle. Except for the need for an exact size when fitting the rope around something, the method of working is the same.

Prepare the end of the rope and bend it into an eye of the size required. For a practice eye, do not make the loop too small. Arrange the open end strands so they point across the lay of the standing part of the rope, with two ends at the front and the other one behind (Fig. 4-2A). This first assembly is important. Be careful not to put the parts together the other way around, with the two strands pointing the same way as the lay. There is another splice started that way, but it is not one for use in rigging. Regard the side with two ends crossing as the front.

Open a space between strands by twisting a soft rope (Fig. 4-2B) or by lifting one strand at the front with a spike. With many ropes it is possible to withdraw the spike and insert the tucking strand before the gap closes. Otherwise it is necessary to

push the spike in far enough to allow the strand to go through the gap alongside it. It is the central end strand that goes under one strand of the rope (Fig. 4-2C). There is no need to pull much through at this stage. Note where the end comes out. The other front end strand has to go in where that end comes out and pass under the next main strand. Notice that it goes in on the side of the first tuck towards the loop (Fig. 4-2D). Do not tuck it the other side of the first tucked strand.

There are now two end strands under two main strands, so there must be a main strand without anything tucked under it. Turn the splice over and locate this main strand. Lift that main strand and tuck the remaining end so it goes in across the lay (Fig. 4-2E) in the same direction around the rope as the other end strands. A common fault when learning is to tuck the third strand the wrong way.

If tucking has been done correctly there will now be one end strand projecting from each space between strands in the standing part (Fig. 4-2F). Pull through in turn until all of the ends have been brought up with the same tension and the temporary seizing is close to the standing part. Adjust the positions of the ends so they all come out on the same level around the rope. Satisfy yourself about tension and level before moving on to the next stage or you may find difficulty in completing the splice tightly and neatly.

Further splicing consists of tucking each end in turn "over and under one." Lift a main strand on the side of the first tucks away from the eye and tuck the appropriate end strand over the adjoining main strand and under it (Fig. 4-2G). Move around to the next space and tuck there with the next end. Try to go in at about the same level as you tuck this and the third end strand. Keep the tucks as close to the first tucks as possible. It is very easy to tuck so the ends are almost pointing straight along the rope. That is wrong. They should go around the rope at about the same angle as the lay of the rope, but in the opposite direction. As you complete the second round of tucks by pulling the ends tight, press them close to the first round.

Make a third round of tucks in the same way, so each end now goes over and under three main

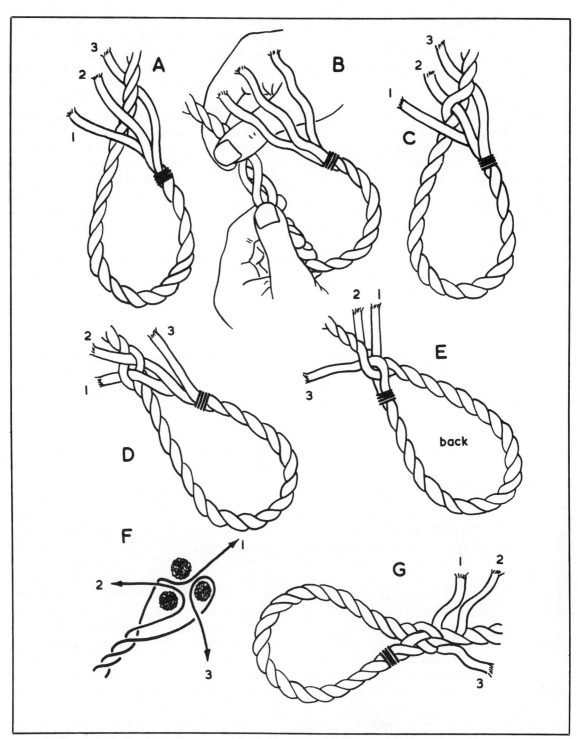

Fig. 4-2. Steps in tucking an eye splice.

strands in turn (Fig. 4-3). In most natural fiber ropes that will be sufficient, but with the more slippery synthetic ropes it is advisable to tuck once or twice more. All of these tucks with the full thickness of end strands are called *whole tucks*.

Sometimes a splice is left with just the whole tucks, but for neatness it is usual to make a *taper tuck*, or sometimes two taper tucks. This is done with thinned strands. Scrape away some of the fibers in each strand with a knife. Do this mostly on what will be inside the strand when tucked. Remove fibers at different levels to produce the taper so when another tuck is made, only about half the thickness will be nipped under the next main strand in each case. Tuck all three tapered ends as tightly as possible. Besides giving a neater appearance to the splice, tapering also provides strength. It is an engineering principle that an abrupt change of section is a weak point, so the taper avoids that.

Cut off any surplus ends that are left, but do not cut too close. Natural fibers may be left as cut, but if it is a very hairy rope there may be many long fibers projecting around the splice. They can be cut or burned off with a flame. Where you cut the ends of synthetic strands they can be fused by careful work with a flame, but be careful not to melt any part of the spliced rope.

Even with careful tightening the tucked part may not be very smooth. Older books tell you to roll the splice underfoot. That may have been satisfactory for a seaman who had not been ashore and was probably in bare feet on a wood deck, but it is inadvisable under most circumstances as grit could be forced into the rope and this would do damage. It would be better to roll the splice between two boards.

A splice will settle down after it has been under load. Tucked strands may pull back slightly. It is unusual to do anything to a splice to cover it, but sometimes the cut ends are covered with a seizing, put on like a whipping. If that is to be done, give the splice a good stretch first and put the seizing on when you have the rope stretched between two supports. Wax both the rope and seizing twine as

Fig. 4-3. An eye splice in three-strand rope, with the ends tucked three times.

Fig. 4-4. An eye splice around a thimble, with the end strands tucked once.

you do the work. Adhesive tape is sometimes put on instead of a seizing, but that may not be considered very seamanlike.

Eye Splice on a Thimble

If the eye has to fit very closely around a solid object, the method of splicing only differs in the need to make the first round of tucks in the right place for the splice to draw up tight. The most common application in rigging is in enclosing a thimble in the splice. This relieves the rope of wear if it is attached to a shackle or other hard object. It also strengthens the rope by keeping the end of the loop in a good curve. If an unprotected end of an eye is pulled around something small, like the pin of a shackle, the rope is forced to a tight curve, which could weaken or break some of the fibers within the bend. When preparing rigging, it is always advisable to include a thimble anywhere that it would be acceptable.

Prepare the rope as for a free eye. Wrap it around the thimble with the temporary seizing brought close to the standing part of the rope. Tuck the central front strand under the nearest convenient main strand close to the thimble. If the splice is large enough, the main strand can be lifted in position and the end tucked, but if it is a small splice or the object has deep grooves, note where the end strand will have to go and take the thimble out so the end is more easily tucked. Try the assembly with that end strand pulled close. If the fit is reasonable, continue tucking the other end strands. If the fit is not as you want it, the solitary tucked strand can be slid further away or closer before the other end strands are tucked. Adjustment after more ends are tucked is not so easy.

All three end strands can be tucked loosely without the thimble in place. See that they all project in the same plane around the rope, as described for the open splice. Draw them tight around the thimble (Fig. 4-4). If the fit is satisfactory, cut away the temporary seizing and draw up the ends in turn as tightly as possible. From this point, tuck each end strand over and under one main strand in turn, as already described. Continue to complete the splice in the same way.

An interesting application of the eye splice in both forms is in the making of a *toggle line* (Fig. 4-5), where the open eye is made of a size to slip over the toggle endwise and the whole thing is useful for securing a coil of rope or a rolled sail.

Eye Splice with Collar

Any normal eye splice is thick below the eye and may taper to the normal thickness of the rope. For many purposes this is satisfactory, but if the eye has to be drawn as closely as possible to a block or fairlead there is an advantage in keeping the normal size of rope as close to the eye as possible, so there is no risk of the thicker part jamming through a restricted opening. This means that there has to be an alternative to the normal tucks along the rope, while keeping sufficient strength in the splice. Working a collar around the rope with the end strands will have this effect and provide decoration as well. The strength should be about the same as a normal splice.

Allow rather more length of unlaid ends than you would for a normal splice, so you have enough for handling. Start by tucking in the normal way for one round. Pull tight and make sure all the ends project on the same level around the rope. From this stage you have to make a decorative collar knot around the rope with the three end strands. There are some alternatives, but the one described is a *manrope knot*, which is at least as easy to make as any of the others.

Take each end under its neighbor and up through the loop formed (Fig. 4-6A), going around the rope to the right. This formation is called a *wall knot*. Note that the ends finish pointing upwards. Draw the parts moderately tight and even, then continue above it to make a *crown knot* going around the same way, but this time passing the ends down through the loops (Fig. 4-6B). Draw this to the same tension as the wall knot, so the crown is resting on the wall, with the ends angled downwards.

Each end will be alongside a turn of the wall knot. Tuck each end against its turn of the wall knot. This will bring it pointing up towards a turn of the crown knot. Tuck there as well. The result will bring the two knots together with doubled strands, so as they are tightened they look like a continuous three-plait or a Turk's head around the rope. Use the point of a spike to draw up the slack until the surplus can be pulled up by the ends. Do this a little at a time until the final collar shows parallel strands all around. When you have all the parts as tight as possible, cut off the ends (Fig. 4-6C).

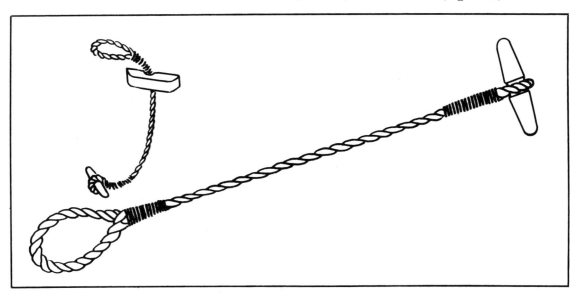

Fig. 4-5. Toggle rope made with eye splices.

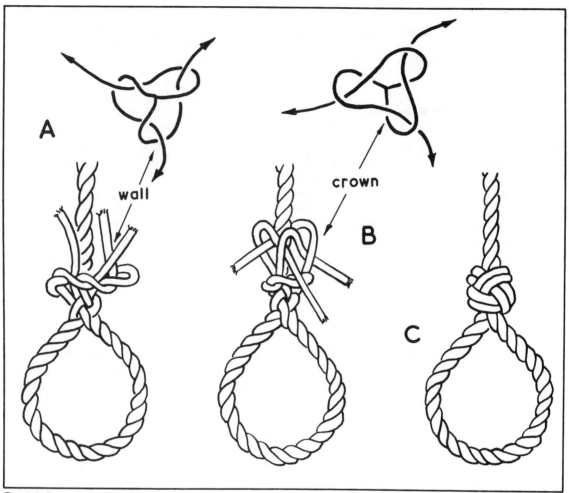

Fig. 4-6. Eye splice with collar.

Eye Splice Variations

The method of making tucks in an eye splice can be adapted to other requirements. A fork can be made by joining the end of one rope into the side of another. This is called a *branch splice* (Fig. 4-7A). What you are doing is making an eye splice, except the two parts of the fork are not part of the same length of rope.

A loop can be put in a rope by using a *cut splice*. The two ends overlap by the amount to make the loop, then the ends are tucked into the opposing standing parts in the same way as making the tucks of an eye splice (Fig. 4-7B). This is useful where a loop is needed to slip over a spar, with ends going away from opposite sides. For most purposes the sides of the loop are the same, but they do not have to be. There could be more at one side and this may be called a *horseshoe splice*. That form might be better for a rope used to fit over and restrain a tiller.

A loop put into the side of a rope is called a *cringle*. There are ways of making it by working around with a single strand, but the strongest joints are made by tucking in the same way as for an eye splice (Fig. 4-7C).

DOUBLE-ENDED SPLICING

The looped splices just described are mainly suitable for applications where the ends have to project towards opposite sides. If the two parts have to come in about the same direction, the eye is better made in a different way. An example is in the double sheets needed for a foresail.

With three-strand rope there is a quick way of making such an eye, which may be called a *brummel*

eye or a *guy-line hitch,* from its use in joining ropes to tents. Lift one strand near the eye and pass the other side of the rope through the gap. Do the same a little further along with the part that has just gone through (Fig. 4-8A). It is possible to do this with braided rope that is not too tightly made. Push a

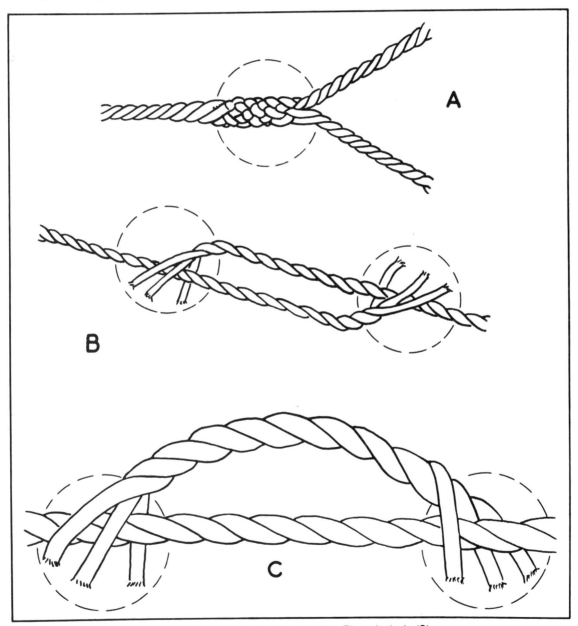

Fig. 4-7. Variations on eye splice tucking: branch splice (A), cut splice (B), and cringle (C).

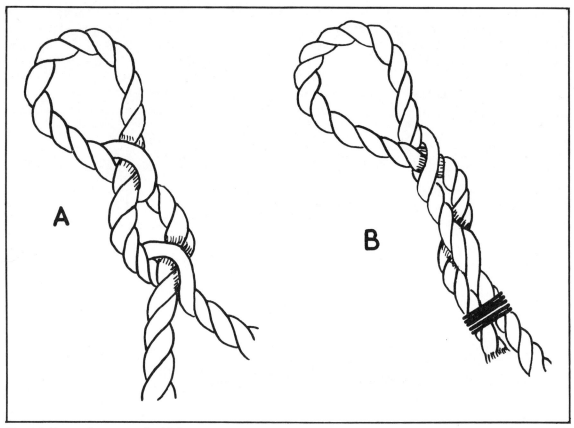

Fig. 4-8. Brummel eye or guyline hitch.

spike through the center each time to make a hole large enough for the other part.

The two parts may be brought close together to lock the splice and they can be covered with a seizing to give a neat appearance. A variation is sometimes used to make a quick eye in the end of a rope. For the best results the main part is passed through what will be the end, far enough back for that to be tucked, then the end is passed through the main part. Sometimes the splice is made by tucking the end twice through the standing part. That is not as strong and it is advisable to seize the end to the standing part (Fig. 4-8B).

Where a central eye is needed in braided rope, particularly for such purposes as a foresail sheet that may have to be shackled to the sail, a thimble has to be enclosed and the rope may be unsuitable for opening to push opposite parts through. In that case it is better to seize the two parts together.

There are two possible seizings. A round seizing should be satisfactory for the sheets of small craft, but for larger boats it is better to use a *racking seizing*.

For a round seizing use waxed twine. Make a slip knot around the parts of the rope. This could be done with a figure-eight knot (Fig. 4-9A). Continue to wrap around tightly. With a thimble to enclose it is best to work towards the eye, but leave room to get on somewhere between ten and fifteen turns. (Fig. 4-9B). This is a situation where a marline-spike hitch should be made to provide a stronger pull every two or three turns. A single set of turns would only be strong enough for a light application. Put a half hitch around one part of the rope to hold the turns, then go back over them with a second layer. Do not overtighten the second layer or parts

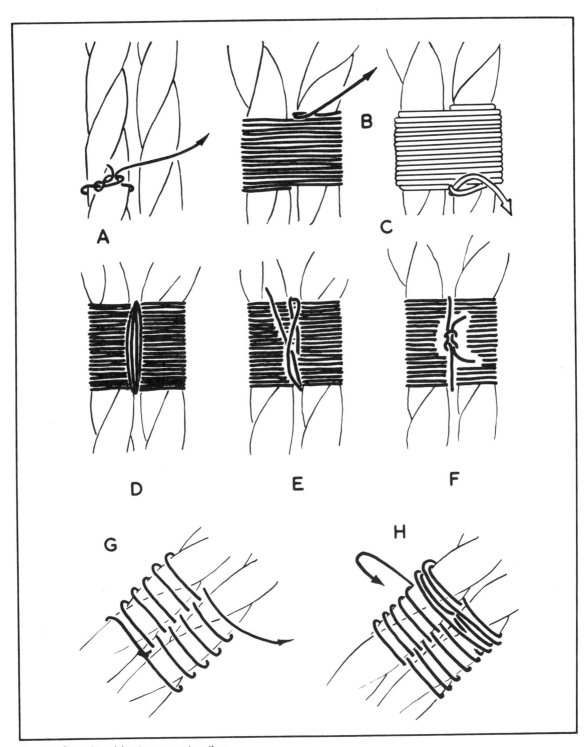

Fig. 4-9. Steps in seizing two ropes together.

of it may pull down into the first turns. When you get back to the start, put a half hitch over one part of the rope to hold the turns (Fig. 4-9C).

The seizing is further tightened by putting on *frapping turns* (Fig. 4-9D) lengthwise between the parts of the rope. Get these turns tight as you progress, using the marlinespike hitch to apply strain. You may have to use a needle to pass the end through close to a thimble. It is possible to put on the last two frapping turns in the form of two jamming half hitches, forming a clove hitch over the round turns (Fig. 4-9E). That is not enough to completely lock the turns, but one way of final locking is to make a clove hitch with the end through them after taking a turn around the nearest part of the rope. Another way is to leave a length of the original end projecting from the first slip knot and bring this up over the frapping turns to tie with a reef knot to the final end (Fig. 4-9F).

A racking seizing differs from the round seizing in the way the first turns are put on. Start in the same way with a slip knot, but then work the line in a figure-eight fashion around the opposite parts of the rope (Fig. 4-9G). This is shown open for clarity, but in fact make the turns close together. Get the turns on with moderate tightness, then use the point of a spike to pull more tension progressively along the turns. Go back over the first layer with another layer of turns put on like a round seizing. This time there are gaps due to the figure-eight formation and the second turns may fit into them (Fig. 4-9H). Finally, put on frapping turns in the same way as completing a round seizing, so externally it is not easy to see which seizing has been used.

BRAIDED ROPE SPLICES

Rope with a plaited or woven pattern on the outside casing is convenient to use on a boat and it is pleasant to handle, but it presents problems in splicing. Some of it cannot be spliced and the only way of dealing with the need for an eye is to bend the rope back into a loop and seize the parts together.

One improvement on a simple seizing is to sew the parts of the rope together first. This might be called a *Flemish eye*, but it does not have much in common with the old-time splice of that name. Bend back enough to form the eye and a length of end to go alongside the standing part—how much depends on circumstances. There could be a length equal to about ten times the diameter kept full section, and a further length of half as much again that is opened into straight fibers that can be scraped to a taper (Fig. 4-10A). Draw the neck of the eye together tightly. Go one way with large stitches and come back over them with more (Fig. 4-10B). Spread the tapered ends of the fibers around the standing part and half hitch with twine over them. Tension the rope so the parts settle down, then go all over the joint with a tight *serving* (Fig. 4-10C). Put this on like a long seizing, using a marlinespike hitch at intervals to apply plenty of strain. It may help to hold the turns to make half hitches at intervals. For large ropes and stouter serving line it will help to use a *serving mallet*, which may be just a grooved board with the line taken around it (Fig. 4-10D). The leverage with this can be considerable and care is needed to put on enough strain, yet not so much that you break the line.

THREE-STRAND CORE SPLICE

If some braided rope is examined it will be found to have the braided casing around a three-strand rope core. This type of rope is usually soft and flexible, so it is possible to work the casing back from the end far enough for a small eye to be spliced in the core. Some of the casing may have to be cut away, but no more should be removed than is necessary. It is better to push back all you can.

Prepare the three-strand core for splicing in the usual way (Fig. 4-11). Make the splice with the normal tucks, but taper the strands slightly after the first tucks, so the whole splice has more taper than usual. Work the casing back over the completed splice so it covers the tucks, then put a short seizing over its end close up to the eye.

DOUBLE-BRAID ROPE SPLICES

Most braided ropes used on pleasure boats are actually a form of double braid, with one tube of plaited construction inside another. The whole

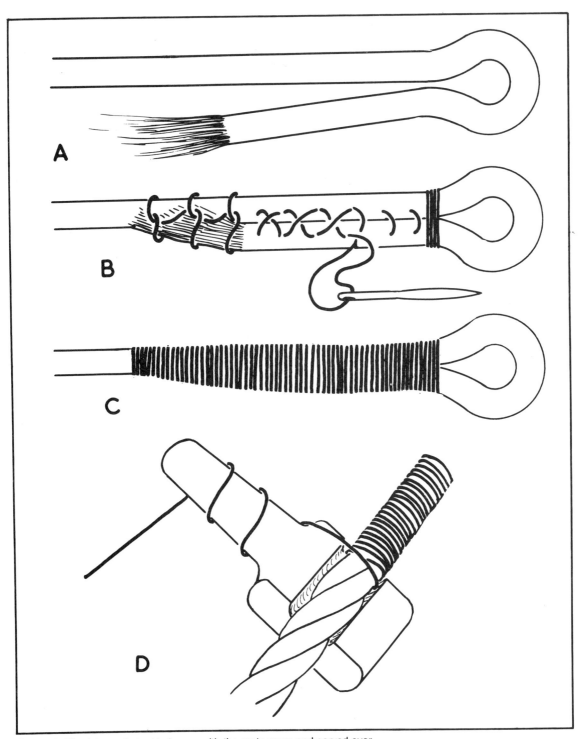

A

B

C

D

Fig. 4-10. Flemish eye in braided rope, with the parts sewn and served over.

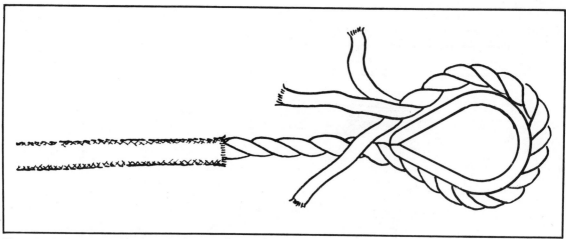

Fig. 4-11. Three-strand core braided rope prepared for an eye splice.

thing is fairly loose and flexible and this form permits a different type of splicing. The instructions for splicing that follow are based on information provided by the Samson Cordage Company of Boston, Massachusetts.

The spike and knife needed for ordinary splicing will have uses, but there are other tools needed for these special splices. One is a special fid (Fig. 4-12), which is metal, with a hollowed end into which rope can be pushed. A marking on the fid is used to indicate lengths on the splice. Different sizes are needed, according to the rope diameter (see the key to Fig. 4-12). As the fid has to go into and through the rope, there needs to be pusher, that is just a handled rod that will fit into the hollowed end of the fid alongside the piece of rope. Metal rod

less than 3/16-inch diameter will suit all sizes of fid. For temporary seizings while splicing this rope, adhesive tape can be used. There has to be some marking of the rope and a wax pencil is convenient for doing this.

There are several splices possible with double braided rope, but only the eye splice is likely to be needed. End-to-end splices are rarely needed, but there is a need, in rigging, to to able to join this type of rope to wire rope. That splice is included in the next chapter.

SAMSON EYE SPLICE

This is the eye splice recommended by the makers of double braided synthetic rope. The actual construction of the splice is difficult to visualize. The

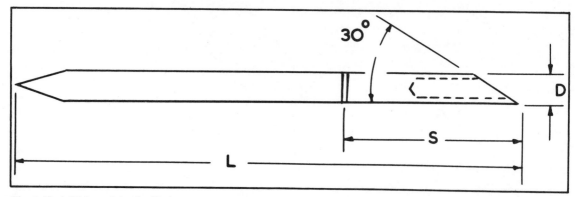

Fig. 4-12. A fid for splicing braided rope.

Table 4-1. Fid and Rope Sizes.

Rope diameter	Fid diameter (D)	Fid length (L)	Short section (S)
¼	7/32	5½	2 1/16
5/16	¼	6¾	2½
⅜	5/16	7¾	2⅞
7/16	⅜	9½	3 9/16
½	7/16	11	4⅛
9/16	½	12¼	4¼
⅝	9/16	14	4½
¾	11/16	16	4¾
⅞	13/16	19	5
1	15/16	21	5¼

sheath goes around the eye one way and the core goes around the other way, then the ends are buried inside each other in the body of the rope. The result is a strong neat splice that has all its construction hidden. A marked fid of the appropriate size is essential to make the splice. See Table 4-1.

Prepare the rope by marking distances with the fid. Put a mark one fid length from the end, then allow the amount needed for the eye and make another mark. From this go about five fid lengths and make a temporary slip knot, put there to restrict movement of the casing, which should not be allowed to slide too much (Fig. 4-13A). At the second mark on the casing, open the weave of the outer casing and extract the core from there to the end (Fig. 4-14). Smooth the cover from near the knot to check that there has not been any slipping. Slide the cover back from this point about one-third of the fid length and make a mark on the core. Make more marks from it along the core at a distance equal to one fid and its short section, then another short section (Fig. 4-13B).

Push the fid into the core at mark 2 and pass it through with the aid of the pusher so it just emerges at mark 3. Bunching the core casing on the fid helps in getting it through. Put the end of the outer casing in the hole in the fid and jam the end of the pusher into it (Fig. 4-15). Push the fid and the outer cover

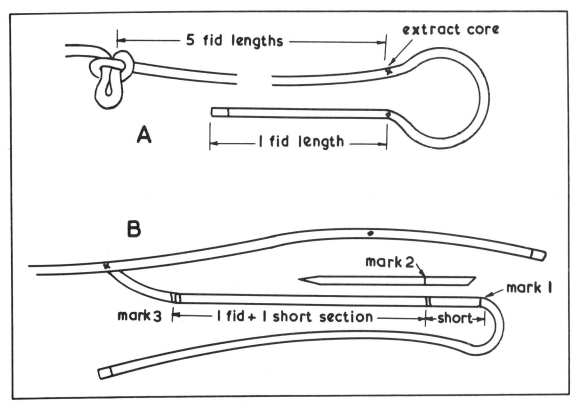

Fig. 4-13. First steps in making a samson eye splice.

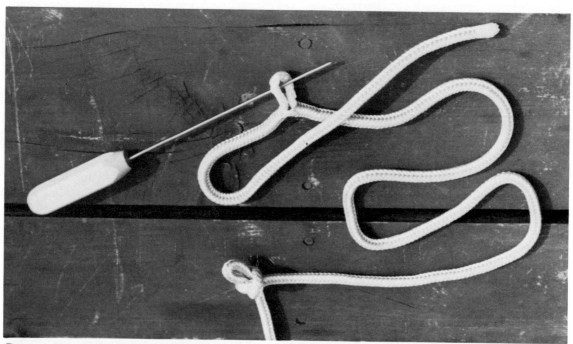

Fig. 4-14. Extracting the core is the first step in making an eye splice in double-braided rope.

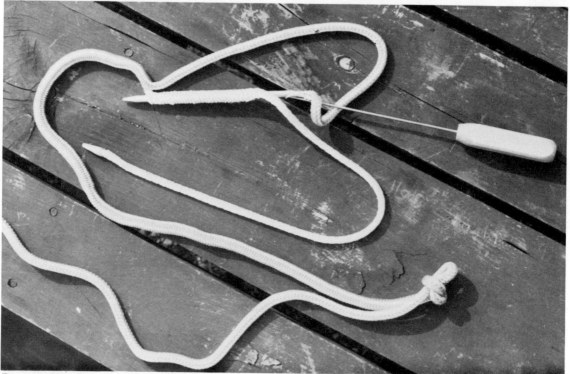

Fig. 4-15. The cover, fitted into the fid, is passed through the core of a double-braided rope with a pusher.

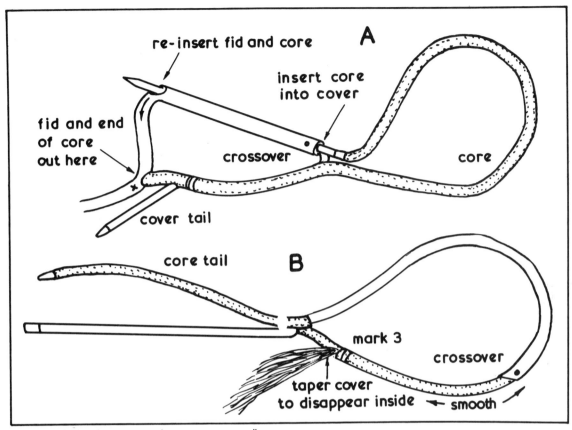

Fig. 4-16. Making the crossover in a samson eye splice.

through until the first mark on the outer cover almost disappears into the core. Remove the tools and leave the end projecting.

The next step is to push the core through the cover. Enter the point of the fid at the first mark in the cover and push it through to emerge at the mark indicating where the end of the eye is to be. If the eye will be quite a large loop, and much further around than the length of the fid, take the fid and its following core out through the casing at any convenient point. Pull this much through and re-insert the fid in the same place to push it on a further stage (Fig. 4-16A). Pull the core end through until it is tight and stroke the casing to get its tension right, with the crossover tight in both directions.

You now have to make the end of the cover disappear inside the loops. Unlay a short distance and cut the yarns to different lengths to get a ta-pered end (Fig. 4-16B). Smooth both sides of the loop away from the crossover and these tapered covered ends will disappear into the rope at mark 3 (Fig. 4-17).

The cover has to be drawn over the core and crossover. Hold the rope tightly at the knot and *milk* the cover by gripping and stroking away from the knot (Fig. 4-18). This action will cause the cover to move around the loop. Continue doing this until the whole eye is enclosed in the cover. Smooth the eye towards the core tail. Cut that off reasonably close to the cover, but there may be a short piece left. Pull at the top of the eye and the end should disappear into the rope. Untie the knot and even the cover pattern by smoothing and stretching the whole rope in shape (Fig. 4-19).

If the eye has to be made around a thimble, that should be inserted after the core and casing are

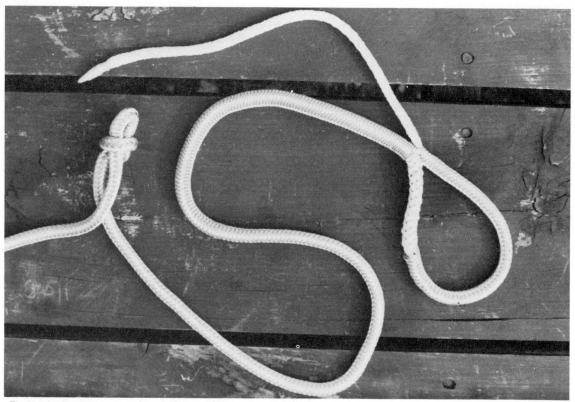

Fig. 4-17. With the cover buried in the core the splice is ready for the final stage.

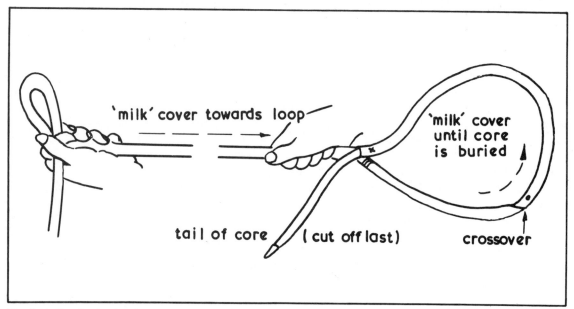

'milk' cover towards loop

'milk' cover until core is buried

tail of core (cut off last)

crossover

Fig. 4-18. Drawing back cover to enclose the splice.

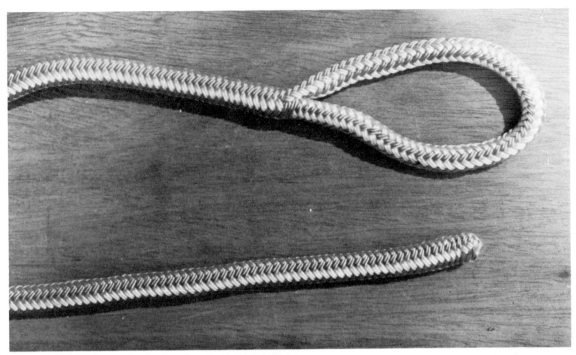

Fig. 4-19. Complete eye and back splices in double-braided rope.

fitted into each other, but before the loop is drawn to size. Avoid excessive tightness at that stage, as the cover has to be drawn around the loop over the thimble in the final stage.

New double braided rope should splice easily. If used rope seems rather tight for making this splice, soaking in water for a few minutes will soften and lubricate the fibers.

Chapter 5

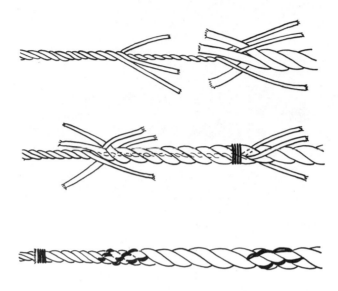

Wire Ropes

WIRE ROPE IS INCREASINGLY USED IN THE RIG-ging of sailing craft. If standing rigging is not rod, it is wire on all boats except the simplest, small open boats. Flexible wire rope is also used for some running rigging. In halyards, it has the advantage of being non-stretch, so sails can be set up tight. Synthetic fiber rope is almost non-stretch, but where the tightest result is required, wire is used. Wire is not as flexible as fiber, and it is common practice to add a fiber rope tail to a wire halyard for convenience in handling, so wire does not have to be dealt with at a cleat until a sail is almost full hoisted. This necessitates some special splicing, described later.

With the stiffer iron and mild steel ropes of the past, it was comparatively easy to make splices. The more flexible, high-carbon steels used for nearly all wire ropes today (whether stainless or plain steel protected by galvanizing or other process), are not so amenable to splicing. It is usual to use some other form of terminal arrangement for the end attachments of wire rigging. It is possible to splice modern seven-strand wire rope, but it is inadvisable to attempt to splice nineteen-strand wire rope. In most circumstances it is better to use some other method of dealing with the end of a wire rope. A rigger should be able to make an eye splice in seven-strand wire rope. Other splices on which the old-time seaman was proud to show his skill are not worth bothering about today.

EYE SPLICES

Old books contain descriptions of a large number of wire eye splices. The broad differences are in the direction of tucking. Some are against the lay in the same way as in the fiber rope splices. Others are tucked with the lay and may, in fact, have each end taken many times around one main strand. Other differences are in the arrangement of the first round of tucks. There was one school of thought that said it did not matter how you tucked a wire splice, as long as you got in plenty of tucks—some compensation for those of us who find that a wire splice does not work out as neatly as planned.

It is easier to make a neat job of a splice tucked with the lay, but tests have shown that a properly-made splice tucked against the lay is stronger and therefore preferable. The only wire splice worth mastering today is an eye, tucked against the lay, as described here.

Although the technique of making an eye splice in wire may seem straightforward, the main problem is not in getting things in the right places, but keeping the wire under control. The eye may be a free one or around a thimble. In practice there is nearly always a thimble, and the splice is easier to make with one, so a practice splice is best made around one. The points of a metal thimble can sometimes be bent back for easier working, then hammered back into shape after splicing. With a plastic or cast metal thimble you have to work within the points.

If the wire has to be cut from a longer length, put a safe seizing each side of where the cut is to come. Unrestrained steel wire will unlay rapidly if left to itself. Iron wire is not so bad. Thinner wire can be cut with wire cutters having a plier action, but for thicker wire it is better to use a cold chisel and hammer it over an iron block (Fig. 5-1A).

PREPARATIONS

Go back a good distance from the end to get a sufficient length of strands for tucking. You must allow for a little waste to have enough of the ends to grip. A length of about 9 inches for a ¼-inch diameter rope is about right. Put on a temporary seizing at this point and another to mark the distance around the thimble (Fig. 5-1B). Waxed thread made into a West Country whipping will stay put on the rather slippery metal.

Each strand now has to be prevented from unlaying. Leave them in the end seizing until you are ready to withdraw each one by gripping with a pair of pliers quite close to the end. One way of securing an end is to grip between two pairs of pliers and twist tightly in the direction of the lay (Fig. 5-1C). With most wire this will hold for the duration of the tucking.

Another way of sealing an end is to have a small amount of molten solder in a can over a flame and another can containing flux. Dip the end in the flux, then into the solder briefly. Hold it out until the solder goes dull, showing it has set. If the wire is greasy, clean it before soldering.

With larger wires you can whip with electrician's tape (Fig. 5-1D) or with thread (Fig. 5-1E). In smaller sizes the thickening at the ends would be a nuisance in tucking.

The wire must be held tightly around the thimble. Do not try to rely on a hand hold. There are special wire-splicing vises that are essential for large ropes. For small wire it is usually possible to get the wire tight by hand pressure and secure it with twine or improvised clamping.

Start by putting a tight seizing around the top of the thimble to hold the wire in close (Fig. 5-1F). Bring the two sides close into the thimble and put on more tight turns with a figure-eight action (Fig. 5-1G). Taper wood blocks in a machinist's vise will help (Fig. 5-1H). A more portable splicing vise can be improvised from a rigging screw or turnbuckle, with some wood or plastic packings (Fig. 5-1J).

It is possible to use an ordinary round spike, but wire has to be tucked alongside the spike, as the parts would spring back and close the gap too quickly after its withdrawal. A screwdriver pushed in and turned on edge makes more room for tucking. Even better is a spike with a groove ground along it (Fig. 5-2). Other spikes are made with sections like a woodworking gouge.

Some wire can be opened with a direct push of the spike, but it is better to enter the point along the lay (Fig. 5-3A) and twist to get it under a strand (Fig. 5-3B). Be careful not to dig into the heart of an adjoining strand or lift wires from it. Some riggers prefer to push the spike through the opposite way to which the strand will be tucked. Care is needed all the time to avoid kinks in the tucking strand. If that happens with fiber rope, the fault will pull out, but in wire the kink (Fig. 5-3C) may close and finish with a hard angle that cannot be removed. If a kink appears to be forming, twist the wire in the direction that will unwind it (Fig. 5-3D), while there is still a large curve. Pliers will have to be used to pull strands through.

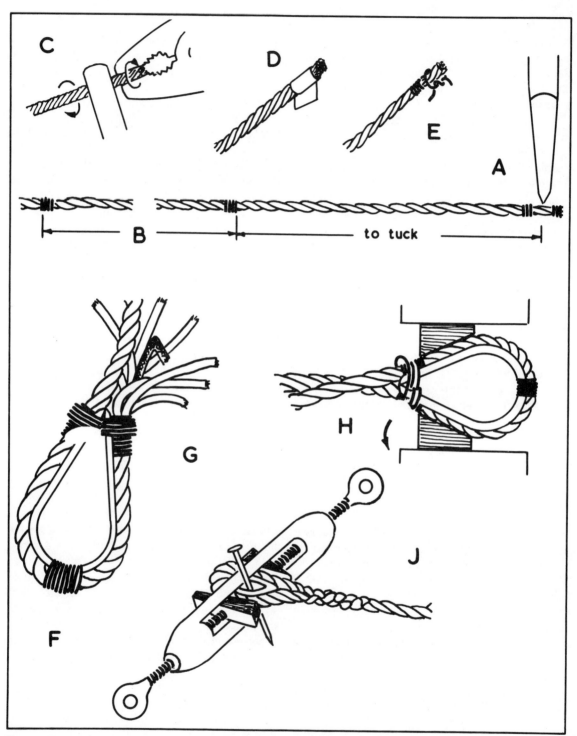

Fig. 5-1. Preparing seven-strand wire rope for making an eye splice.

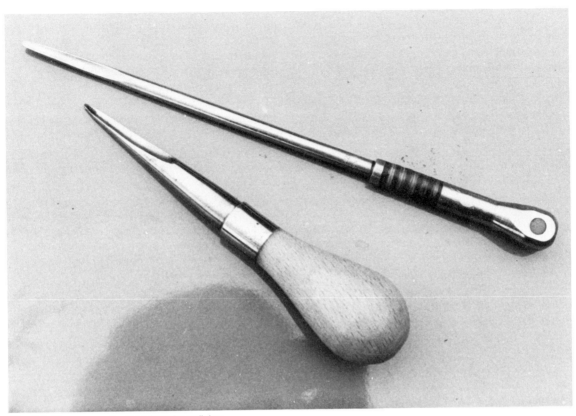

Fig. 5-2. Two grooved spikes for wire splicing.

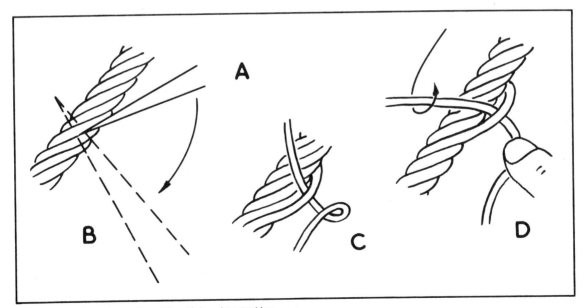

Fig. 5-3. Opening wire and avoiding kinks when tucking.

71

The six outside strands will have a wavy shape due to the lay. A wire heart strand can be identified by its straightness. In the best eye splice the wire heart strand should be included centrally within the tucking and alongside its standing part. If the heart strand is fiber there is no need to tuck it, and it may be cut off.

All of that may seem a lot of preparation before actually splicing, but it is essential if you are to get a good result. Trying to skimp on preparations may make the further work longer or even impossible.

TUCKING

Arrange the ends so there are three outside strands on the front of the standing part, pointing across the lay of the main strands, and the other three behind. If the heart is to be tucked, bend it back out of the way between the two groups of three. Lift a convenient main strand and put the upper end under the heart strand (Fig. 5-4A). Allow space between this and the thimble for the other two strands to be tucked.

Take the end nearest the thimble and tuck it into the space where the other end strand comes out, but go under two main strands against the lay. Arrange the remaining front strand to go in the same place, between the two that are tucked and only under one strand (Fig. 5-4B). Use the spike and pliers to work these tucked parts close down to the thimble. Turn the splice over and keep the heart strand out of the way. Note where end number 3 goes in. Tuck the other strands in turn in the same way, with each going under one main strand (Fig. 5-4C). Keep these tucks close down to the thimble.

There should now be one of the six outer strands projecting from each space in the main rope, with the heart strand alongside one of them. In most wire ropes the splice will have opened to a sort of cage. Do not be in a hurry to close it. Press the heart into a convenient space in the splice so it goes alongside its own standing part in the center of the rope and projects higher up (Fig. 5-4D). It will help to avoid confusion between the many strands if the heart is laid along the rope and temporarily seized to it out of the way of further tucking.

Draw all of the projecting ends tight with

pliers. It is helpful to have a large screw eye in the bench and to pull through that (Fig. 5-4E). So far as is possible, get the ends equally tensioned and in the same plane around the rope (Fig. 5-4F).

If the wire has opened very much it helps if you now get it into a more compact form before further work. Hammering on an iron block is usual, but that is harsh and may damage the wires. It would certainly remove galvanizing. A lead hammer on a lead block is better. Or use a plastic-faced hammer or a wood mallet on the bench top.

Further tucking is done in the same way as in fiber rope splicing, with each end taken in turn over and under one main strand against the lay. Try to tuck at about the same angle around the rope as the angle of its lay, but in the opposite direction. It is easy to get wire tucks very elongated. After a round of tucks, go around tensioning with pliers and coaxing the tucks close to the previous ones. After each round of tucks with the outside strands, bury the heart a stage further, pushing it into the center of the splice at the space where it is already emerging. Do not take it over any outside strands. Draw the tucks to the same level and use a hammer or mallet again.

It is usual to make a total of four tucks with all ends, burying the heart at each stage. After these four tucks the heart may be cut off and its end pushed into the middle of the rope. Wire cannot be satisfactorily tapered like fiber rope, but the splice can be given a taper by taking alternate ends and tucking them once more. Some riggers prefer to make these last tucks over one and under two.

With the ends still projecting, stretch the splice and hammer it into shape. Do this sufficiently to get a round and even shape, then cut off the ends close to the splice and hammer it again.

With the older wires it was usual to cover the splice with tarred strips of cloth (called *parcelling*) and wrap over this tarred twine, as a protection against damp and to resist rust. With stainless steel this is no problem, but the projecting ends may scratch hands, so it is still common to cover part of the splice. For small wire the parcelling may be a few turns of electrician's tape. Leave the first two or three tucks exposed and cover the rest of the

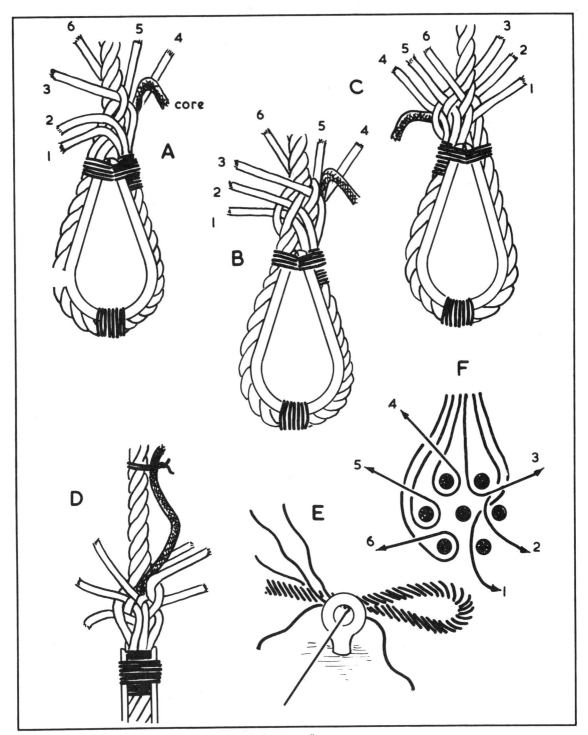

Fig. 5-4. The first round of tucks in a seven-strand wire eye splice.

splice and a short distance on to the plain part of the rope with tape covered by serving.

MECHANICAL SPLICES AND TERMINALS

The alternatives to splicing the ends of wire rope can be divided into those that require equipment not usually possessed by the individual rigger, and those that can be fitted with ordinary tools. There are many places where mechanical splices can be done, and it is often most convenient to have the wire supplier make up the wire rigging parts to your sizes or do a mechanical splice or add suitable terminals himself. Many standard pieces of marine hardware are made so one of the methods of attaching wire can be used without the need for shackles or other attachments. This results in a neat, streamlined fitting with minimum wind resistance or projections that could cause trouble.

The commonest method of attaching a terminal or closing an eye splice is called *swaging*. The single wire rope or the two parts brought together

from around an eye are enclosed in a metal tube, which is then squeezed under considerable pressure so the walls of the tube get pressed into the spaces in the wire and an extremely close mechanical joint is formed.

For single wire terminals there are a large number of ends that may have eyes or other ends to join to rigging screws or other fittings (Fig. 5-5A). For an eye, the tubes make a neat sleeve next to the thimble (Fig. 5-5B). The metal of the part to be squeezed is stainless steel of a grade that permits shaping, while having a good resistance to salt water. For the tubes on an eye splice the metal may be copper, which may be plated with zinc or other metal.

Two methods of compression are commonly used. In one type the fitting is squeezed between two rotary dies, with several passes necessary to get a good tight round section. Another method uses a split tubular die that revolves round the fitting while under pressure, to give a smoother

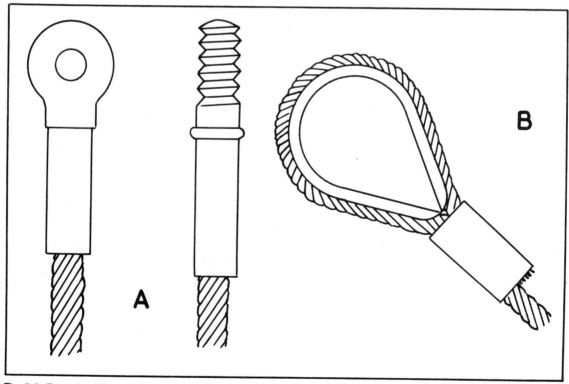

Fig. 5-5. Examples of swaged ends on wire rope.

surface. There is a hand operated tool, with an action like bolt cutters, for closing the smaller types of copper sleeve. Swaged fittings are common and generally satisfactory. However, they should be examined occasionally as they are liable to develop small cracks after being under load for some time. They are then suspect and should be replaced.

A variation on the swaged metal tube is a type using copper sleeves, which are squeezed with a plier-type hand tool in a series of local presses, that crimp the sleeve on to the wire. There may be some settling of such a joint under load, but the suppliers claim high strength in a properly made joint.

SCREWED TERMINALS

There are at least three types of terminals intended for nineteen-strand rope that are fitted with a screw action. These can be attached without the need for special equipment or even a bench and vise. Norseman, Loos, and Sta-Lok are trade names. Properly fitted, any of these attachments should be as strong as the wire rope. Although usually only for 1 × 19 wire, it is possible to get them for 7 × 7 and 7 × 19 wires.

The piece of wire rope is taken through a closely fitting end bore in the terminal casing. The outer strands are then unlaid, leaving the inner strands to go through the bore of another conical shaped piece. The outer part of the fitting has a matching internal taper. The outer strands are fitted around the conical part and the assembly goes back into the fitting and a screw arrangement tightens the whole lot together (Fig. 5-6). When finished, the assembly makes a neat terminal end to

the wire. The parts can be used again, except that a new conical wedge part must be fitted (Fig. 5-7).

There are detail differences between the makes and they may not all be the same quality stainless steel, so it is necessary to check that the fitting matches your needs. Each fitting is designed to suit one diameter rope and it cannot be adapted to other sizes. So far as possible, it is wise to settle for one diameter and one type of wire throughout the boat.

There may be slight settling after the first use. Slacken the lock nut on the terminal and tighten the terminal part further, if it will go. Re-tighten the lock nut. Some means of securing this nut should be provided. One is a heat-shrink plastic tube, which slides over and can be made to shrink and grip the nut and adjoining parts with heat from a flame or electric element.

POURED TERMINALS

Some of the oldest terminals are made with solder poured around the wire in a hollow metal fitting. These were used for larger, commercial wires and, even if available in suitable sizes, they tend to be clumsy for many of the pleasure boat wire rope sizes. Common solder does not have an affinity for some metals, but it will unite with most stainless steels and the zinc coating of galvanized steel.

A fitting for pouring has a conical inside above a bore that matches the wire rope (Fig. 5-8A). The wire end must be clean and free from grease. If there is a rope heart it should be cut off below the fitting, or the charring will interfere with the flow of solder. The strands are separated into their wires, which are spread within the fitting (Fig. 5-8B).

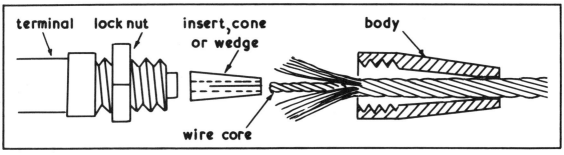

Fig. 5-6. The parts of a screwed terminal for wire rope.

Fig. 5-7. Parts of a Norseman wire rope terminal: a locking plastic sleeve, the top with a knurled locknut, the internal cone, and the main body.

Soldering flux has to be put in the socket and around the wires. It helps to heat the socket, while it is supported with its top upwards, to near the melting temperature of solder, which is not very high. Solder is melted in a ladle and poured in. Tapping the fitting gently helps the solder to flow in and the solder to escape. Sufficient solder should be poured to fill and possibly stand a little above the fitting. When the joint is cold enough, wash off surplus flux.

WIRE CLAMPS

There are various types of clamping arrangements for wire rope that depend on a squeezing action with screws. The usual type for steering cables for outboard motors are flat with the wire, which may be plastic-covered, put between the plates in grooves, then pressure applied with several screws. For rigging, the clamps are more often a form of U-bolt. These rope clips or cable clamps are made in sizes

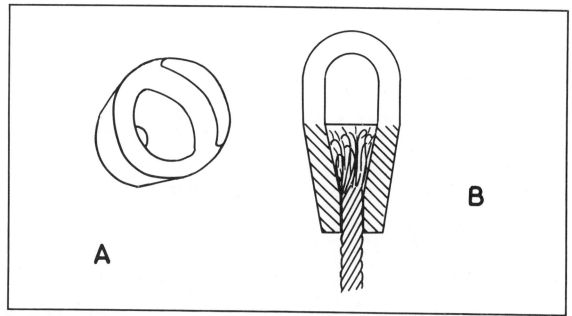

Fig. 5-8. Poured terminal for wire rope.

76

Fig. 5-9. Two clamps for wire rope.

to suit different diameters of cables and the size chosen should be a reasonable fit if sufficient strength is to be achieved.

No one would claim that a cable clamp is anything but an emergency fitting or at least one to be put out of sight, but these clips are useful stock for a rigger making repairs or setting up temporary wire rope rigging. The usual form (Fig. 5-9) has a cast block with the U-bolt through it and two nuts for tightening. It is unwise to depend on a single clip. Two might serve, but it is better to settle for three, preferably positioned alternate ways (Fig. 5-10A). The exposed wires should be covered with tape to prevent scratching. If only one clamp is to be used, it may be possible to turn the end back into the clip (Fig. 5-10B). Any slipping then would have a tightening effect on the loop.

ROD RIGGING ENDS

Rod may be regarded as solid wire, but in the sizes used for boat rigging it cannot be bent like wire and is not large enough to be treated as metal rod to have screw threads cut in it.

In one method of commercial production the end of the rod is enlarged to form a head. This is called *cold heading*. An end fitting has to be put

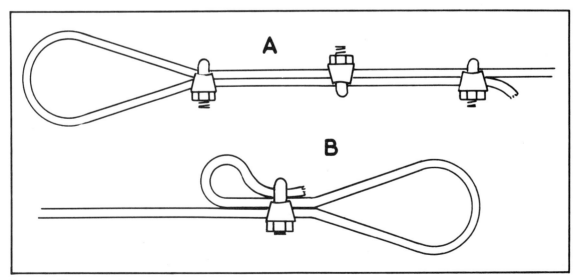

Fig. 5-10. Clamps on wire rope.

over the rod, then the rod end is enlarged to about twice the size of the rod so it cannot pull back through the close fitting bore (Fig. 5-11A). A variation is a screwed sleeve (Fig. 5-11B) to enter a rigging screw.

It is possible to get a conical wedge for a Sta-Lok fitting so it will take rod rigging instead of wire, allowing an end to be put on without special tools.

FIBER TO WIRE SPLICING

A fiber rope tail to a wire rope is usually there for convenience in handling. When the load is taken the fiber rope should be clear of the cleat and free from strain. This means that the fiber rope must be strong, but not as strong as the wire rope to which it is attached. In any case, the fiber rope will be of greater diameter than the wire rope. It is possible

to make a form of short splice if the fiber rope is three-stranded, but a long splice is better and essential if the fiber rope is braided. It will also follow better over a sheave.

For a short splice, cut the heart out of the wire rope and pair the outer strands by temporarily seizing them together. Put a temporary seizing on the wire rope far enough from the end to allow for tucking and some extra for pulling through. Prevent the ends of the strands from unlaying by using one of the methods described earlier.

Prepare the fiber rope by putting on a temporary seizing to prevent unlaying, then taper the sealed strands to about half thickness at the ends. Bring the two ropes together with a pair of wire strands in each space of the fiber rope (Fig. 5-12). From this point tuck each of the pairs of wire strands into the fiber rope against the lay by going

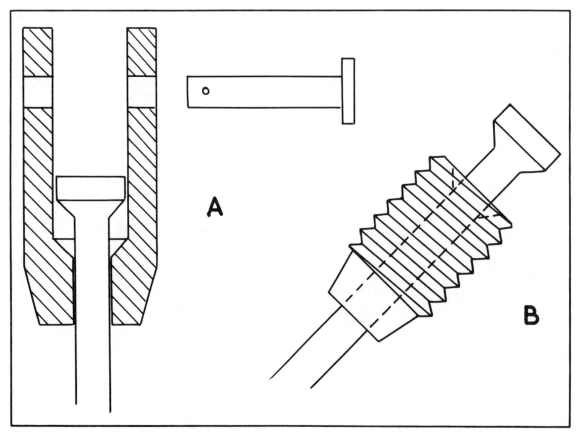

Fig. 5-11. End fittings for cold-headed solid rigging wire.

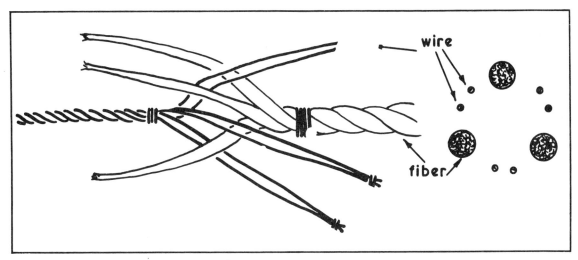

Fig. 5-12. A simple method of splicing wire to fiber rope.

over the adjoining fiber strand and under the next one. Do this with all three pairs of wire strands fairly close to the temporary seizing on the fiber rope. When all are level and tight, do this again. Three sets of tucks should be enough. Cut off the temporary seizing.

Now tuck the fiber rope into the wire rope, but this time take each end over two and under two of the wire rope. Do this three times and cut off the ends of the fiber rope strands and seal them. With the wire rope strands, take one strand of each pair and tuck it once more to provide tapering. Draw the wires tight and cut them off.

This type of short splice can only be done reasonably well if the diameters of the wire and fiber ropes are not vastly different, otherwise there has to be excessive tapering of the fiber strands. If there is much difference in the sizes of the ropes and a short splice is still wanted, it is possible to make it by tucking with the wire strands only. Much depends on the suitability of the wire and fiber ropes, particularly of the fiber, which has to be opened, tapered, and relaid. Some synthetic rope is difficult, or impossible, to put back together again after the original construction has been disturbed.

Unlay the fiber rope up to a temporary seizing for about twenty times the diameter of the rope, or a little further, but try to keep the twist and waviness of each strand as much as possible. Taper each

strand by scraping away fibers, mostly from the inside. Rubbing with wax will help to keep the scraped fibers in place. Lay up the tapered strands and put on a temporary seizing an inch or so from the end.

Prepare the wire as before, into three groups of two, then bring the rope ends together as before. Start tucking the pairs of wire strands over and under one into the fiber rope. Continue tucking until you have passed the limit of the tapered part of the rope. Each pair of wires should be tucked at least six times. Continue for a tapered tuck with one of each pair of wire strands.

With both methods it is possible to bury the wire ends in the fiber rope, but they have to be retained by sewing. Twist open the fiber rope and push an end into the center, then use thread and needle to sew the wire to the inside of a fiber strand. Do this with the other wires at slightly staggered positions.

LONG SPLICE: WIRE TO THREE-STRAND FIBER ROPE

This splice is preferable to a short splice, particularly if there is much difference between the sizes of rope. It will pass around a sheave easier and this is usually a requirement of a fiber rope tail on a wire halyard. The long splice differs from the short splice in having the wire strands tucked individually at two different positions.

Unlay the fiber rope for a greater distance than would be needed for the short splice. Taper the strands. Unlay the wire rope for a much greater distance—up to 150 times its diameter (about 36 inches for a ¼-inch rope). Use seizings where necessary to keep the rope in check. Take three alternate wire strands and lay them together as a three-strand rope, using up about half their length. Keep the other three out of the way and mate the ends of the twisted strands with the fiber rope (Fig. 5-13A). For compactness in illustrating the parts of the splice, they are shown closer than they would be in practice. Put a temporary seizing over the junction.

Lay up the fiber strands around the three-strand wire part, as far as the other three wire ends and arrange these with the ends fitting into each other (Fig. 5-13B). From this point the wire ends are not tucked over and under one, but each is wrapped around the adjoining fiber strand. Do this four or five times at each position. Cut off the wire ends or sew them in, if preferred.

Lay up the remains of the tapered fiber strands around the wire rope and seize the end firmly and permanently (Fig. 5-13C). If you wish, there could be a serving over the tucked parts or over the whole splice.

LONG SPLICE: WIRE TO BRAIDED FIBER ROPE

Double braided rope is used in preference to

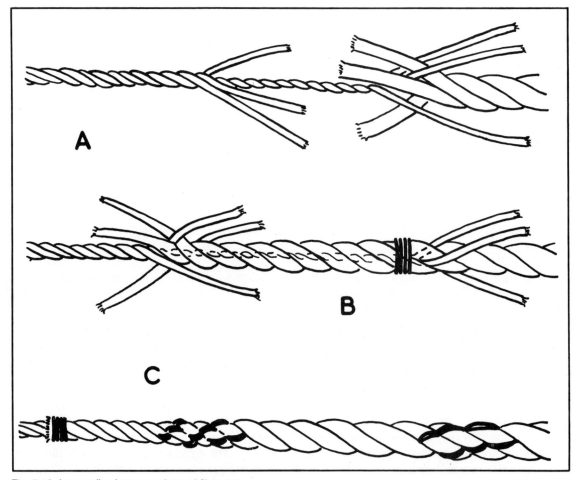

Fig. 5-13. Long splice between wire and fiber ropes.

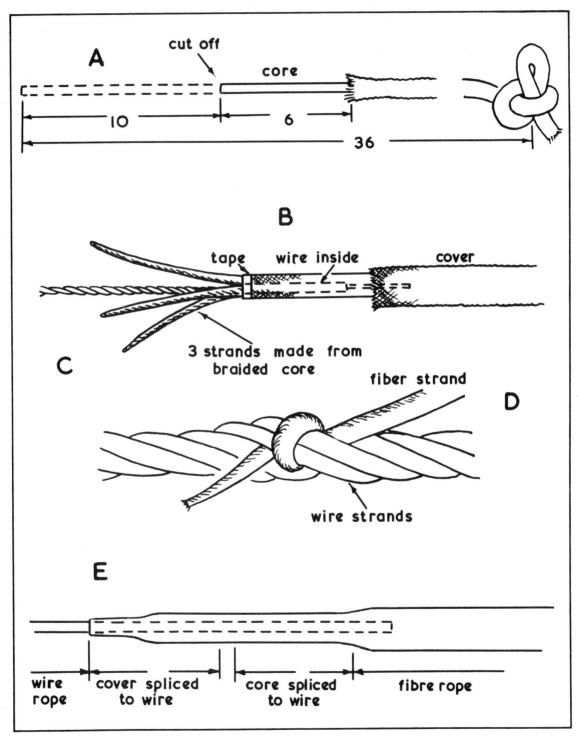

Fig. 5-14. Splice between wire and braided fiber ropes.

three-strand rope for most purposes on many sailing craft, so the rope tail on a wire halyard may have to be made of that. This involves a different method of splicing. The finished splice is comparable in bulk to that with three-strand rope. In the usual arrangement the wire rope diameter is about the same as the diameter of the heart of the double braid fiber rope. The sizes quoted should suit the usual sailing boat rope sizes, but might have to be increased for very large ropes.

Knot the fiber rope about 36 inches back from the end to limit the amount of movement of the casing during splicing. Slide back the casing, without cutting it, but cut off about 10 inches of the exposed core (Fig. 5-14A).

The wire rope does not have to be tucked and you can seal the ends together with solder or other means, but take care not to increase the rope diameter as that would cause a bulge in the splice. To get a tapered effect, the central heart wire may be allowed to continue while the outside strands are cut back and soldered to it. There could be further tapering by cutting back alternate outside strands. The wire ends might be held with electrician's tape instead of solder, providing it is not built up too bulky. Once the wire is enclosed in the fiber rope there should be little fear of movement.

Open up about 5 inches of the inner braided sleeve, picking it out into its separate fibers. Push the wire end into the core. If the rope core is very tight, it may be necessary to unlay more of the inner sleeve to reduce the pressure. Make sure the wire goes in centrally (Fig. 5-14B).

Tape around the braided core that has been unpicked. Divide these ends into three groups and twist them into strands with the aid of wax. Taper their ends (Fig. 5-14C), which have to be tucked into the wire. The method can be used with seven or nineteen strands. Tucking is done under pairs of wire strands. This uses all the laid strands of seven-strand wire rope, but the pairs should be selected evenly around the outside of nineteen-strand rope.

Tuck a fiber end under two wire strands, then go back around the pair again (Fig. 5-14D). Do this with each fiber end under a different pair of wire strands. Pull tight, then either continue around the same pair of wire strands or go over two wire strands and do the same again at the next two wire strands. This should be sufficient, but you can make a further set of tucks if they seem desirable. Cut off the ends.

Work the cover over this part of the splice and take it along the wire until all slackness has been taken out. Put a temporary tape around the cover about 5 inches from the end and unpick the cover from there. Separate what you have picked into three strands in a similar way to how you treated the inner sleeve. Tuck these into the wire in the same way as was done there. The wire then has the fiber rope tucked into it in two places, with their locations as shown (Fig. 5-14E).

That completes the splice. You can put a serving over its end, where tucks are exposed. The other parts are covered by the casing. Release the knot further along the rope and stroke the casing smooth. The total length of the splice is not important, providing there is a short length of untucked wire rope between the places where the fiber rope ends are tucked.

If the fiber rope is single braided, the core is proportionately thicker since there is no inner sleeve. The outer fibers of the core will have to be kept out and used to twist into the tucking strands, but otherwise a splice to wire can be made in a very similar way.

If it is a rope with a braided sleeve over a three-strand rope core, the wire can be spliced into the core in the way described for a short splice, then the cover drawn over it. If the wire-to-fiber core splice is adequate, the end of the cover can be seized to the wire rope. If more strength is needed, the end can be divided into three parts and tucked into the wire, as described for the other long splice.

Chapter 6

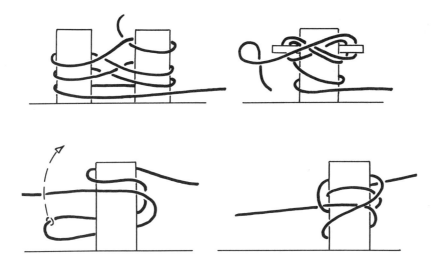

Rope Handling

MUCH OF A RIGGER'S WORK IS CONCERNED WITH long lengths of ropes in a variety of sizes. Most of the ropes are in diameters easily dealt with, but some anchor and mooring cables may be quite large. Modern synthetic ropes are usually more flexible and pliable than some of the older natural fiber ropes. Tangled ropes have no place on board; this applies to the lightest lines as well as the more substantial ropes.

New rope usually comes on a reel and it should be left there until required. It should be unrolled, not drawn off sideways in loops that will disturb the lay. Disturbance of the lay can happen in other ways. It may be due to use, or misuse, and the twists have to be eased out. In an extreme case there may be kinks. Handling and twisting while you work along the rope will get twists out and move any disturbances towards the end, where the rope will twirl to rectify itself. Braided rope does not have a lay to bother about, but some twisting may have to be corrected.

COILING

If you just pick up a length of rope and start coiling it in one hand you may find a resistance to forming coils as you progress, because you are imparting a twist to the rope. Coiling should be done in the direction of the lay. That means making the loops clockwise with normal righthanded rope. To do this, hold the rope end in the left hand, palm upwards, and put loops into it with the right hand. As you put each loop in place, give it a slight twist in the direction of the lay (Fig. 6-1A).

If you are coiling braided rope, do not twist as you coil. Instead, let the loops take a slightly figure-eight form as you put them together without a twist (Fig. 6-1B).

If there is more rope than you can coil in your hand, it will have to be coiled on the deck or floor. You could start with a few turns made in the hand and put them down, or you can start directly on the floor, working around in the same way as you would into the hand, and giving the slight twist with the lay

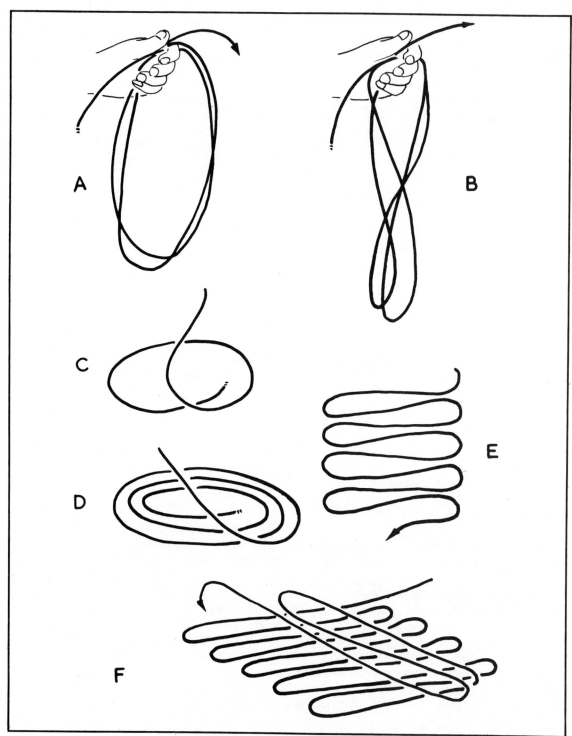

Fig. 6-1. Fiber rope may be coiled in the hand (A,B) or on the deck (C,D). It can be flaked down (E,F) so as to run out easily.

as you put down each complete turn (Fig. 6-1C). If there is a lot of rope to be coiled down, make three or four turns on the deck around each other, then start back above them from the outside in with the same number of turns (Fig. 6-1D). Continue in this way until the coil stands up like a cylinder of rope three or four turns thick, with little risk of falling over.

The alternative to coiling down is to *flake* the rope, particularly if you want to be certain that it will run out quickly when required, as with an anchor warp. If an anchor warp was allowed to run rapidly from a coil it would become snarled. If you are dealing with a high rig and you want to be able to pull up a rope cleanly from the deck, flaking will insure a clear flow when the rope is drawn from a distance.

Start flaking from the end that will be inboard or is attached to something. The end that will be pulled, as when an anchor is let go, will run out from the top. Lay out the line in a series of loops (Fig. 6-1E). There will probably have to be more loops than you can put down in one layer in the available space. Make a second layer of loops across the first (Fig. 6-1F). If there is still more line to be put down, make the third layer across the second and so on until all the line has been used up. An experiment with a spare length of line will show how a long piece can be made to run out quickly and smoothly. The line for a rocket lifesaving apparatus is laid out in this manner in a tray.

COILING FOR STOWAGE

When a rope is out of use it should be secured in a coil in a way that prevents it coming adrift, yet readily available for use when required.

One simple way is to make up the rope into coils in the hand, then use the end to hold the turns together. Hold the coils together with enough projecting from the hand. Twist a half hitch into the end (Fig. 6-2A). Hold this behind the coils and pass the end through the coil and through the half hitch (Fig. 6-2B). You can carry or hang the coil by the projecting end. If a bight is passed through instead of the end, that can be used for hanging.

Another way is to use the end to make two or three crossed half or marline hitches around the bundle (Fig. 6-2C). Clove hitches or rolling hitches could be used. This is suitable if you want to keep the coil round.

A tighter way of coiling for stowage brings the sides of the coil closer together. Use the final end to put on several turns (Fig. 6-2D), working away from the end that will be hung. Push a bight of this end through the top of the coil (Fig. 6-2E) and turn it down on to the coil. The effect is to put on a half hitch above the other turns, leaving the end projecting (Fig. 6-2F). If the rope is to be hung, leave enough of the end so it can be looped or knotted on a hook, rather than hung by the coils.

Another way of coiling finishes with an upwards loop for hanging. Leave enough of the working end to make a half hitch. Continue around and pass a bight formed with the end through the half hitch (Fig. 6-3A). Pull tight so the bight finishes upwards (Fig. 6-3B) for hanging.

There could be marline hitches all round or part way round the coil (Fig. 6-3C) if it is to be stored flat. If it would be more convenient for stowage to have the coil long and narrow, the marline hitches could go over the turns (Fig. 6-3D). The final turn, or the only one if securing in one part is all that is needed, may be locked by going around (Fig. 6-3E) and tucking a loop for easy release (Fig. 6-3F).

CLEATS

Most ropes on a boat have to be secured, or *made fast*, to a cleat or some other solid object that functions in a similar way. Making fast may also be called *belaying*. A rope is belayed when turns are put on, then it is made fast when something is done to prevent them coming off. The reverse of making fast is to *cast off*. A surprising amount of the security of an attachment is due to the friction caused by the many turns. A half hitching or other finishing action does not actually have to take much load.

At one time any marine hardware catalog showed a few cleats of standard design and any choice was mainly concerned with size. Now there are a great many cleats and related holding devices, so the choice for a particular purpose may not be

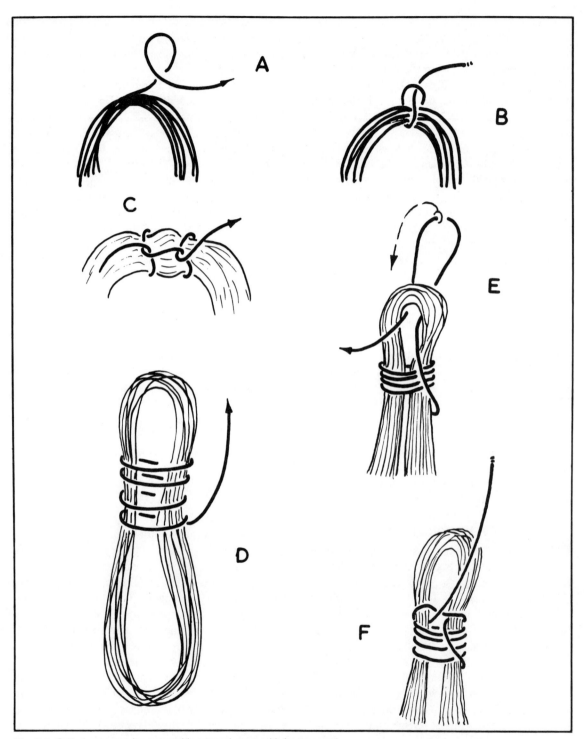

Fig. 6-2. Coiled rope can be secured in several ways with its own end.

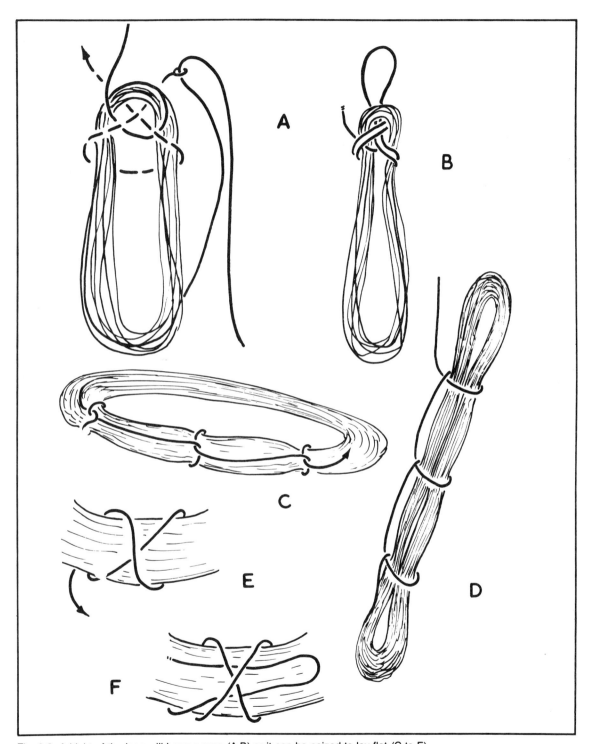

Fig. 6-3. A bight of the loop will hang a rope (A,B) or it can be seized to lay flat (C to F).

very obvious. It is important to have the cleat large enough to take enough turns of rope. An undersize cleat may seem neat, but it could be dangerous if it does not allow rope to be made fast properly.

Cleats and other fittings on older vessels were made of wrought iron. After its initial slight coating of rust it has a surprising resistance to further corrosion, as can be seen by the fittings on trading craft a century old. Wrought iron is no longer obtainable. Mild steel or cast iron will both corrode rapidly if unprotected. In more recent times fittings made from one of these metals have been galvanized with zinc, which protected until it wore away. Bronze fittings were considered superior and they are still a good choice, as the right alloy has a good resistance to corrosion in a salt atmosphere. They look good if kept polished or they may be plated. More recent choices are stainless steel and salt water resistant aluminum alloy.

It is also possible to have cleats and other fittings made of wood. They have to be slightly bulkier than the equivalent metal fittings and they have to be treated with oil or varnish. They have a traditional appearance and have the advantage of not being difficult to make. They can be customized to suit particular needs.

A cleat is a solid block with two extending horns (Fig. 6-4A). There are many detail differences, but the important requirement is the pair of horns. A larger version may be called a *bollard* and it may have a hole through it (Fig. 6-4B). *Belaying pins* are not so common today, but they provide a means of belaying ropes to get a grip similar to that of a cleat. The traditional belaying pin was turned on a lathe with a sort of handle at the top and a parallel part to pass through a hole (Fig. 6-4C). If a line had to be let go in an emergency, the pin could be knocked out upwards to spill the rope, no matter how complicatedly it had been made fast. A modern version may be a wood or metal peg put through

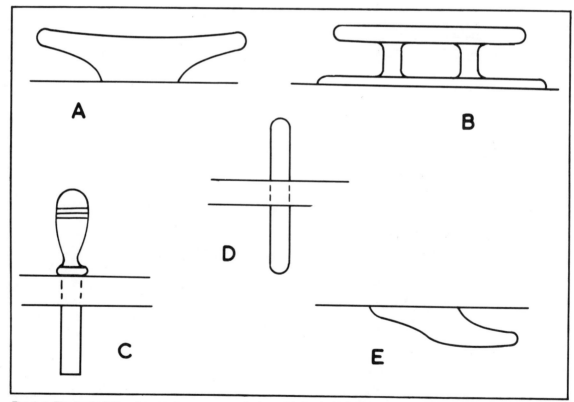

Fig. 6-4. The basic fittings for securing ropes are cleats and bollards (A,B,E) or belaying pins (C,D).

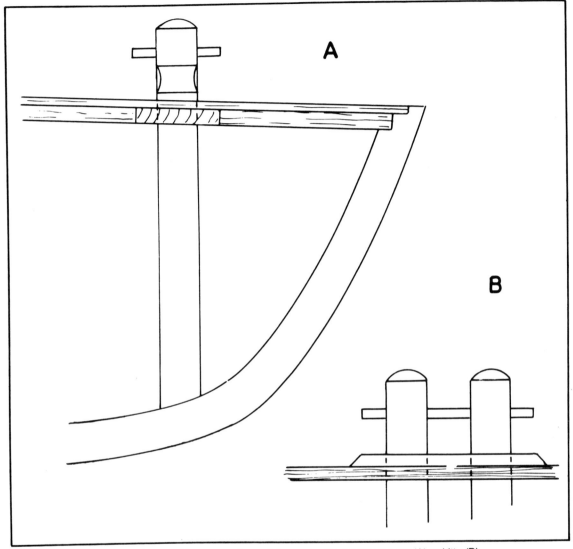

Fig. 6-5. For a strong place for attaching a rope forward there may be a samson post (A) or bitts (B).

near the edge of a mast thwart (Fig. 6-4D). Sometimes there is only a peg projecting below. Half a cleat may be called a *thumb cleat* (Fig. 6-4E).

Cleats and bollards are designed to attach to a surface. For the strongest attachment, particularly on the foredeck where the strain of a towing hawser may have to be taken, it is better to have some holding arrangement that goes through the deck and spreads the load to other points. A single substantial post in this locaion is called a *samson post* (Fig.

6-5A). It may be just a projecting post, but more often there is a metal rod through it, which may be called a *stag's horn* or a *norman*. Instead of one post, there may be a pair, called *bitts,* which may be united by a metal rod through them (Fig. 6-5B). In both cases, the rod converts the post(s) to something like a cleat, so the rope can be belayed in a similar way. If there are no bitts or a samson post to take a towing strain, a mast that goes through the deck may be the most secure attachment point for a rope. If a mast is deck mounted or is a modern, light aluminum hollow section, there may not be much strength for this purpose.

A samson post (or bitts) must go through a reinforced part of the deck and be securely attached at the bottom to the stem or hog. Loads may also come from the side, so besides the normal structure of the decking, a king plank should go fore and aft under it and there should be bracing carried out to the gunwales.

Cleat Attachment

It is in the attachment of cleats and bollards that some designs are unsatisfactory. Wood screws should only be regarded as normal where it is impossible to use a through fastening and the load is comparatively light in a direction about square to the screws (Fig. 6-6A). If the screws are taken as deeply as possible into hardwood and the cleat is drilled to take sufficient (usually four) screws the holding power is then usually ample. A pull in the direction of withdrawal should be avoided (Fig. 6-6B). The screws should normally be of the same metal as the fitting.

It is better to bolt through, but the load must be spread on the other side. Normal size washers are not good enough alone, particularly in fiberglass decking on a small boat. The spread is best taken with a wood pad larger than the base of the cleat, with its edges faired off (Fig. 6-6C). A suitable pad may be molded into a fiberglass deck, or if it is added below, it might be bedded in resin. Even with the wood pad, it helps to use oversize washers under the nuts or provide a metal plate to take up all the bolt holes.

With boat construction using a soft core between two layers of fiberglass, bolting directly would merely compress the skin. If the boat was built with the intention of a bollard being put at a certain place, there may be a piece of hardwood in the core at that point. Otherwise the only way to prevent compression is to include a metal tube on each bolt (Fig. 6-6D). The length of the tube should be slightly less than the thickness it is going through, so the slight compression it permits will ensure a close fit.

Some deck fittings are provided with a stud to go through the deck as part of the construction. A neat and secure way of attaching is with a screw from below into the base of the fitting (Fig. 6-6E). This has the advantage of less projection inside a cabin. With a single screw arrangement there may be small projections under the base to press into the deck and prevent the fitting from turning. It is important that the screw length is arranged so it has enough turns in the base for security.

Where security depends on a nut on a screwed part, something should be done to lock the nut. Stiff nuts, in which there is a spring or fiber insert to resist loosening are simple. A second, thinner lock nut may be used, but that increases the amount of projection. A modern simple treatment is an epoxy adhesive locking treatment. Smeared on the thread, it sets and locks the joint, but it is still possible to force it apart with a wrench.

Cleats or bollards attached to decks should be bedded in joint compound. Some joint compound may be put on bolts, particularly through wood decks. This not only keeps water from leaking through, but it prevents the accumulation of moisture that could cause rot. If the material is fiberglass, some of the resin used in fiberglass work could be used for bedding. Wood screws should be driven into pilot holes no bigger than necessary and they might be lightly greased before driving.

One problem with wood screwing comes in the attachment of cleats to softwood masts. Spruce, or other soft wood, is chosen for its lightness, but it does not offer much grip to screws. Screws should not be too thick or long, as that might weaken the mast. One way to provide strength is to drill oversize holes at each screw position, so a hardwood plug can be glued in, then the screw driven into that (Fig. 6-6F).

Belaying to Cleats

Providing there is a steady pull on the standing part, a simple half hitch will hold on a pin (Fig. 6-7A) or on one horn of a cleat (Fig. 6-7B), providing the working part is trapped under the standing part. Even better is another turn to trap the end with a half hitch on the other horn (Fig. 6-7C) or opposite

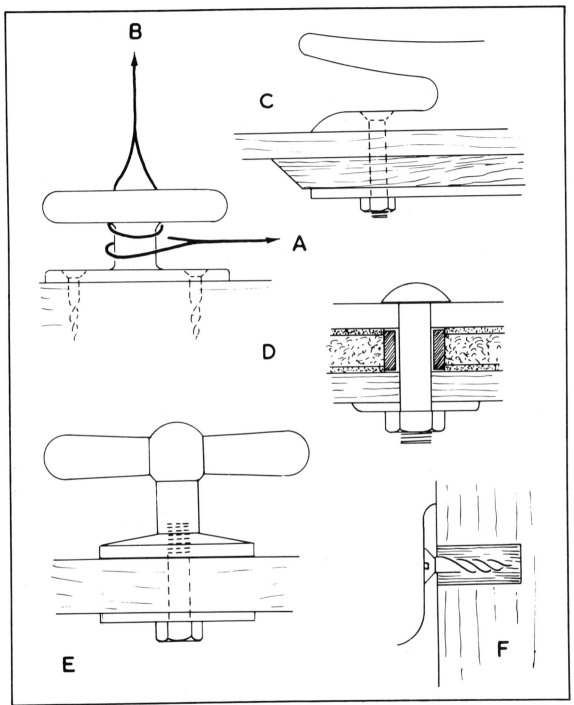

Fig. 6-6. The load on wood screws should be across (A) and not in the direction of withdrawal (B). Reinforcement is advisable (C). Use a tube to avoid compressing cored fiberglass (D). A part may be screwed from below (E). A soft mast may have to be plugged (F).

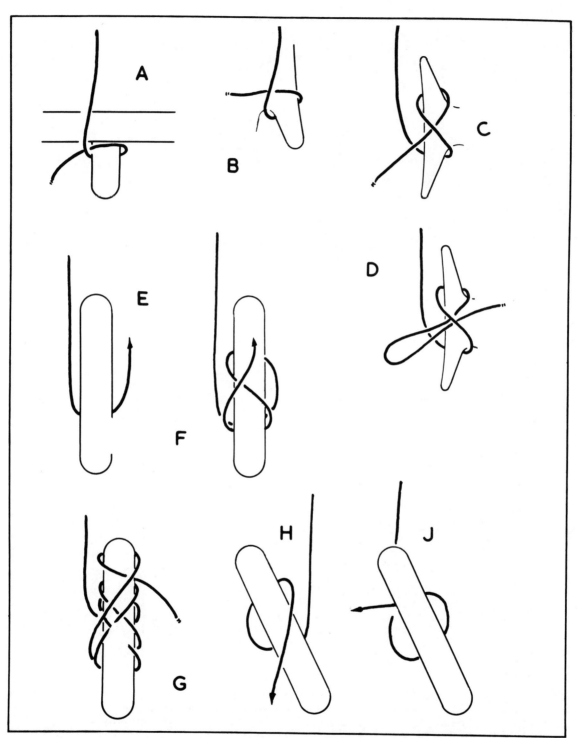

Fig. 6-7. A rope to a cleat or pin holds mainly by friction of many turns and any hitches are for final securing.

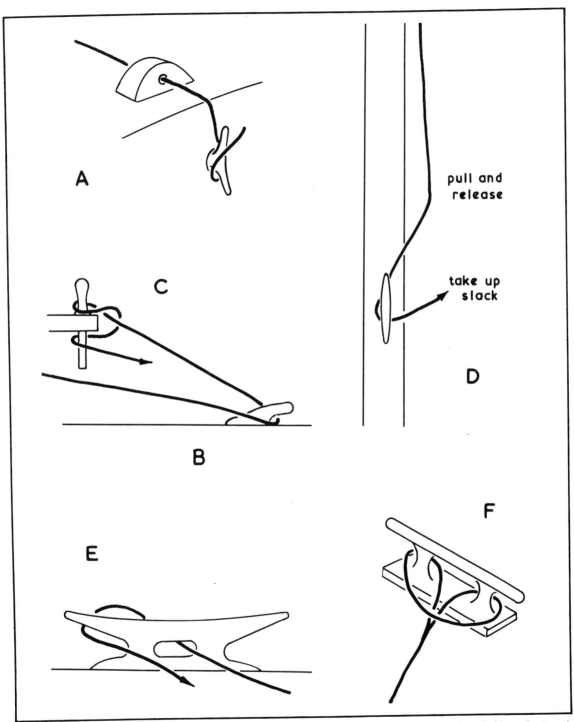

Fig. 6-8. Leading a line so there is friction before the cleat (A,B,C) aids its hold. A halyard can be tensioned with a pull outwards (D). A hole through a cleat allows secure mooring E,F.

side of a belaying pin. If you want to be able to cast off easily, make the half hitch with a bight (Fig. 6-7D).

It is more usual to take the strain with more turns around the cleat. After the first turn, it is better to work in a figure-eight manner (make S or Z turns). Enclose the horn opposite to the direction of pull first (Fig. 6-7E). Other turns cross each other (Fig. 6-7F). How many turns you put on depends on the load and the size of the rope in relation to the cleat. The turns may be all that are needed to take the load. To prevent them coming off, finish with a half hitch, preferably on the upper horn or the one towards the direction of load (Fig. 6-7G).

A cleat may be mounted at an angle to the direction of pull. This provides a better lead to the standing part when the first pull is taken. The rope is better led around the cleat in the direction shown (Fig. 6-7H). If it is brought in from the other side, the working part is trapped (Fig. 6-7J) as it goes round and is more difficult to tighten.

In many parts of the rigging the rope has to come directly to the cleat, but if something can be arranged to direct the pull, it may be easier to get a good tension. Such a device is a *fairlead,* of which there are many patterns. A simple example is a block of wood with a hole in it to guide a halyard over the cabin top to a cleat (Fig. 6-8A). It could be a thumb cleat (Fig. 6-8B) to alter the direction of a line to a cleat or belaying pin (Fig. 6-8C). It is then possible to take up the strain around the thumb cleat and hold the pull while making fast to the belaying pin.

In larger, modern sailing craft rope may be pulled by winches, but where the maximum pull has to be obtained by hand, there is a method of *swigging* on the halyard. A strong pull is put on the rope brought under the cleat. This is held while the other hand is used to pull outwards further up on the standing part (Fig. 6-8D). As the standing part is allowed to return, anything gained is drawn up by the hand holding the end around the cleat. Then securing turns are put on.

If the cleat of bollard has a hole through it, that

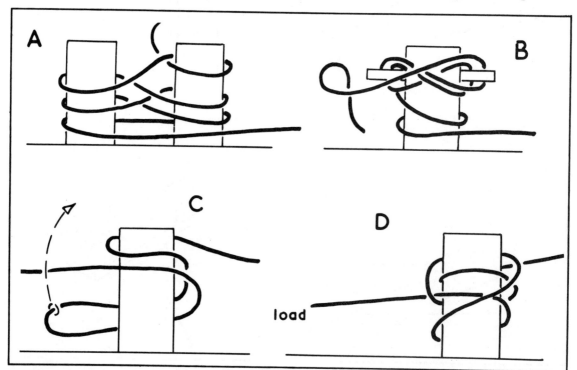

Fig, 6-9. A tow rope can be secured to a post or bitts with many turns so it can be easily released.

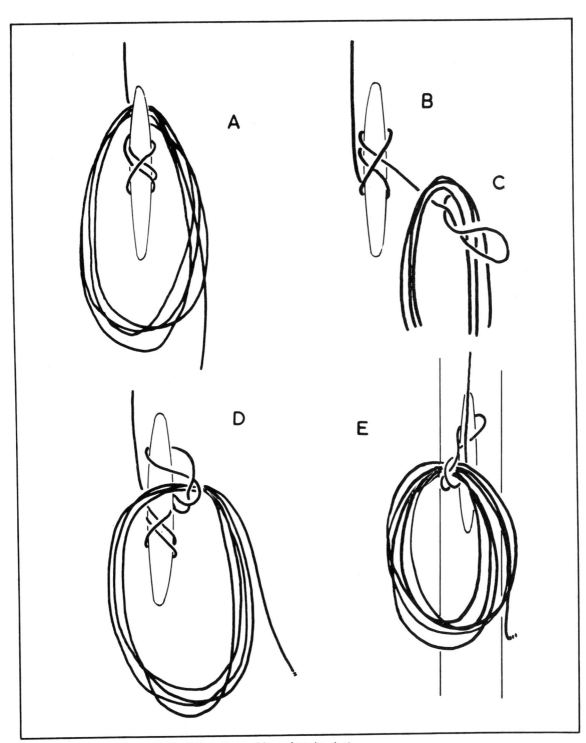

Fig. 6-10 The fall of a halyard should be coiled and hung from its cleat.

serves as a fairlead. A line may be brought to it through the hole, then turns put on around the horns in the usual way (Fig. 6-8E). If the line has an eye in its end, as it might for a mooring line, the eye may go through the hole and be doubled back over the horns (Fig. 6-8F). A smaller eye may go through and over one horn, then in either case, more turns can go around the cleat if necessary.

The two parts of bitts and the bar across a samson post, can be treated in a similar way to the horns of a cleat. For towing or mooring it is usual to put on a large number of turns so the load is taken by the friction they cause. A final half hitch does not pull up so tight as to be difficult to let go. With bitts, figure-eight turns are built up (Fig. 6-9A). With a samson post a few turns go around the post before figure-eight turns at the top (Fig. 6-9B). A method of securing to a samson post that will not jam uses a loop of the end of the rope around the standing part (Fig. 6-9C). This can be done after a few turns, then more turns put on and the process repeated.

ROPE TAILS

When a rope has been attached to a cleat there is usually a surplus to be dealt with. This is particularly so with halyards. When they have done their job of hoisting sails there is more than half the rope left coming from the cleat. A short piece may be left loose, but otherwise something must be done about

it. Sometimes there is a bin or bag to hold the rope tail, but it is more usual to gather up the rope in a coil and secure it. It must be possible to cast off the rope and let it run out, so the method of stowage must be uncomplicated. Jamming the coil of rope between the standing part of the halyard and the mast is sometimes seen, but this is not considered seamanlike.

When surplus rope is coiled it should be done from the cleated part outwards, not the other way round. Coiling back from the end may cause it to twist or kink. If coiled the other way it should be possible to drop the coil on the deck when you have to cast the turns off the cleat and it should run out without trouble. If there is a long enough horn on the cleat the coil may go over it (Fig. 6-10A), but this is not very secure under usual sailing conditions.

It is better to do something to hold the coil to the cleat. One way is to coil outwards from the cleat, leaving a short piece there. Hold the coil in one hand while reaching through it with the other to grasp where the rope comes from the cleat. Pull this through the coil (Fig. 6-10B) and twist this loop (Fig. 6-10C), before putting it over the horn of the cleat (Fig. 6-10D). Normally the twisted part goes over the horn in front of the standing part, but there can be some extra security if the twisted part goes behind the standing part before putting it over the horn of the cleat (Fig. 6-10E).

Chapter 7

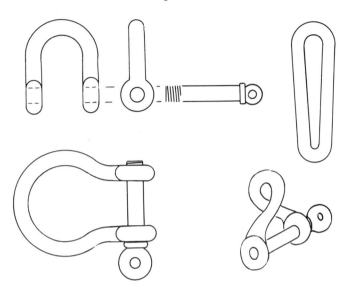

Hardware

THERE HAVE BEEN CONSIDERABLE DEVELOP-
ments in the design and variety of hardware
for boats since World War II. New items for particular purposes come in many sizes and
patterns—so much so that anyone with a long experience of boat rigging may wonder how much is
necessary and how much is an attempt by manufacturers to entice purchasers with the latest gadget.
There have certainly been advances in the design of
equipment for racing sail craft, where something
elaborate and more complicated may be justified if it
can be seen to make any operation faster. For many
purposes on cruising craft, the long-established
types of fittings may be better and cheaper.

We will bring together those basic items of
hardware, or *chandlery*, with some idea of their
uses. You can see their functions and relate them to
other variations you may be considering for a particular boat. Anyone unfamiliar with available hardware for sailing and power boats should obtain a
catalog from one of the larger suppliers and use it as
a reference book for identifying items. If the

catalog's information on a particular part is related
to those described in this and other chapters, it will
be possible to assess the suitability of a special
design when balanced against the proposed use of
the boat being rigged.

The material and finish of hardware affects the
cost considerably. The latest gadget in the most
expensive finish can be quite costly. An examination of the hardware used on a commercial boat will
show how to get the results needed with the
minimum amount of simple equipment. There may
be few commercial sailing craft, but you can find
similar gear on some fishing craft. Wooden parts
may be difficult to buy today, but many of them can
be made with only a moderate degree of carpentry
skill. Galvanized iron may not be available or considered desirable, but for general purposes there is
no need to buy expensive plated bronze, when
something at an intermediate cost will do equally
well. Fortunately, stainless steel can now be fabricated into many more items and where it is available in a piece of hardware, it is a good choice.

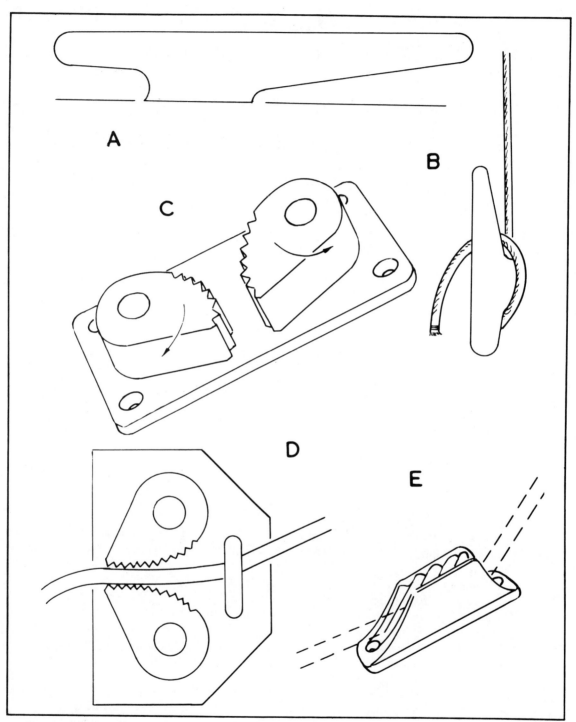

Fig. 7-1. A jamming cleat may be made similar to a plain one (A,B). A cam cleat grips between sprung serrated cams (C,D). A clam cleat uses tapered teeth (E).

JAMMING CLEATS

With ordinary cleats, having two identical arms a rope has to be locked by putting on a half hitch. If it is a situation where the rope may need to be cast off quickly, the action of removing the hitch is a delay. There have been several cleats produced that will lock the rope, but the basic *jamming cleat* has the underside of one arm tapered so the rope can be trapped under it (Fig. 7-1A). The load is taken around the other side, then the action of putting the rope across at the tapered side will lock it by friction (Fig. 7-1B). This is suitable for sail sheets, which can be cast off quickly when going about and taken up again with the minimum delay on the other tack.

Another version of a jamming cleat may be metal or plastic. The rope leads through a tube and is locked by lifting it into a tapered slot (Fig. 7-2). The rope remains in the tube when it is released, so if there is a knot in its end, it does not run away. This is useful in places like foresail sheets, where the sheet on the lee side can be left ready to be taken up again after tacking.

A popular version of a jamming cleat or rope stopper is a *cam cleat*. Two cams are sprung towards each other and given teeth to grip a rope that goes between them (Fig. 7-1C). The teeth are not sharp enough to cut into the rope and in many cleats the cams are plastic, which is not so rough on the rope. Besides independent cleats, the arrangement may be built into other things, so the rope leads into the cams directly from coming around a sheave or some other operation. Cam cleats are often provided with an eye or other arrangement to lead the rope fairly to the cams (Fig. 7-1D). Release is by jerking the rope back and up slightly to clear the jaws.

A *Clam cleat* is the trade name of a cleat that uses a wedge action and serrations to get a grip like a cam cleat, but without moving parts (Fig. 7-1E). The rope is lifted and pulled clear to release the grip.

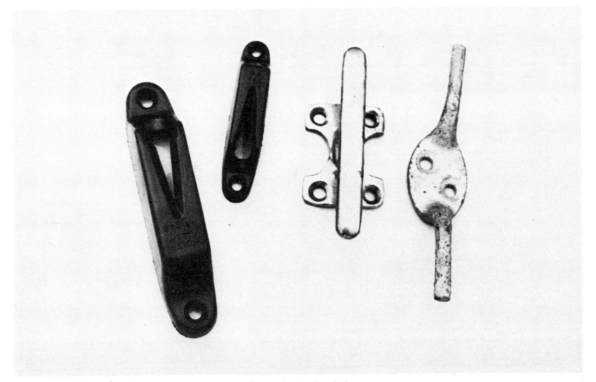

Fig. 7-2. Two slotted jam cleats, a plain bar cleat, and a flag halyard cleat.

WOODEN CLEATS

A simple, serviceable wooden cleat can be made from close-grained hardwood. First draw the outline, then drill through the curved inside corners (Fig. 7-3A) before sawing into the holes to remove the waste (Fig. 7-3B). Finishing is then a matter of smoothing and rounding, with a chisel or file, followed by sanding. That basic shape is satisfactory, but there can be some curving in both directions (Fig. 7-3C). Care is needed not to cut down too much. Grain lines from the horn should go right across for strength (Fig. 7-3D).

Wooden jamming cleats are effective and kinder to the rope than metal and some plastics.

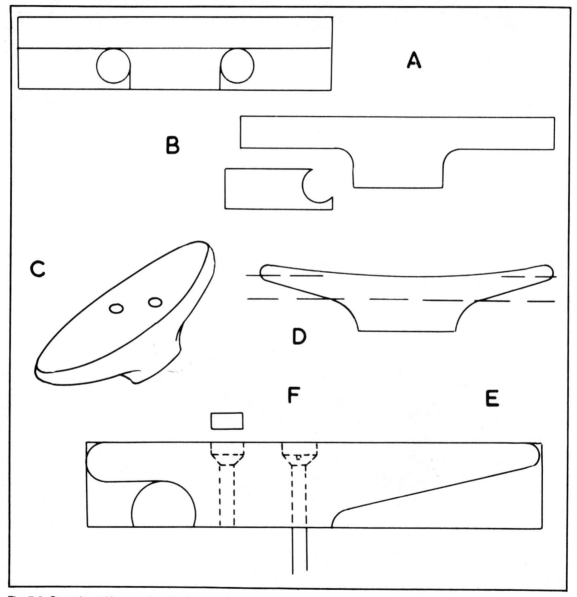

Fig. 7-3. Steps in making wooden cleats.

One can be made in the same way by drilling (Fig. 7-3E). The whole of the ordinary side may be made with a large drill, then the wood shaped with a round file or a gouge.

In all wooden cleats the appearance can be enhanced by sinking bolt heads so they may be covered with wood plugs (Fig. 7-3F). Avoid breaking through all grain lines when hollowing the top of a cleat. It is also advisable not to sink heads so much that you drill away enough to weaken the wood. Deeply countersinking the heads is suitable for bolts that tighten on the other side, but if the cleat is to be held with wood screws, it is better to only countersink them at the surface in case later tightening is necessary. If a wood cleat is to be mounted on a wood surface, you can glue it there, both for strength in addition to screws and to prevent water from becoming trapped behind it.

FAIRLEADS

Any device that directs the run of a rope is a fairlead. Simplest is a block of wood or plastic with a hole in it (Fig. 7-4A). There could be a row of holes if several ropes are involved, as they may be when halyards are led over a cabin top to cleats in the cockpit. The holes should be well rounded in section (Fig. 7-4B) to not chafe the rope.

A traditional alternative to the hole through a block of wood is called a *bull's-eye fairlead*, which is a well-rounded block of hardwood (or plastic), held down by a U-shaped piece of round metal rod (Fig. 7-4C), either to a base plate, which is screwed down, or with bolt ends. Even simpler is the U-shaped piece without a wood insert. Both arrangements may be incorporated into blocks or cleats so as to control rope direction as close to where it is needed as possible.

Another type of fairlead is used for mooring ropes in particular and is mounted on the gunwales. It may be a closed elliptical opening (Fig. 7-4D), with ears extending for bolting down. The rope end needs to be passed through, but the closed form resists any tendency of the rope to lift, as it might if the boat rises and falls with the tide. Open fairleads are more usual (Fig. 7-4E), so the rope can be dropped in, possibly after the load has been taken and the rope is under tension.

It is better if the gap between the jaws is no more than necessary for the rope to drop in. These fairleads may be handed with angled slots for use on each side of the bow, where it is assumed a mooring rope will lead forward to the dock. These fairleads are not intended for the anchor warp. That has to lead over, or close, to the stem head. The fairlead there may be a deeper arrangement with a roller included (Fig. 7-4F).

To resist lifting of the rope, open fairleads may have staggered jaws, so the rope has to be dropped in with a slight twist, making it unlikely to lift out unintentionally (Fig. 7-4G). Fairleads, particularly in large sizes, have rollers built into the sides, to ease the pulling of ropes and reduce friction on them.

For small craft, such as open sailing boats, there is no need for much elaboration and a fairlead may take the place of a block. A useful gunwale-mounting fairlead, in wood, plastic, or metal, looks like a handle (Fig. 7-5) with the load taken around the higher and larger side. This can take care of a foresail sheet. Where sails may be changed and the lead have to come at a different place to get the best set of the sails, this or a bull's-eye fairlead may be mounted on a gunwale track so it can be moved fore and aft to the best position.

Chafing can be a problem. If a boat is left moored for some time, particularly where it is subject to the effect of tide, wind, and the wash of other craft, the rope will rub against the fairlead and the outer fibers may wear through. In a long-standing and neglected position, the fibers may finally wear to the stage where not much rope is left and it breaks. In the past, chafe was taken care of by *worming, parcelling,* and *serving.* Worming is putting a light line around and between the strands to get a rope section more nearly circular. Parcelling is wrapping with cloth. Serving is a long seizing of small line. The serving took the first of the wear and probably had to be renewed more frequently than the user would wish. Today it is simpler and better to use flexible plastic tube or hose, usually polythene, either colored or transparent.

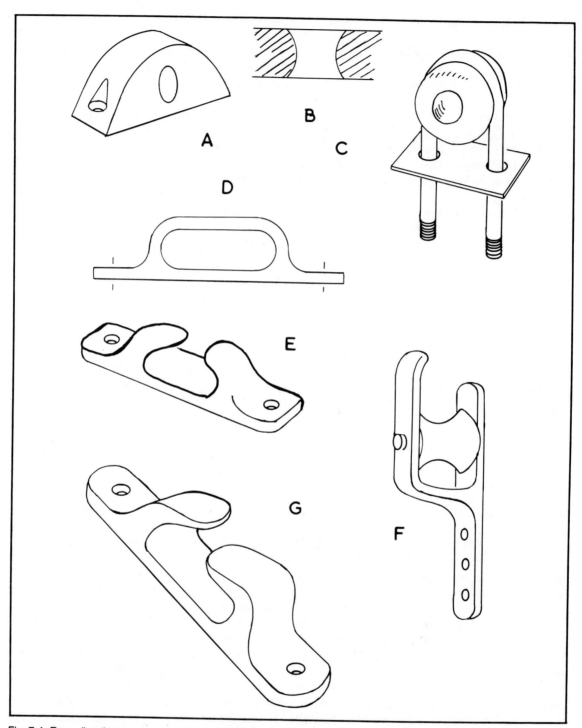

Fig. 7-4. Rope direction may be controlled by fairleads, such as a hole in a block of wood (A,B), a bull's-eye (C), or at the gunwale through shaped fairleads (D,E,G). A roller is used at the stem (F).

Fig. 7-5. A fairlead for small boat jib sheets.

on, soak it in hot water so it can be sprung on. If it resists springing on, soak it in hot water to soften it. The cut should remain closed under most circumstances. If it is a rope through a fairlead, have the tube long enough to extend either way to allow for movement. This also does something to reduce the abrupt bend in the rope as it goes through the fairlead. Too hard a bend tends to cause internal friction in the rope and may break some fibers.

Similar lengths of plastic tubing can be put on part of the standing rigging where running rigging may cross it—as with sheets around shrouds. Where the tubes are nearly upright, as in sheets on shrouds, they will stay in place by gravity. For a mooring rope, or elsewhere that might slide out of position, there can be holes made in one end of the tube to take twine that is then seized around the rope. If the tube is a fairly close fit on the rope, its end can have a few slits cut along it so a tight seizing around the tube will compress it on to the rope.

It is best if a tube can be slipped on, but if the end of the rope would not admit the tube or is inaccessible, the tube may be slit lengthwise with a knife so it can be sprung on. If it resists springing

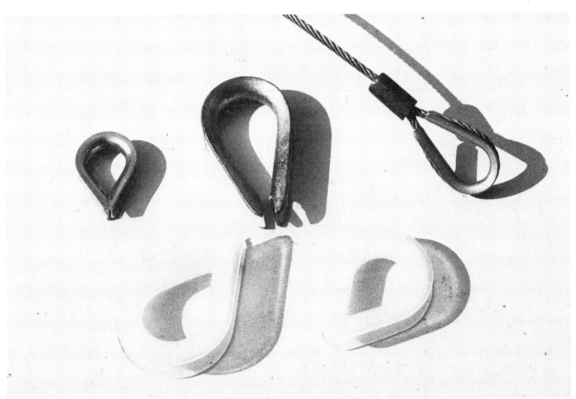

Fig. 7-6. Two metal and two plastic thimbles, and a metal thimble used in a swaged wire rope splice.

THIMBLES

Wire and fiber rope ends are strengthened and protected with thimbles. Thimbles have already been mentioned in connection with eye splices. Their purpose is to protect the loop from chafe and to keep it to a moderate curve under load. Without the thimble the end of the loop would pull to a close small curve that might damage the rope by fracturing wires or fibers.

At one time brass thimbles were common, but unless they are quite stout, they may pull out of shape under load. Galvanized iron was used for both fiber and wire ropes, but today it is better to use stainless steel on wire rope and either this, or nylon or other plastic, on fiber rope. Round thimbles have been used on rope, but it is better to use the common heart shape (Fig. 7-6). The width of the score, or groove around the thimble is most important. This should be a fairly close match to the rope. If, for instance, a ¼-inch rope was put around a thimble with a ⅜-inch score, it would tend to flatten under load and be weakened slightly.

SHACKLES

The common form of linkage is a *shackle,* if there is no other special provision. The ordinary shackle is often called a *D shackle* (Fig. 7-7A). The pin passes through one side and screws into the other side.

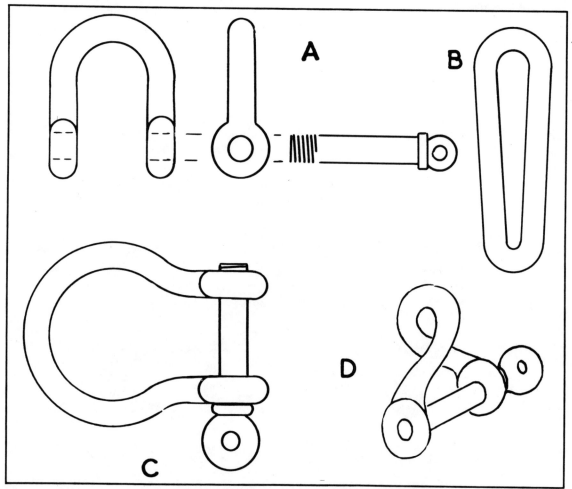

Fig. 7-7. Shackles may be in many shapes. Their screwed pins may be turned with a slotted key (B).

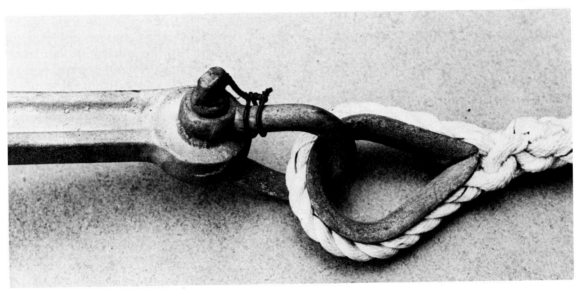

Fig. 7-8. The screwed pin of a shackle should be wired to prevent loosening.

Fig. 7-9. A shackle with a screwed pin and two with quick-release keyed pins.

The eye in the pin is not really intended for pushing the point of a spike through for turning, although that is often done. It is better to tighten a shackle with a pair of pliers or with a shackle tool or key, which is a slotted plate (Fig. 7-7B), sometimes provided as part of a clasp knife. The hole is there for wiring the pin to prevent it unscrewing. Wire through the hole is then looped around the side of the shackle (Fig. 7-8).

If the shackle has a more open curve it may be called a *harp* or *bow shackle* (Fig. 7-7C). For places where the two parts to be joined have to come at right angles to each other the shackle may be twisted (Fig. 7-7D). Shackles can also be obtained in a long pattern, where more clearance between the parts being joined is required. In the traditional form of shackle, the pin and the round part forming the loop are the same diameter.

Some shackles are now made from flat strip stainless steel as well as being forged from that material. Both types may have a key pin arrangement instead of a screw. The key handle on one end of the pin allows turning without a tool. On the other side there is a slot beside the hole to pass a retaining peg, which rests at the other side in a groove, to lock the shackle closed (Fig. 7-9). When the pin is withdrawn it cannot fall out because of the retaining peg hitting the side. Such an arrangement allows an easy attachment or release of a sail from a halyard.

Snap shackles are a different form, intended to give a quick release, possibly while under load, and a way to make a connection without losing tension. In the usual form the retaining pin is kept in place with a spring. There are many forms of attachment to the rope. It can be a fixed or swivelling ring to take a splice, or it may be arranged as a sail hank with holes for sewing to a sail, as when the leading edge of a foresail has to attach to and slide on a forestay.

In one snap shackle, the opening part pivots at its extremity (Fig. 7-10A), then they fall open to release without jamming (Fig. 7-10B). Another type has the pivot to one side (Fig. 7-11), but the pin is sprung in a similar way.

Another snap shackle opens from the side and is released by pressing a disc (Fig. 7-10C). This is not so much a rigging device as a clip for a lifeline. Another variation of a shackle is a *pelican hook* (Fig. 7-10D). Its particular use is where the last bit of tension has to be put on. When the opened hook is engaged with a ring and levered back to be secured, it draws the parts closer together.

Carbine hooks are comparatively recent arrivals on the boating scene and have come over from mountaineering. The hook goes on the end of a line that has to be quickly and securely attached to something else (Fig. 7-12). The opening part is springloaded and is arranged to link with the fixed part. This is a modern version of the older spring clips, which were usually fitted with springs that rusted. A more advanced version has a spring-loaded sleeve to guard against accidental opening (Fig. 7-10E).

Rather similar is a *link shackle*, which is shaped like a chain link, but with a screwed connector at one side (Fig. 7-10F). It can be hand tightened or the hexagonal sleeve can be locked tight with a wrench.

Another form of linkage between parts is a pair of *Brummel hooks* (Fig. 7-13). They may also be called *Inglefield* or *Englefield clips*. While not intended for heavy loads, they are ideal for quickly attaching or disengaging signal flags to their halyards, or they may be arranged on fender lanyards. When the two slit parts are crossed squarely to each other they will pass through each other, but at any other angle they will not come apart.

EYEBOLTS AND PLATES

If a block or other fitting has to be mounted flexibly to the deck or elsewhere, it is shackled to an eye. For a light load the eye may be in the form of an *eye plate* or *fender eye* (Fig. 7-14). This is held down with two, or preferably four, wood screws or small bolts. The name of fender eye comes from the use of the plates in providing attachment points for the lanyards from fenders hanging over the side. A fender eye could serve as a fairlead for a length of light line.

For a more secure attachment there is an eyebolt that goes right through (Fig. 7-15A). If much direct pull is expected, something with a

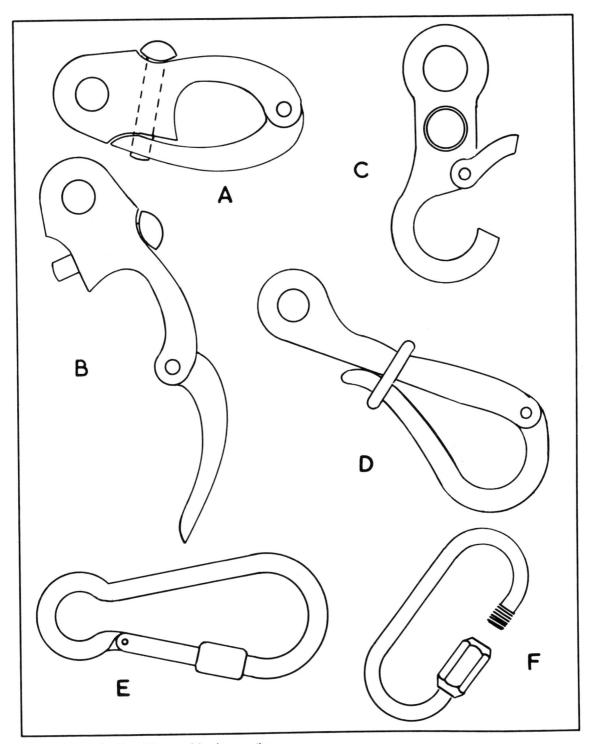

Fig. 7-10. Snap shackles all have quick-release actions.

Fig. 7-11. Two snap shackles.

Fig. 7-13. Brummel hooks with swivels on one part of each pair.

bigger area than the usual washer supplied should be arranged to take the pressure under the nut. A ring bolt is an eyebolt with a ring loosely included (Fig. 7-15B). The ring is not always round, but usually is, for attaching a small boat tow rope or similar line.

An alternative to a ring bolt is a *U bolt* (Fig. 7-15C), where the load is spread between two ends instead of the one bolt.

For light applications there are *eye straps* or *lacing eyes* (Fig. 7-14). They are used to take the lacing line from covers, but they may take shackles

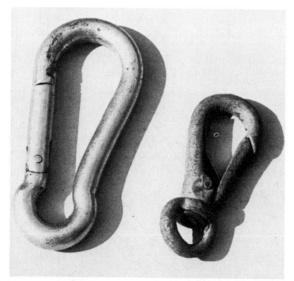

Fig. 7-12. A carbine hook, compared with the earlier type of spring hook.

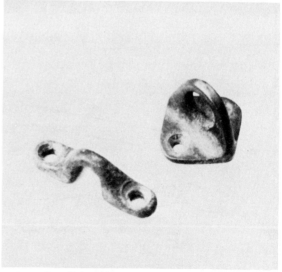

Fig. 7-14. A looped fender eye and an eye plate.

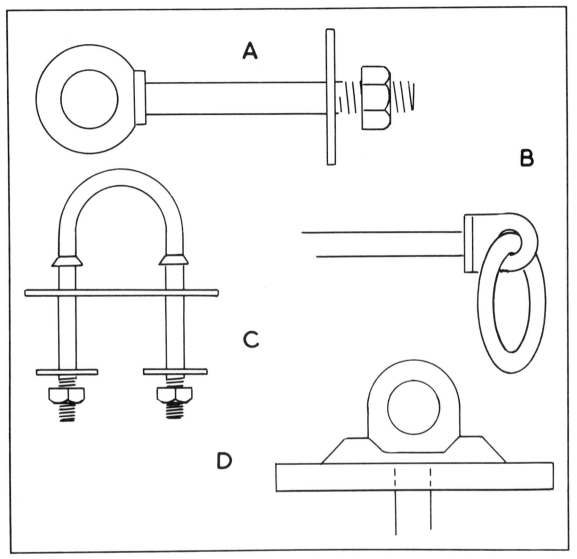

Fig. 7-15. An eyebolt (A) may have a ring added (B). A U-bolt provides an alternative to an eye (C). A deck plate protects a swinging block.

from light rigging lines. The older type is cast with a round neck and a pair of screw holes, but others made from strips are rounded for stiffness and may have extra screw holes.

A deck plate is more like a substantial eye plate, but large enough and strong enough to take the pull of the main sheet tackle. Some are arranged to limit the fall of the block when the tackle is unloaded, so it does not knock against the deck (Fig.

7-15D). Where a larger load has to be taken the attachment may be an eye bolt, but padding is arranged around it to protect deck and block from each other.

RIGGING SCREWS

Many parts of the standing rigging of a boat have to be tensioned. At one time this was done by gaining a purchase by hauling lanyards through holes in

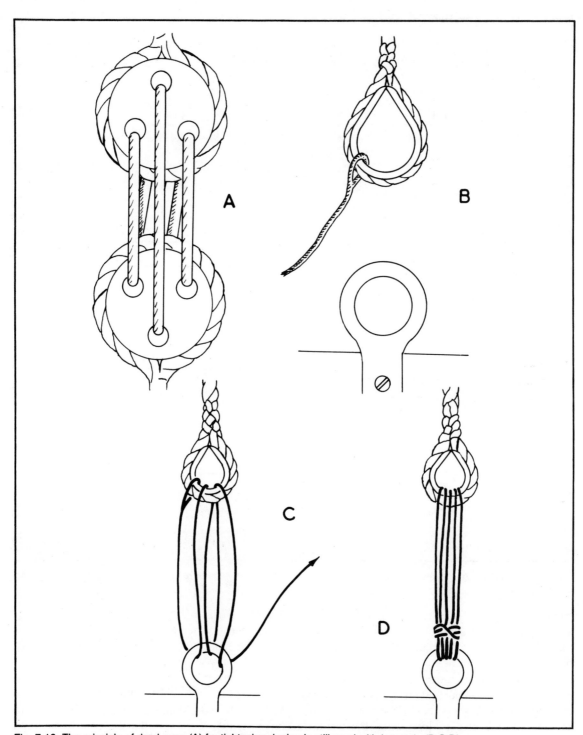

Fig. 7-16. The principle of dead eyes (A) for tightening rigging is still used with lanyards (B,C,D).

pieces of wood called *dead eyes*. In the days of square-rigged sailing ships this was the usual way of setting up shrouds. Even if the method is unlikely to be used today, the principle should be understood. The outside of each dead eye was grooved to take a spliced eye in the rigging rope, then the lanyard attached to one dead eye was rove through holes and hauled tight (Fig. 7-16A). The theoretical mechanical advantage of going backwards and forwards through many holes was considerable, but the friction involved reduced it.

An arrangement that is similar in principle is still used for the shrouds of small open sailing boats. The strong point on the gunwale is known as a *shroud plate* or *chain plate*—the latter name coming from the fact that in a square-rigged ship that area was called the chains. The usual shroud plate has an eye at the top, then a strap going down far enough to take several screws or bolts into the hull below the gunwale (Fig. 7-17).

The shroud should finish in a thimble a short distance above the top of the shroud plate. Ideally, the two openings should be about the same size (Fig. 7-16B). A lanyard is spliced to the thimble on the shroud and should be long enough to put on plenty of turns—six or eight would be reasonable. Reeve the lanyard backwards and forwards through the openings (Fig. 7-16C). Haul this tight, probably a few turns at a time, then finish with a clove hitch around the turns (Fig. 7-16D). With flexible smooth line, it should be possible to put on a considerable strain in this way, as the friction to be overcome should not be excessive.

It is more usual today on larger craft to tension with the aid of screws, usually in the form of rigging screws or turnbuckles. In the simplest and most easily understood form there is an open body with internal threads at the ends, one end being right handed and the other left handed. If the screws that fit do not turn, but the body is turned, the effect will be to increase or reduce the distance between the attachment points at the ends of the screws (Fig. 7-18A). The ends of the screws may have eyes, jaws, or other attachments for rigging to be joined on. Less common are *straining screws*, where there is only a screw adjustment at one end and the other

has a swivel (Fig. 7-18B).

Tubular *turnbuckles* or rigging screws are more popular, as they are more streamlined, with less projections, but the principle is the same. The screws pass into a tube and there may be a slot where their ends can be seen or just a hole across the center so the tube can be turned with a rod or spike passed through. There may be a lock nut on one or both end screws, so the turnbuckle can be prevented from unscrewing. In larger sizes the ends of the tube may have flats to take a wrench for turning it.

If the turnbuckle ends are merely eyes, shackles are needed to engage with shroud plates and the eyes in the shrouds. If there are jaws there may be a clevis pin through (Fig. 7-18C), or it could be a nut and bolt or a screw pin as used in a shackle. In any of these cases a direct attachment to an eye or hole in a plate is possible.

It is also possible to get screwed ends with a Sta-Lok or Norseman terminal included for direct attachment to wire rope, giving a neat and uncluttered assembly (Fig. 7-18D). Suitable ends can be swagged on wire.

It is important that a rigging screw should not be able to loosen in use. Lock nuts at one or both

Fig. 7-17. A shroud plate and a stem plate for a small boat.

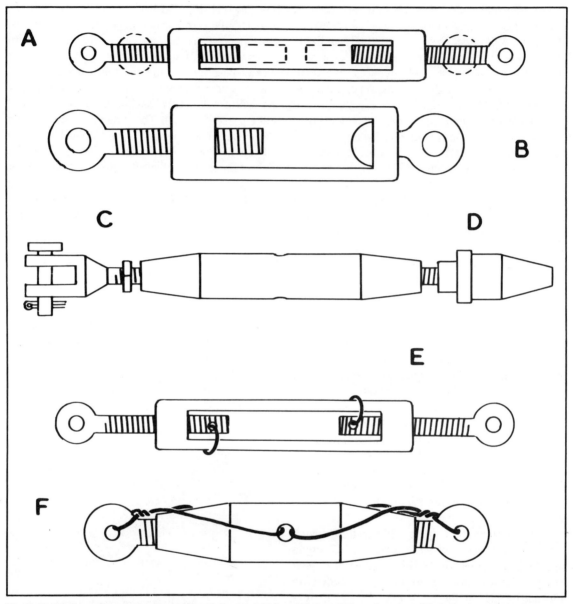

Fig. 7-18. Rigging screws or turnbuckles use left- and right-handed threads for adjustment (A). A simple one may have only one screw (B). Ends to join to rigging may be included (C,D). Screws may be locked with nuts, rings, or wire (E,F).

ends should prevent this. If there is only one lock nut (usually on a right hand thread), let this be on the end attached to the wire rigging. If that end is prevented from turning, there cannot be any loosening at the other end attached to a shroud plate or other rigid fixing.

Some rigging screws have the inner ends of the screws drilled to take split rings, that can be put on to hold the body against turning (Fig. 7-18E).

If there are no locking arrangements provided, the turnbuckle will have to be wired. Use a non-corrodable wire and twist with pliers so the ends

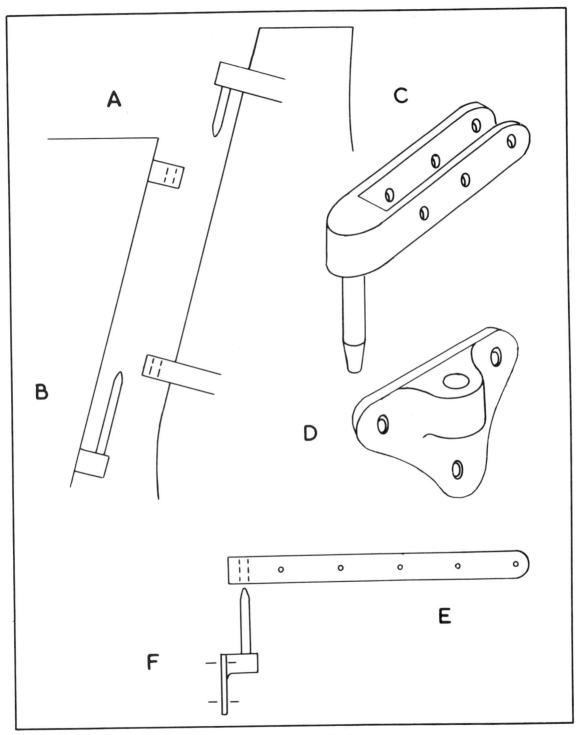

Fig. 7-19. A rudder is hung by gudgeons, with holes; and pintles, with pins.

and the body cannot turn much in relation to each other (Fig. 7-18F).

One way of covering the end and further locking a lock nut is to use a piece of heat-shrink plastic tube. It slides over, but when you heat it with a flame or in any other way, it will shrink and conform closely to the part it is around. If you need to open the joint later, it will have to be cut off and cannot be re-used.

GUDGEONS AND PINTLES

There are several ways of hanging a rudder on the stern of a boat, but in many craft where it is outboard and capable of being lifted off, there is an arrangement of pins in holes to provide the hinge arrangement. Parts with pins are *pintles*. Parts with holes are *gudgeons*. For larger craft and those where the rudder post goes through the hull, the rudder hangings are specially fabricated. For boats with the rudder on the transom or stern post there are stock fittings.

In a common arrangement there is a pintle pointing down at the top of the rudder to engage with a gudgeon bracket on the boat (Fig. 7-19A), then a pintle on the boat engages with a gudgeon near the bottom of the rudder (Fig. 7-19B). Usually the lower pintle is longer so it can be engaged first when the rudder is being located.

In use there can be considerable torsional loads on a rudder, particularly when the boat is sailing in a beam wind and the rudder is being used to prevent leeway and keep the boat on course. Consequently, attachments have to be strong. At the top the pintle has straps on each side of the rudder as long as it allows (Fig. 7-19C). The gudgeon bracket to take it usually has three bolts through the transom (Fig. 7-19D). As the lower part of the rudder is usually wider, the straps are longer on that gudgeon (Fig. 7-19E) and the mating pintle bracket has three holes for screws (Fig. 7-19F).

Chapter 8

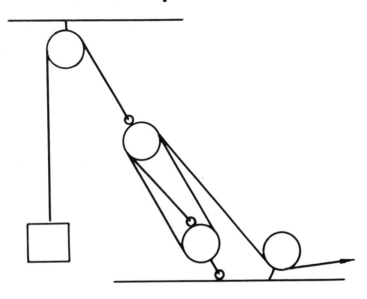

Mechanical Aids

THERE IS A LIMIT TO THE EFFORT ANY ONE PERson can exert. If he is to make a direct pull he will reach a point where he just does not have the strength to pull any more. If he is to hoist a load he will find that more than a certain amount cannot be managed. One way of getting more power is to have more men helping. With large sails, there could easily be too much direct weight for one man to hoist and if the wind is trying to fill the sail as well, the load on the halyard becomes very much more. In the days of square-rigged sailing ships there may have been space for many men to tail on the halyard and get the sail up, but in today's average sailing boat there are neither the men nor the space to allow this. This is only one example. Breaking the anchor from the bottom may need more power, and handling the sheets of even a modestly canvased boat may need more power than one man can exert by a direct pull.

There are other situations where the actual lift or pull may be within the strength range of a man, but for the best effect the final tightening has to be more than he can apply. As with the previous examples, he needs assistance of some sort. This is particularly so with the sails of racing craft, where, to get the best results, sails must be hoisted tightly and sheets hardened in precisely.

PURCHASES

When there is an arrangement that allows a load to be moved greater than the effort applied there is said to be a *mechanical advantage* or a *purchase*. This is not something for nothing. If a small load moves a large load, the small load has to be moved a proportionately greater distance than it moves the larger load. The product of load and distance are the same in both cases. This is called *work*. As an example, if a pull of 50 pounds moves a load of 100 pounds, the 50 pound pull will have to move 2 feet for every 1 foot the load is moved. This means that there has to be a balance between a reasonable distance and the reduction of effort. In the case of a main sheet, it would be possible to arrange tackle so the sail could be pulled in by a small child, but he would be filling the cockpit with an enormous length of rope in the process. Similar reasoning applies to devices that use a crank handle, where practical limits have to be balanced against the desire for easy operation.

FRICTION

Another consideration is friction. You cannot operate any mechanical device without friction, which has to be overcome. With modern equipment it is possible to reduce friction to quite a small amount. A plain wheel on a plain axle can be eased by lubrication, but there will still be some friction to overcome that could be noticeable, especially in a series of wheels. If the wheel is given ball or roller bearings, the friction is reduced to a point where it has little effect.

There is also internal friction within the rope. When rope is bent around a wheel or even over an edge, fibers towards the outside of the curve have to stretch, while those inside are compressed. Those around the center, called the *neutral axis*, do not stretch or compress, but the total effect within the rope is for fibers to need to slide against each other. This sets up friction, which has to be overcome.

A severe example is the improvised rope purchase (Fig. 4-5C), where the rope under load is bent around another part of the same rope, so the curve is quite tight. It may be almost as severe in a deadeye (Fig. 7-16A). In both cases there is also the friction due to the rope rubbing over a non-rotating surface. It would be better to have a wheel, but at the original size that would be too tiny to be very effective.

Internal friction is greater when the curve is small (Fig. 8-1A) and is much less on a large curve (Fig. 8-1B). This means that it is always better to take a rope around a large wheel than a small one, but there are obvious practical limits. You cannot set an exceptionally large wheel in a mast for a halyard, nor have big wheels in blocks for a sheet. However, the point should be remembered and the largest diameter wheel that can be used should always be preferred. The friction on the axle is little different between large and small wheels. There is

such a difference between the surface friction of a rope on a rotating wheel (Fig. 8-1C) and sliding over a curve of the same size (Fig. 8-1D), that the latter arrangement should be avoided when rigging a boat.

How much friction to allow for depends on the arrangement and its complexity. When estimating it is reasonable to think of a loss of 10 percent, so if what you plan to use will move 500 pounds, treat it as actually being 450 pounds, although with modern equipment you will probably do better than that.

The user of a sailing boat is not so concerned with timing—at least not as a precise measurement. *Work*, meaning the product of load and distance, becomes *power* if we add time to it. Thus, if a man manages to lift 50 pounds through one foot in one second, or any other combination of the three factors with the same product, that is in fact what may be considered one man power. One horse power is about eleven times as much.

BLOCK AND TACKLE

The word *pulley* may seem the obvious name for the grooved wheel around which a rope is taken, but to a seaman it is a *sheave* or maybe *shiv*. The assembly containing one or more sheaves is a *block*—just that, not "pulley block," which is more of the shore term. An assembly of ropes and blocks makes a *tackle*, which many seamen prefer to pronounce "tayckle." Most modern blocks are combinations of plastic and stainless steel, but many still use wood for cheeks, which is kinder to anything it may knock against. The parts of an all-metal double-sheave block will serve as a guide to the usual names of pulley parts (Fig. 8-2A). Traditional blocks were of wood, with a rope *strop* taking in the sheel of the block and a thimble, by using a tight seizing between them (Fig. 8-2B). If suitable minimum-friction bearings are used, there is no reason why this type of block should not be used on craft where a traditional appearance is wanted.

The rope strop is made from a single strand of rope, slightly longer than three times the intended circumference. Take it from the rope without disturbing the wavy shape produced by the lay. Start twisting into itself (Fig. 8-2C) until you have gone

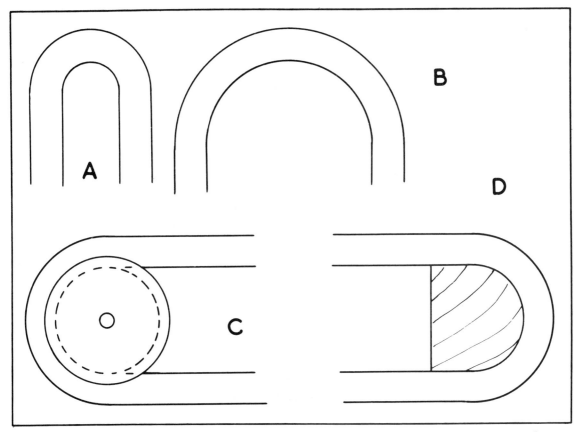

Fig. 8-1. There is more internal friction in a rope with a tight turn (A) than in a larger curve (B). Friction over a wheel (C) is less than over a solid curve of the same size (D).

round three times and the ends meet so you have a continuous three-strand rope (Fig. 8-2D). If you want the strop as an independent thing, then the ends should be tapered and tucked, but on a block you can arrange the ends to be covered and held by the seizing.

The simplest block has just the eye at one end, but for making up into a tackle at least one of the blocks must have an eye at the other end as well. Notice that the *swallow*, through which the rope is *rove* is wider than the gap at the other side of the sheave. You cannot reverse a block. For much of the work in rigging a boat there are blocks with the load taken by stainless steel that extends to form the eyes, while the cheeks are plastic laminates or wood. This construction is preferable to all-metal blocks (Fig. 8-3). Some plastic sheaves on metal

axles do not require lubricating, but in other blocks it should be possible to remove the pin occasionally for lubrication and servicing.

Sheaves are designed for particular sizes of rope. There is some tolerance, but ideally the curve of the cross section of the groove should be only slightly larger than the rope it is intended to take. Where a fiber rope tail on a wire rope has to go around the same sheave, the groove has to be a compromise and sheaves are made with a deeper groove for the wire part. Wire suffers more from being made to go around too small a curve than does fiber rope. The ideal sheave for wire is usually much bigger than can be accepted because of practical problems. It should preferably never be less than 24 times the diameter of the rope. For 7 × 19 stainless steel wire rope, which is the most flexible

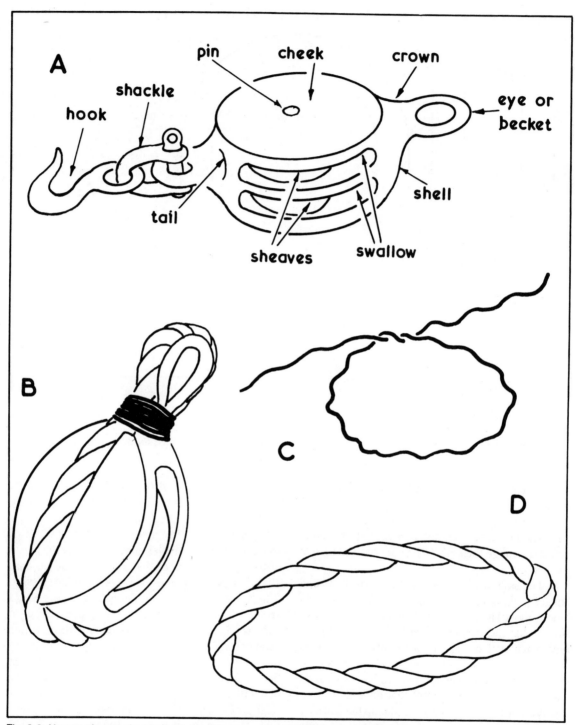

Fig. 8-2. Names of parts of a block (A). Traditional wooden blocks have rope strops (B,C,D).

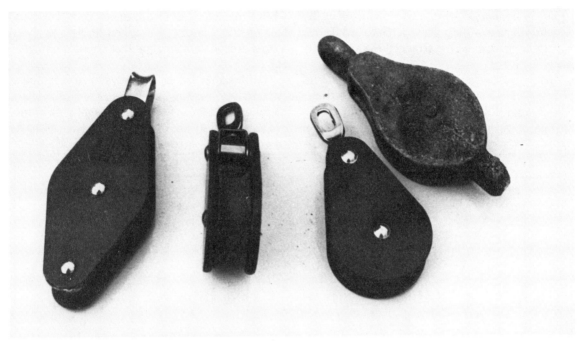

Fig. 8-3. Three stainless steel plastic-faced blocks compared with a galvanized iron one.

RATIOS

and the usual choice for running rigging, that would mean a 3-inch sheave for ⅛-inch rope. In some places you can have that, but if the sheave has to be smaller, you must accept that there will be more internal friction and a greater risk of wires parting.

Tackle is used to vary the ratio between force and distance. If you have one sheave and reeve a rope through it, the direction of the rope is altered, but there is no gain in purchase (Fig. 8-4A). In fact, you will have to apply slightly more weight to the pulling end to overcome friction, so there is a slight loss. This is the case in the common arrangement of hoisting a sail, with the halyard over a sheave near the masthead. If the sheave is on a block attached to the load and you pull back from that there is a theoretical mechanical advantage of two to one (Fig. 8-4B). You do not normally want to apply a pull by lifting, as it is easier to pull down, so the rope may be taken through another block to alter its direction (Fig. 8-4C). The mechanical advantage is still the same, as the second block is only altering the direction of the rope. In fact, this arrangement is more usually arranged with the end of the rope below the second block, but the effect is the same (Fig. 8-4D).

That arrangement of two single blocks gives a mechanical advantage of two to one. If the same assembly is reversed, the advantage is increased to three to one (Fig. 8-4E). As in the earlier assembly, we do not want to pull upwards, so there can be a second block to alter the rope direction (Fig. 8-4F) or the top block can be made into a double one (Fig. 8-4G). If that assembly was reversed, the mechanical advantage would be increased to four to one.

How does that come about? There is an easy way to discover the theoretical mechanical advantage. Count the number of the parts of rope coming from the moving block, and that is the ratio. If the tackle made up of two single blocks is reversed there will be three parts coming from the moving block, where the other way around there were only two. If the tackle made up of a double and a single block is examined, a similar gain in ratio by turning round can be seen. Older users of tackle may talk of *rigging to advantage,* when a tackle is used in the direction that gives the greater purchase, while it is *rigging to disadvantage* if arranged the other way round.

A rigger may find many uses for an assembly of two single blocks with rope tails and called a *handy billy* or *jigger* (Fig. 8-5). It may not form any part of the final rigging of a particular boat, but it is useful when a temporary strain has to be taken. The rope tails or lanyards can be attached to parts or even wound around another rope that needs a stronger pull.

Although a mechanical advantage may seem attractive in reducing the effort needed, remember the amount of rope to be pulled through. With a ratio of 4:1, with every one foot you lift the load you have

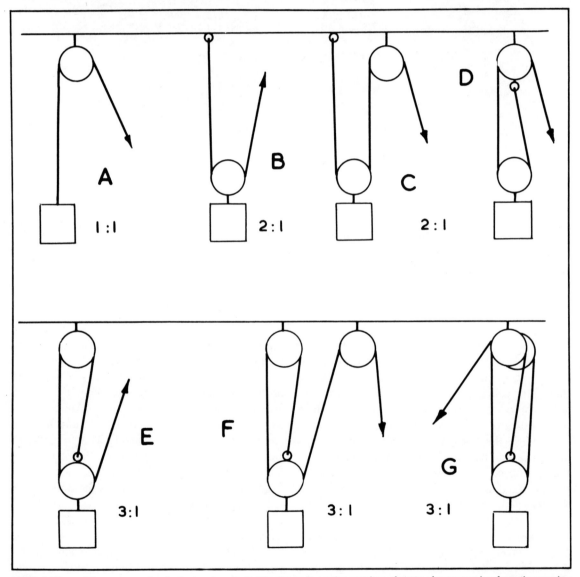

Fig. 8-4. The purchase or mechanical advantage in tackle depends on the number of parts of rope coming from the moving block.

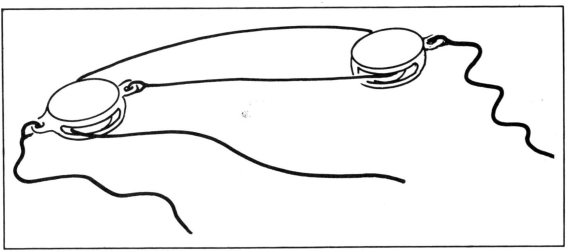

Fig. 8-5. A handy billy is a general-purpose tackle with rope tails for attaching where needed.

to pull through 4 feet of rope. For convenience, do not use a mechanical advantage greater than is actually needed. This is a consideration on arranging main sheets, where the boom may have to be hauled in without undue delay and an exceptional amount of rope to be handled may cancel the value that a high advantage gives. In some boats there may be alternative sheet arrangements for different wind strengths.

TACKLE NAMES

Older books on seamanship contain a great many names for different arrangements of tackle. Many of these are obsolete, but there are a few related terms that should be understood. If there is a rope through a single block that merely changes its direction that is a *whip*. If the single block is at the load it is a *runner*. Two single blocks make a *gun tackle*, from its use in handling the guns of a sailing fighting ship. A single and a double block make a *luff tackle*. A double and a treble block make a *winding tackle*, but it is unusual on a modern boat to go as far up the scale as that. A rope on the end of a block may be a lanyard, but the rope that comes from a block is a *fall*.

There are arrangements where one tackle pulls where there is already another tackle. This happens when a handy billy is added to get more pull on an existing tackle. In that case the purchase is the product of the two tackles. If there is already a ratio of 2:1 and you add another tackle of 2:1 the result is 4:1.

A rather similar arrangement is seen when tackle is used on a sail halyard. There is no mechanical advantage where the halyard goes over the mast sheave—it is only forming a whip—but add a single block to the fall and you get a 2:1 advantage (Fig. 8-6A), whether the rope is pulled directly or led via another block to the cockpit or elsewhere (Fig. 8-6B). If you need a greater pull, there can be a double block at one end for 3:1 or 4:1 (Fig. 8-6C). In some assemblies of tackle the thickness of a normal double block may be a nuisance. Instead, one sheave can be put below the other and this may be called a *sister block* or a *burton* (Fig. 8-6D), but the effect is no different.

That name may also be used when two single blocks are used to get 3:1 ratio. To distinguish, this may be a *single burton* or a *Spanish burton* (Fig. 8-6E).

A *snatch block* is arranged with one cheek to hinge open so the block can be put on a rope without using its end. This may have some uses during rigging work, but is not usually part of permanent rigging.

Although it is easier to pull downwards than upwards, the amount of effort a man can then employ is limited by his own weight. He could reach

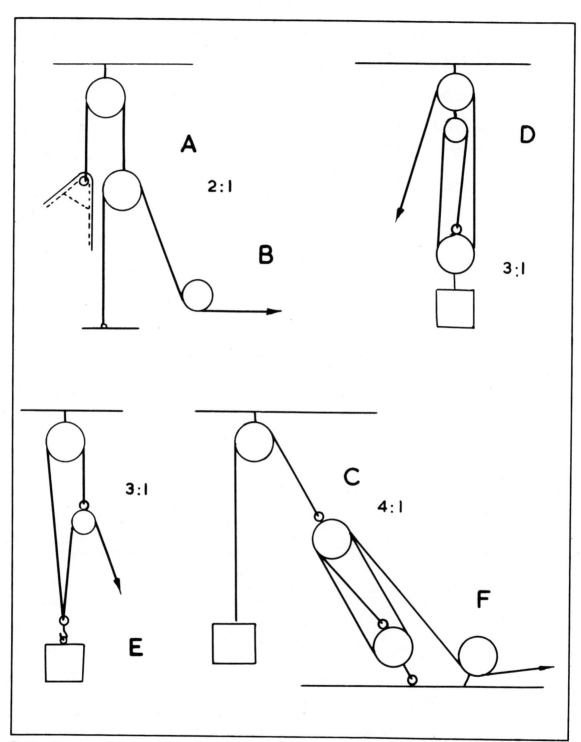

Fig. 8-6. Compound tackles provide purchase compactly.

122

a stage where he is lifted off the deck. It is better to have a lead block (Fig. 8-6F) so the pull is taken nearer horizontal, with the feet braced. If help is needed, it is easy for another person to share the pull in that direction.

SAFETY

In theory the rope used in a tackle need only be proportional in size to the mechanical advantage. In a 4:1 tackle it need only have one quarter the cross-sectional area of the rope being pulled, but in practice it is never as small as that. There are practical considerations, such as the rope being thick enough for comfortable handling. The margin of safety is therefore quite large. In practice, the parts of a tackle may be thinner than the main rope, but usually not very much so.

If a tackle is made up temporarily, the end of the rope can be attached to the ring of one block with a round turn and two half hitches. For a more permanent assembly the rope should be spliced around a thimble and shackled to the eye of the block. The other end of the rope should be whipped and a knot put in it to prevent it running out of the blocks.

Usually when tackle is used the end will be held or secured elsewhere, either knotted or held by a cleat or a belaying pin. Sometimes it may be more convenient to secure the rope at the tackle, particularly if it is temporary and the fall will soon have to be used again. The method of securing is called *choking the luff*.

To do this, put the free part of the fall under a turn that would be pulling into the throat of a block if the load was allowed to run (Fig. 8-7A). That may be all that is needed for a temporary hold, but a bight of the fall can be used to put a half hitch above the block (Fig. 8-7B). It could be continued with a second half hitch to make a clove hitch in the bight.

A strong pull by the load could cause the part of the fall nipped under the turn through the swallow to pull in and jam, particularly if there is much clearance around the ropes there. An alternative to avoid this risk is to use the bight of the fall to make a clove hitch around the parts between the blocks (Fig. 8-7C). The first method locks the tackle exactly as set, and this may be important if the amount the load has been pulled matters. There would be a little backlash in the last method as the clove hitch pulls tight around the block.

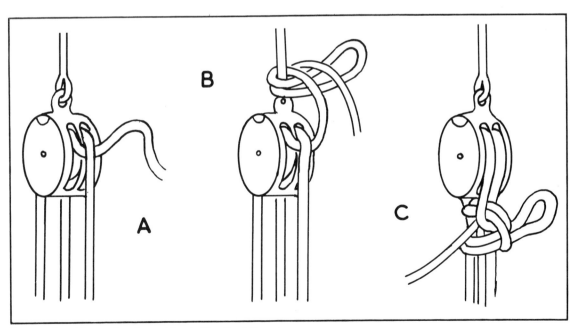

Fig. 8-7. A tackle may be stopped by choking the luff.

LEVERS

It is possible to gain a mechanical advantage with a simple lever. If a bar rests on a *fulcrum* so one end extends much more than the other, a heavy weight on the short end can be lifted by comparatively light pressure on the other end (Fig. 8-8A). If the fulcrum is moved to the end and the weight brought to the same side as the handle, the effect is the same (Fig. 8-8B). If the handle is four times as far from the fulcrum as the weight, the effort needed is one-quarter of the weight, but the handle has to be moved four times as far as the weight is moved.

There are a few applications of levers in the permanent rigging of a boat. One is found where a backstay to the gunwales has to be let go quickly on the lee side and quickly set up again when that becomes the weather side on the next tack (Fig. 8-8C). Throwing the lever over leaves the stay limp so it does not interfere with the sail, yet the reverse action tensions it without the need for adjustment.

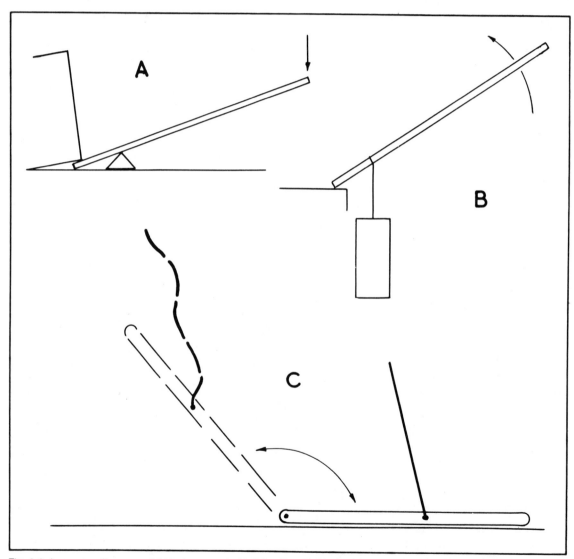

Fig. 8-8. Leverage allows a weight to be moved with little effort (A,B) or a lever can be used to release a load (C).

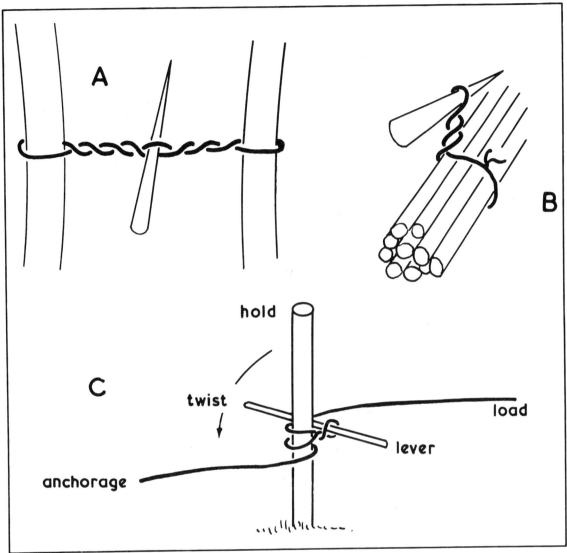

Fig. 8-9. A Spanish windlass tightens by twisting a rope (A,B) or it can be used to move a load (C).

Temporary levers can be used by a rigger to move or lift things too heavy for handling directly. Something may be levered and then blocks put under the bar to hold it in place while other work is done. A simple application is the use of a spike through two holes in parts that have to be drawn into position for a bolt to be put through.

One application of the lever is seen in the *Spanish windlass,* of which there are at least two variations. If two parts have to be drawn closer together and are parallel or nearly so, several turns of line may be wrapped around and the ends knotted. Put a lever through and twist, to put on considerable squeezing pressure (Fig. 8-9A). If the load has to be held, the end of the lever may be wedged against something or it can be seized to the turns.

If a bundle has to be drawn together, there can be several loose turns around, then twist the lever in them (Fig. 8-9B). This is similar to the first aid

125

tourniquet and may also be called *log lashing*, from its use in drawing bundles of logs together ashore.

The name is also used for a surprisingly powerful improvised windlass, that will pull a heavy load a short distance. Have a stout pole with its end pushed into the ground, if ashore, then hold the top so it is reasonably upright. Have one end of the rope securely anchored and the other attached to the load. Put the lever through with a few turns of the rope, then start to twist the lever around the pole, (Fig. 8-9C). This will draw the load along and tilt the pole, which will have to be repositioned if the load has to be moved far.

WINDLASSES AND WINCHES

If the rope under load is taken up by winding it around a drum, which is turned by hand or power, the device may be called a *winch* or a *windlass* and to some people the names are interchangeable. It is probably more in line with modern thinking to use the name windlass for the apparatus for working the anchor cable or a mooring line, while a winch is used for working running rigging. The first usually has its drum horizontal, while the winch drum is upright. In the old days of square riggers the men walked around a windlass, not a winch, and you are not necessarily wrong today to use either term for either apparatus.

In its simplest form the rope is wound on to a drum directly coupled to a crank handle. The mechanical advantage is then the ratio between the length of the handle and the radius of the drum (Fig. 8-10A), or more correctly the radius of the neutral axis of the cable to the drum. The longer the handle the greater the advantage but as with other apparatus, the effort may be less, but the distance the hand has to go around the circumference of the handle swing is proportionately greater. You do not get something for nothing. There is obviously a practical limit to the length of the handle that can be accommodated. In some winches a lever is used instead of a handle. As it only needs a limited movement instead of a full circle, it can be rather longer (Fig. 8-10B). It could be taken out and put into a new slot, or it may swing to a new position with a ratchet to provide drive. In both cases the drum has to be locked between movements.

The next step is to gear the drum. This is particularly necessary if there is electric power because an electric motor has to rotate rapidly, even if the drum of the windlass needs to turn much slower. As a simple example there could be two mating gear wheels, with one twice the size of the other. If the handle is attached to the smaller one, there is a mechanical advantage between the two wheels of 2:1, with the handle having to be turned twice for one revolution of the drum. Suppose the handle is six times the radius of the drum, the ratio due to that is 6:1, which has to be multiplied by the other ratio to give a ratio of 12:1 (Fig. 8-10C). There could be a further pair of gears to give an even better ratio for a stubborn load. Some hand anchor winches have two places where the handle can be fitted, so either of two ratios can be used according to the load.

Sheet winches are now made in great variety, with various gearing and the handle position either above or below. In one type the gear ratio can be altered by changing the direction of turning the handle. A ratchet handle may be provided, so it does not have to make a complete circuit, or there may be a ratchet in the winch. If gearing is provided, it is within the drum, although the principle is the same as that shown in the diagrammatic example.

A *snubbing winch* is one where the drum is provided, but no handle, and the tension on a sheet is provided by a direct pull on the fall after a few turns around the drum.

A halyard winch may be mounted on the mast (Fig. 8-10D). With a small drum and a long handle, considerable work can be done, so the halyard may be set up very tightly. With this and some other winches used for running rigging, care is needed not to use so much power that the rope is damaged or even broken. With most winches the handle can be removed. This is important, otherwise unintentional free rotation could be dangerous, especially if the handle flies away.

With the usual vertical drum of a sheet winch the rope comes from the load to the lower part of the drum and turns go on above it. The fall is held and pulled by hand as the turns build up while the winch is turned. Be careful that the turns go on evenly and do not ride over each other. There is a limit to the

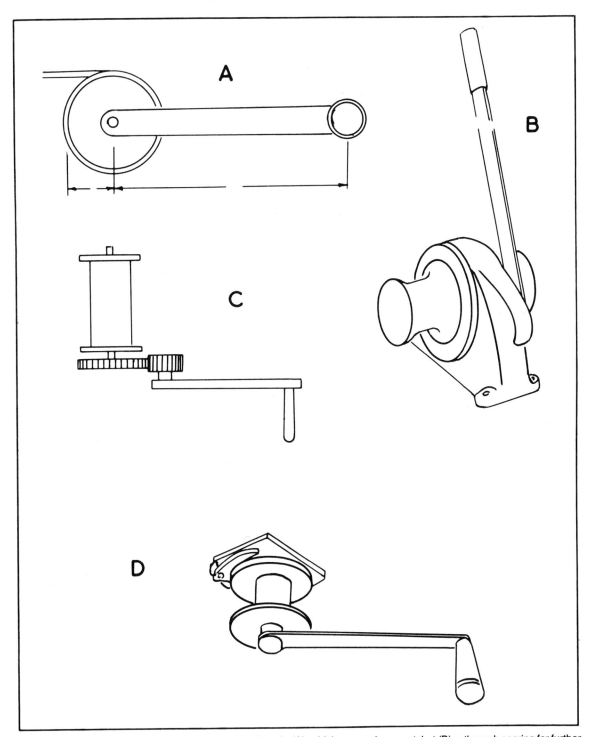

Fig. 8-10. There is a mechanical advantage in a long handle (A), which can work on a ratchet (B) or through gearing for further advantage (C) in a windlass. A simple windlass may have a pawl to prevent it running back (D).

capacity of a drum and turns should not be allowed to build up a second layer. If there is a tendency to ride up, the lead of the loaded part is probably wrong and the rigger may have to relocate blocks or fairleads.

An anchor windlass is usually on the foredeck. If it is hand operated it is more likely to have a lever than a crank handle. This makes a more compact unit that does not stand too high above the deck, but it is comparatively slow-acting because of the long leverage. In many smaller craft the windlass breaks the anchor out of the bottom, but it is then brought to the deck by pulling the cable directly by hand.

If the windlass is electric, there has to be an internal gearing to get a slow turn of the drum from the fast motor. A worm drive gives a good step down, but there may be other gearing. It is usual for such a windlass to have a drum for fiber rope as well as a *gypsy*, which has a pattern around it to match the links of the anchor chain. To allow for the modern arrangement of a fiber rope cable for most of the length and only a short piece of chain next to the anchor, there are drums grooved for rope as well as chain.

For some purposes it does not matter if the chain links vary slightly in size, but if the chain has to be used with a windlass having a gypsy, the two must be matched. Chain that has the links made to match is called *gauged* or *registered*. A stronger type is *stud link chain*, which has a stud across the center of each link to keep it in shape under load. That will not go on a gypsy intended for ordinary short link chain, so a special gypsy must be used.

By their nature any types of winches or windlasses will put a considerable load on their mountings in use. A rigger fitting them in new construction or where others have not been used before them should check the situation carefully. Through fastenings should be used and these should go through reinforcing parts. On the foredeck the bolts holding a windlass must go into structural members and not just the deck parts. If necessary there must be additional parts below the deck to spread the load. Winches often have to come on the cockpit coaming, which in itself may not be built to take much strain. There will have to be thickening and parts extending where they will put the load on parts better able to take them.

With any device intended to produce a resulting load or pull on some part of the rigging, there has to be an equal and opposite load taken as a reaction to it. If tackle is rigged, the fixed end must be capable of withstanding as much load as the boom, or whatever is being pulled. An eyeplate with wood screws will probably not be enough. There should be an eye-bolt going right through, with a pad or large washer to spread the load at the other side.

Chapter 9

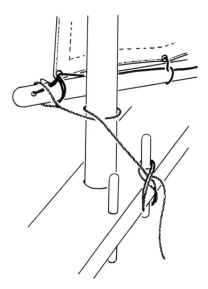

Spars

EVERY SAILING BOAT HAS AT LEAST ONE MAST. There will almost certainly be a main boom and there could be such things as a bowsprit, a bumpkin, and a spinnaker pole, as well as associated things like boat hooks, and oars or paddles. At one time all of these things, collectively termed *spars*, would have been made of wood. Often they still are, but metal, and even plastic, have come into use.

There is a need to keep weight aloft to the minimum, so wooden masts are normally made of the softest woods that have adequate strength. Sitka spruce has been a favorite. Some other softwoods contain more resin that adds to the weight, but the straightness of grain of such woods as Oregon and Columbian pine contributes strength as compensation for the increase in weight. In larger craft the relative weight is not as great, so even more resinous, and therefore heavier, woods have been used for large masts, particularly those in rigs where the mast is expected to provide much of the rigidity within itself, with little or no rigging to support it. For a main boom there is some advan-

tage in weight to help set the sail, and as this is fairly low it does not have such an effect on stability. Although heavier woods are sometimes used for booms, they are more often made of the same woods as masts.

Masts made of aluminum alloy are comparatively recent. Round parallel tubes have been available for a long time, but hollow sections to make tapered masts of any size, with sail track included, have been developed in all the sizes to suit a range of sailing craft. Aluminum alloy masts and other spars have taken the place of wood on many boats. With the masts come a range of fittings and attachments so a comprehensive rig can be set up. Other aluminum sections make booms and other spars.

For the smallest sailing craft, such as canoes, bamboo and other canes have been used for spars. These are unsuitable for larger boats, even when pieces of sufficient size are available. Cane is very light in relation to its strength and size, so there is a case for using it where that property is important. In countries where cane is plentiful and the other woods are rarer, much successful sailing gear is based on canes.

ROUND SPARS

The simplest and most economical rig for a small open boat is based on round wood spars. The mast is a tapered pole and the boom is a parallel pole. If there is a gaff or yard, that is another lighter round pole. For a general-purpose sailing boat, intended just for leisurely sailing or children's use, it is possible to arrange a rig with a balanced lug sail, or something similar, that needs few, if any, bought fittings. In the smallest boat the mast may have sufficient stiffness without stays. In a rather bigger boat they could be fiber rope. A move to wire rigging brings it into a rather more sophisticated type of boat.

For that sort of rig the spars could be merely young straight trees, with the bark peeled off. The old-fashioned drawknife is a useful tool for removing bark, cutting through branches and leveling any slight unevenness (Fig. 9-1). It is advisable to let sap dry out after peeling and before using. Ideally, you leave it about one year after the tree was felled. During the drying time some *shakes* will almost certainly open up. These are lengthwise cracks due to shrinkage while drying. Unless they are very big, they do not affect strength. If you can select a pole

longer than you finally want for the mast you can cut off shakes that open at the ends.

It is more likely that spars will have to be made from square lumber. Select straight stock. If the wood has been seasoned while square and it is still straight, warping is unlikely when you convert it to round. If the spar is to be parallel when finished, as it would be for a boom, boat hook shaft, or spinnaker pole, you first convert it to a regular octagonal section, then take off those eight corners and finally remove all angular parts to make the wood round.

Either draw a square the same size as the wood or work on its end. Draw diagonals and measure half a diagonal. Use that distance to make a mark each way from each corner (Fig. 9-2A). Join those marks and you will see that you have produced eight equal sides (Fig. 9-2B). Mark the lines along the length of the wood. It would be unwise to scratch with a marking gauge as deep scratches might still show on the finished spar. It is better to make a *thumb gauge* by notching a piece of wood to use with a pencil (Fig. 9-2C).

Plane the corners off to these lines. You could do that on a power planer or jointer, but you can do it by hand if the wood is supported in notched pieces on a bench top (Fig. 9-2D). A coarsely set plane will quickly remove softwood and a finer set allows you to work more carefully to the lines.

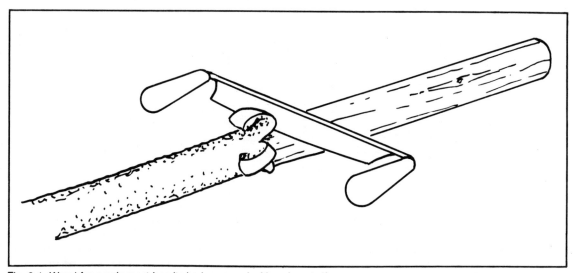

Fig. 9-1. Wood for a pole mast has its bark removed with a draw knife.

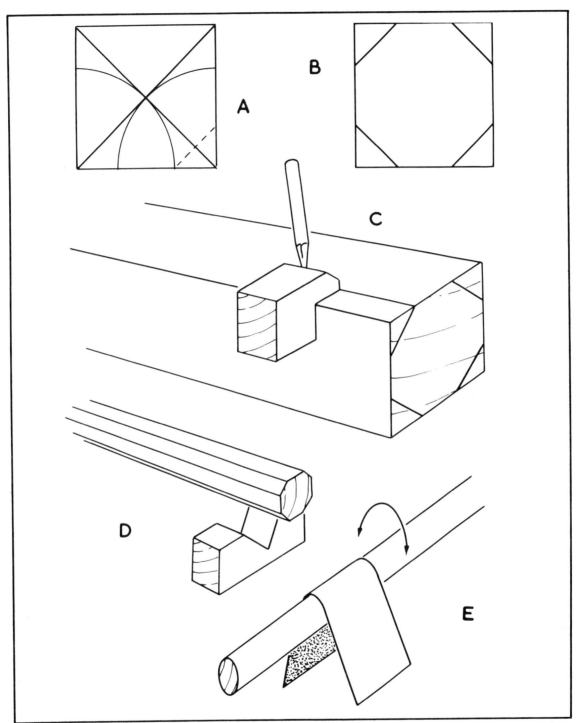

Fig. 9-2. Square wood to be made round is first made octagonal, marked geometrically, then the corners planed off and rounded by sanding.

There is no need to mark the next cuts, but with the spar suitably supported take off the angles so you are left with sixteen fairly evenly matched faces. You may check how much to take off by planing first near one end, but from then on work the full length of the wood. Do not plane just short lengths or you may finish with an uneven appearance. It helps to work so there is a light source on the side of the wood opposite to where you are standing. It could be a window or an electric light bulb. This shows up the ridges from planing and you can see where there are high spots to be taken off with the plane. You may wish to go along with a small single-handed plane while you rotate the spar with the other hand to show up ridges that should be lowered.

Rounding from this stage is done by sanding. Use a fairly coarse abrasive in a strip, so you can pull it backwards and forwards around the wood (Fig. 9-2E). If you rest the wood on padding, you can sit on it to hold it while you work over the part projecting from the bench. With this grip you can easily loosen and turn as required. Do the whole length of the spar in this way. Check that there are no ridges that have been missed. Although the wood will be round, it will be covered with scratches across the grain and these would show through varnish. Remove these marks by using the same coarse abrasive along the grain until you are certain the crosswise marks have gone. For the finest finish follow with a finer abrasive paper used along the grain.

Spruce and other softwoods tend to absorb dirt quickly, particularly just after sanding. If you can, do any other work that is needed on the spar and give it at least one coat of varnish. If the spar will have to wait to be finished, varnish it, even if that will have to be removed later to allow other work to be done. For economy and speed you could put on a coat of shellac to keep out the dirt, but that will have to be rubbed down when the final finish is applied, as shellac is not a marine finish.

A mast will have to be tapered. If it is going through the deck or a mast thwart, the part below could remain parallel (Fig. 9-3A). From there up it needs a slight taper. The best mast taper is not straight. Instead, there should be a slight convex curve along the mast. Be careful not to go the other way and produce a hollow taper.

If you are making a yard, it could be thicker at the attachment point and taper to the ends (Fig. 9-3B). This will lighten the spar and keep strength where it is most needed. A spinnaker pole could be made slightly thicker at the center, putting strength where it is most needed and looking better than a quantity-produced parallel pole.

If you start with a parallel, square piece of wood, mark and plane the tapers first. You then have the problem of marking the guide lines for planing to an octagonal section along tapered length. Mark the octagon at the large end. You can do the same as a guide at the small end, but that is not so important. Make a gauge by driving two stout nails through a strip of wood, with the distance between them the same as the largest size of the wood (Fig. 9-3C). For a better tool put short pieces of dowel rod in holes. With this in position mark where the lines have to come and cut notches there for the pencil (Fig. 9-3D). If you now draw the gauge along the wood with a pencil in a notch, you can twist the tool as the wood gets narrower and so keep the pegs against the sides and keep the line you are drawing the correct relative distance from the edge (Fig. 9-3E). Turn the tool round for the second line or use the other notch. Do this on all four surfaces. From that stage, the finishing of a tapered spar is done in the same way as a parallel one.

FINISHING WOOD SPARS

For a small boat most of the additions to the spars can also be wood. The rigging of a very basic balanced lug sail on a small open boat will serve as an example (Fig. 9-4).

The mast foot should be cut with a tenon to fit a mortise in a mast step over the keelson or hog (Fig. 9-5A). To draw a line around a spar for this or other purposes, use a piece of paper with a straight edge and pencil around it (Fig. 9-5B). To get the tenon in a central position you need marks on the wood diametrically opposite. Use the paper strip. Push a spike or nail through the overlap. When the strip is

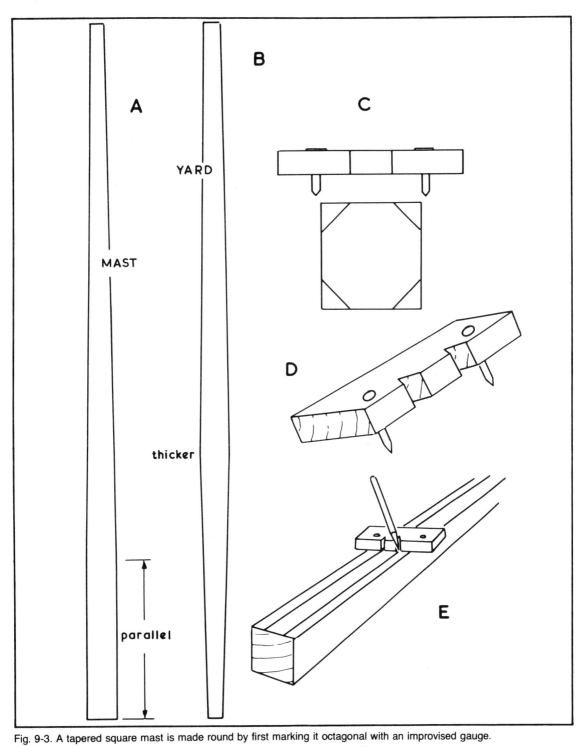

Fig. 9-3. A tapered square mast is made round by first marking it octagonal with an improvised gauge.

133

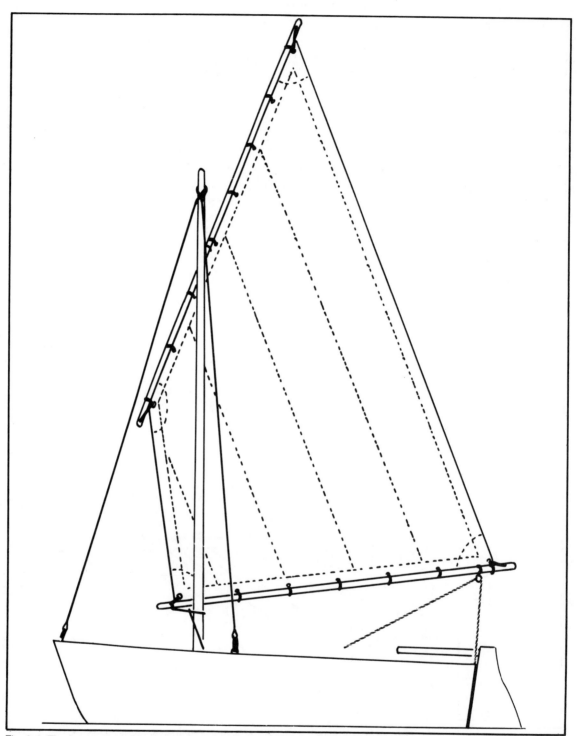

Fig. 9-4. The layout of a balanced lug rig.

134

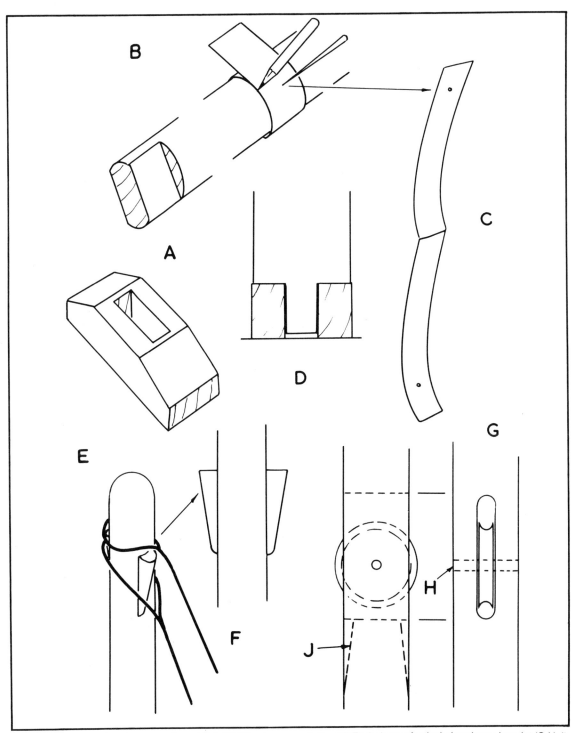

Fig. 9-5. Marking and cutting a round mast (A to D). Chocks support stays (E,F). A sheave for the halyard goes in a slot (G,H,J).

opened out the distance between the holes will be the circumference at that place. Fold the paper so the holes meet and the fold will be at half the circumference (Fig. 9-5C). Put the paper back around the wood and mark where the holes and fold come. Those points will be opposite. Mark the width of the tenon around a centerline and it will be central. When you cut the tenon, it is better for the mast to rest on its shoulders than on the tenon, which should be slightly clear of the bottom (Fig. 9-5D).

The mast should be tall enough to extend up to one foot above where the sheave for the halyard will come. Round the end, then arrange chocks each side a few inches down (Fig. 9-5E). They may be hardwood and screwed and glued in place. Their purpose is to take eyes spliced in the shrouds and forestay (Fig. 9-5F). If the sail is high-peaked, as it should preferably be, there will be no need to worry about the yard clearing the forestay as tack is changed. It may be advisable to try a dummy assembly to check that the position of the mast sheave will allow the yard to swing across.

Use the sheave as a guide to the size of the slot. It is possible to get a sheave already mounted in a metal box, which can be put in as a unit. That may be preferable, but in this case we assume the more economical method will be used. Use a strip of paper, with holes and fold to mark the opposite sides of the two ends of the slot. Allow for clearance above the sheave for the halyard, but the sheave can come close to the bottom of the slot. Drill through the ends from opposite sides and pencil between the holes the width of the slot (Fig. 9-5G). Remove the waste by more drilling with a smaller bit and careful work with a chisel, going about halfway from each side. You can get the inside smooth with a file. See that the sheave fits in easily, but not so loosely that there would be a risk of the rope slipping to one side of it.

The strip of paper can be used to mark where the axle hole has to come at each side, using the sheave itself as a gauge for the height the axle must come. Drill from each side. Use rod of a size to suit the sheave, preferably stainless steel, although it could be brass with a nylon sheave (Fig. 9-5H). If

the rod is driven into the wood, it will not come out accidentally, although it can be driven out if servicing is ever necessary. Ideally, the sheave should be slightly larger than the mast at that point, but if its grooves come within the thickness of the wood, make tapered grooves below the slot so the halyard will run easily (Fig. 9-5J).

The ends of the yard and boom should be rounded and holes drilled to take lacing that will set the sail (Fig. 9-6A). It is unwise to weaken the yard by drilling it for the end of the halyard. It is better to merely knot the end of the halyard around between two small thumb cleats (Fig. 9-6B). Another arrangement uses a *mast traveler*, which is a ring to slide on the mast, with an eye for the halyard and a hook for the yard. In that case there should be a strop (made as described for a block) around the yard, to hang on the hook (Fig. 9-6C). This keeps the yard close to the mast at any height. With the simpler knotting the yard will be kept close when hauled up to the sheave.

For a small boat there is no need to provide a purchase for the sheet, which can be a rope going straight to the hand or through a block on the transom, far enough to one side to allow the tiller to swing. The other end is spliced around the boom and located with thumb cleats (Fig. 9-6D).

In a balanced lug rig there is a tack line at the forward end of the boom—just a short length of line spliced on and held with a thumb cleat (Fig. 9-6E). After the sail has been hoisted, the tack line is used to pull the boom back close to the mast. The method depends on the boat, but if there is a mast thwart, it could be drilled for two belaying pins. Then the tack line is half hitched to the mast and taken down to the pin (Fig. 9-6F). The other belaying pin is used for the halyard. If the arrangement of the boat does not suit belaying pins there could be a cleat each side of the mast to serve the same purpose (Fig. 9-6G).

In this type of rig the sail is usually kept on the spars. At the corners of the sail are grommets or eyelets. Use fairly light line to attach the corners to the spars. Either splice or knot the line to the grommets, then work it through the holes and around the spar. Deal with opposite ends at the same time, so you get an even tension along the

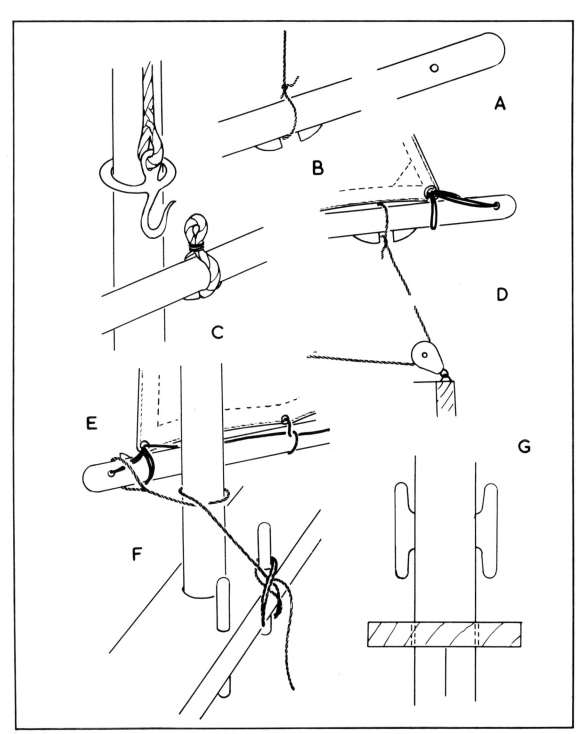

Fig. 9-6. The yard is hoisted by a traveler (A,B,C). The sheet is around the boom (D). The tack line pulls the boom to the mast (E) and may go to pins (F) or cleats (G).

137

spar. Finish with a clove hitch around the turns near the sail (Fig. 9-7A).

It is usual to lace the sail to round spars through eyelets at about one foot intervals. Do this by half hitching along the spar (Fig. 9-7B), not by just wrapping the line around. Be careful when attaching sails to spars that you do not stretch them enough to distort them and see that the sail edge is straight along the spar. It is possible to twist it and to get its edge pulled too tightly, so part of it folds or wrinkles.

If fiber rope stays are used, the two shrouds might be in one length with a cut splice (Fig. 4-7B) over the chocks on the mast. If wire is used it would be better to have separate eyes on the shrouds. Whether fiber or wire the top of the forestay should be an eye. Let the eyes be an easy fit, but not so large that they could slip down the mast if slackened. The bottoms of the shrouds could be attached with lanyards to shroud plates (Fig. 7-16D). The end of the forestay might finish in a similar way, but how it is attached depends on the boat. If there is an eye or hole in the stem head, use that. A shroud plate might be fitted inside the stem.

So the shrouds resist the forward pull of the forestay and keep the mast upright in a lateral plane, locate the shroud plates a short distance aft of an athwartships line across the mast position. How far aft depends on the boat, including its beam as well as its length. The shrouds will stop the boom swinging forward, so must not be led so far aft that it cannot be left out far enough when the boat is running before the wind. On an average 12-foot boat

the shrouds might come about 1 foot aft of the mast. No sail sets flatly and it is the average of the curve which counts. In this case, the boom may be stopped before it is square to the centerline of the boat. The yard will have swung much further and the average angle near the center of the curve of the sail will be right.

When making all the equipment for this sort of rig it is advisable to assemble everything and make sure all is as it should be before final varnishing and possibly before all ropes are spliced and lacing lines whipped. When you have made any adjustments, disassemble completely. Give the spars at least three coats of boat varnish, paying particular attention to the end grain, which is very absorbent in softwoods. Lightly sand between coats for the smoothest finish.

If you use any metal hardware, be careful not to drill too much for screws. Softwoods do not need large holes for screws. For most attachments quite a small hole, less than the depth of the screw is all you need. The screw will then cut its own way in and the fibers pushed aside will help it to grip. If you do find a screw loosens in new work, either replace it with a longer one, if that is possible, or push a few slivers of the same wood into the hole and drive the screw again.

LARGER WOODEN SPARS

There are two main problems with wood when it is used for spars, which become more apparent as the size required gets larger. Solid wood, even when you select the lightest softwood, begins to become

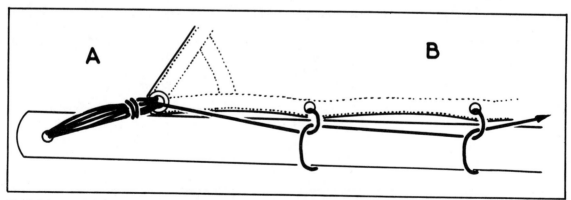

Fig. 9-7. Lacing pulls the sail along its spar and there are half hitches along it.

an appreciable weight in large sizes. Then there is the tendency to warp.

For smaller spars, as just described, it is possible that a natural pole can be selected. This will have the annual rings, which are visible on the end, approximately concentric with the outside of the round spar (Fig. 9-8A). A tree does not build up the rings as true circles as it grows, but they are usually quite near that shape. It is shrinkage as the sap in the wood dries out that causes warping, and this is greatest around the curve of the annual rings. As they go all around, shrinkage cannot pull the spar out of straight, but cracks, called shakes, may open (Fig. 9-8B). Providing they are not very large, they do not affect strength, although they will affect appearance. That does not mean that you will never have such a spar develop a bend or twist, but it is unlikely.

Larger spars will have to be made from sawn wood that is only part of the cross section of a tree. A piece cut from the center of the tree would have the same characteristics as a spar made from a whole smaller tree, but such a piece is unlikely to be available to a spar maker, unless it was specially cut. It is more likely that a spar will have to be made from a square cut from elsewhere in the cross section, as drawn from the stock of a lumberyard. An examination of an end will show the probable shrinkage, if the wood has not already been fully dried out by seasoning. Lines diagonally across a square will cause it to shrink to a diamond shape (Fig. 9-8C) or a circle will pull to elliptical (Fig. 9-8D). This does not give much indication of probable changes of shape in the length, but if you buy new wood from a lumberyard it should be kept for several months, if possible, so you can see if an originally straight piece develops a curve or bend in the length.

With the availability of synthetic resin glues of proved waterproofness has come the possibility of joining strips of wood to make up spars. Laminating in this way is one method of counteracting any tendency to warp. The simplest example is the making of a solid spar from a piece of wood of square section. Before any work is done to shape it, it is cut down the center lengthwise, then one piece reversed on the other and the two parts glued together (Fig. 9-8E). By doing this any tendency of one part to cast or warp in one direction should be balanced by the tendency of the reversed piece to go the other way. This may not always be one hundred percent successful, but it goes a long way towards insuring that the spar remains straight.

In any section, whatever the material, the greater loads are taken near the outside. This is so much so that the center of the section can be regarded as only taking a negligible load. It would be better to remove the center and add an equivalent amount to the outside to gain strength without adding weight. This is a practice in many structural designs as well as in spar making.

If the two parts of a square strip that have been cut and reversed are hollowed before gluing (Fig. 9-8F), the resulting spar will be lighter and just as strong. This technique has been carried much further in the making of hollow tapered wood spars—the work of specialists and not within the scope of a rigger, but you should understand the construction.

ROPE GROOVES

The luff rope of a sail may be attached to slides on a track mounted on a solid mast. There are several versions, but the slides can only be at intervals on the sail, so the leading edge of the sail may curve between slides and not set as perfectly as might be wished (Fig. 9-9A). The sail will set better if the luff rope can slide in a groove in the mast. This becomes possible when a mast is built up from two pieces (Fig. 9-9B). That edge of the mast must be straight, so any tapering or shaping in the length should be done at the other edge. For a smaller sailing boat, cutting the groove may be the only work done on the meeting faces before joining the two parts, but it is more usual to also hollow the mast, so it can be finished to a rounded tapered section (Fig. 9-9C). This is a good aerodynamic shape in relation to the sail, so besides letting the sail set better, due to the groove for the roped edge, it should result in a slightly better flow of air over the sail. Some masts are on rotating steps so they can turn to keep the mast section in the best relation to the cloth of the sail, whatever its angle to the boat.

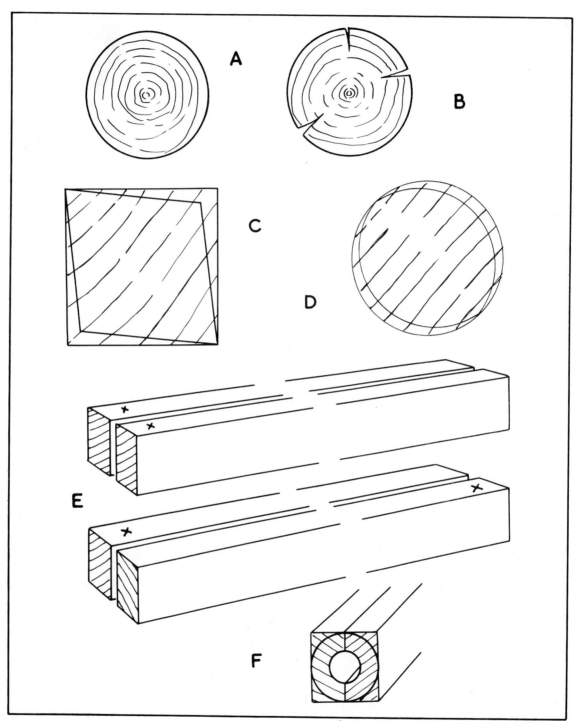

Fig. 9-8. Shrinkage is greater in the direction of annual rings in wood. Cutting and reversing parts or hollowing counteracts much of this.

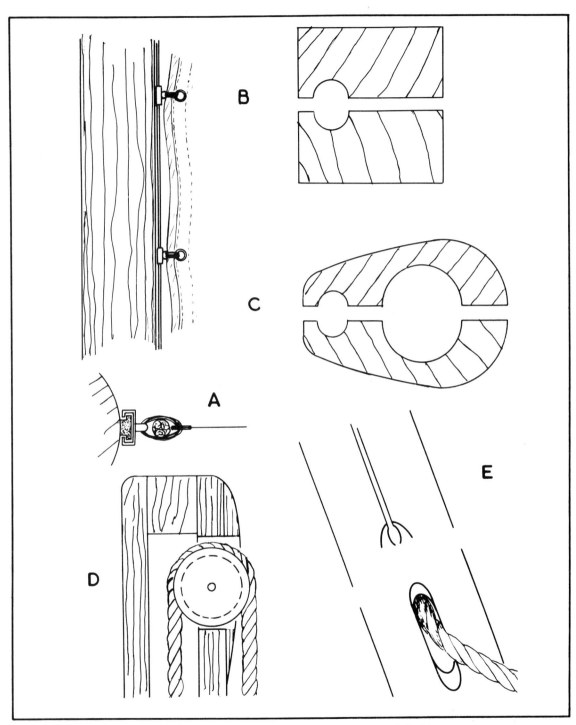

Fig. 9-9. A sail may run with slides on a track (A) or its roped edge go in a mast groove (B,C). A halyard may pass down a hollow mast (D) and out near the bottom (E).

A mast may have adequate strength for most of its length when hollowed, but it is better if top and bottom are solid. As hollowing is usually done by machine and that needs to run right through, a mast may have filler pieces glued back in at the ends. There may also be inside fillers at places where strength is required for the attachment of other hardware.

INTERNAL HALYARDS

It is more usual for the mast to be kept hollow, except at the ends so at least one halyard can be taken through the mast. This means that the main sail sheave at the top is only on the aft side of the mast and the masthead may be modified or carry a bracket for this (Fig. 9-9D). At the bottom the halyard comes out of a slot and the mast may be cut back below the groove to give clearance for the sail rope (Fig. 9-9E). If the halyard is to be led aft there can be a sheave in the slot or below it. If the halyard goes to a cleat further down the mast, it is a simple

slot. There could be considerable wear on the sides of the slot, particularly if it is a wire halyard. There may be sheet metal lining the slot or, more attractively a hardwood, such as mahogany, is let into the sides of the slot during manufacture.

An internal halyard is out of the way of other rigging, so it should not foul when being used. It is also protected from the elements and will affect the aerodynamics of the rig. The rigger has the problem of putting it there.

If there is already a halyard through a hollow mast, but it has to be replaced, bring the end of the new rope to the end of the old one, both being whipped, and draw them together with a needle and twine (Fig. 9-10A). Secure the end of the twine to a strand with a knot and go all around the meeting with diagonal stitches in both directions so you get a smooth enclosed joint. It is worth taking care over this—if the joint comes apart or snags somewhere inside, you are giving yourself extra trouble. With synthetic ropes you may be able to melt the ends of

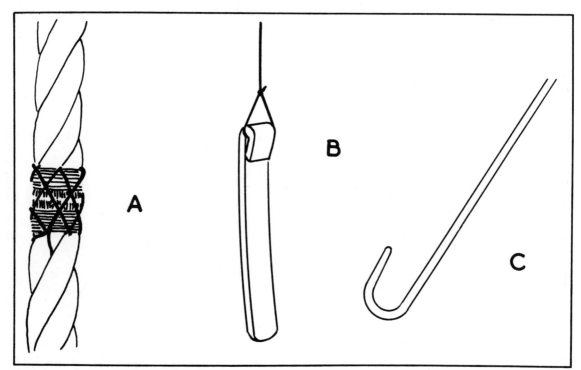

Fig. 9-10. A new halyard can be pulled through a hollow mast attached to the old one (A) or a lead weight may take a line through (B) and be pulled out with bent wire (C).

the rope together strongly enough for one to pull the other through.

If you do not have the benefit of an old halyard to pull through, you have to get a line down the mast so you can pull through the halyard. To do this you have to make up a lead weight, usually called a *mouse*, on a strong, thin flexible line, to lower down the mast.

Cut a piece of strip lead, as wide as will easily pass through the sheave slot at the masthead and out of the lower slot. You will have to compromise between a length that will give plenty of weight and what can be pushed around the sheave. If you have to curve the lead much to get it around the wheel, it may not fall through the hollow very easily. Fishing line can be used, although strong sewing twine is satisfactory. Hammer the end of the lead over the line, which can also be fused or knotted (Fig. 9-10B). Round the free end of the lead so there are no corners to catch inside the mast.

Have a piece of stiff wire with a hooked end ready to pull the line through the slot when you see the weight fall into view (Fig. 9-10C).

Attach the end of the halyard to the line and pull it through. How you do this depends on the line, but make the joint in a way that keeps the end of the halyard straight. You might use a needle and sew centrally into the end of the rope, or it should be satisfactory to have several half hitches and tight seizings near the ends of the rope and the line. If you will not be immediately splicing or doing anything else to permanently stop the rope pulling out of the mast, knot the ends temporarily and make it a practice to always have a knot in the end if the halyard is to be used with just a whipped end.

BOXED SPARS

Another way of building up a hollow spar is to make it in the form of a box section, using four sides (Fig. 9-11A). In its simplest form it has flat outer surfaces (Fig. 9-11B), but there could be enough wood included to allow for more shaping (Fig. 9-11C). The more rectangular section is seen in booms, which also benefit from being grooved for the roped sail (Fig. 9-11D) to give a better set than when slides are used on a track. The more shapely exterior is

better for masts. When such a spar is made it is necessary to see that too much is not taken off the outsides at the corners, otherwise the glued surfaces may be reduced so much that they cannot be expected to hold.

Boxed spars have been made with plywood slides. This allows the sides to be quite thin, yet the crosswise veneers give enough strength in the direction that could be too weak if the sides were thin, solid wood. The only problem with plywood sides is in the possible wear at the plywood edges and water absorption there. The plywood edges should be kept well protected with varnish. In new work edges should be sealed with epoxy glue or some other waterproofing before varnishing.

The ends of boxed spars can be plugged with solid wood glued in. On a boom there would also be inside strengthening blocks where other attachments are to come, such as the sheet blocks or a *boom vang* (Fig. 9-11E). If it is a mast with an internal halyard, inside reinforcing cannot be used. There may have to be some outside strengthening pieces, suitably faired off, where other parts have to join on the plywood surfaces.

SERVICING SAIL GROOVES

One problem that may not be apparent until the rigger tries to fit a sail to a new mast is the presence of glue inside the groove. The maker should have cleared the groove before the glue set, but if that has not been done and glue that squeezed out of the joint has formed small blobs inside the groove, they will be very hard and difficult to get at. The best tool is a small woodcarving spade chisel (Fig. 9-12A). It is narrow enough to pass along the gap for the sail and its end will chip away glue. These tools are not easy to obtain and something similar might be made by hammering and sharpening the end of a piece of tool steel. Even if it is not hardened and tempered, it should stand up to this work.

Another problem is a general roughness inside the groove. A piece of abrasive paper can be wrapped around a dowel rod and pulled along. If much smoothing is needed, use a fairly coarse abrasive paper glued to the dowel rod. This is pulled with a thin line (Fig. 9-12B). You can put pressure

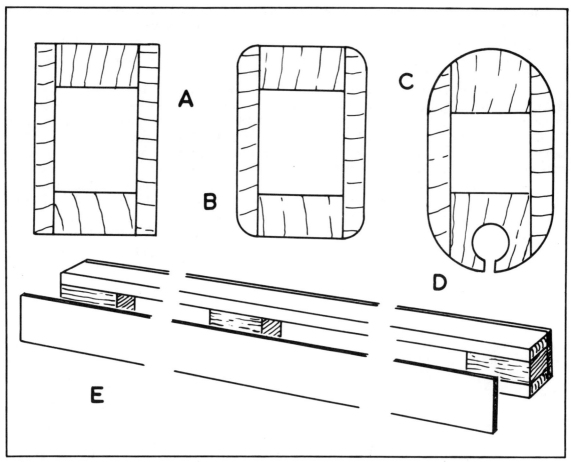

Fig. 9-11. A box-section spar can be built up and rounded or grooved. Blocks of wood may be included where strength is needed for attachments.

on with a steel rule, or something similar, through the slot. With rather less smoothing needed, you can wrap the abrasive paper around the dowel and let the ends project through the slot (Fig. 9-12C). In that way you sand the opening as well as the groove and can pull the paper around to a new position as it gets worn.

Wood spars must be varnished periodically. There used to be special spar varnishes, but now there are general boat varnishes, suitable for all purposes. Unvarnished wood soon absorbs dirt and acquires a grey appearance. Worn places should be touched up to prevent this. A softwood spar will look very attractive when kept protected with several coats of varnish. Rubbing down between coats

can be done with a cloth and a mild scouring powder, such as is sold for domestic purposes.

A neglected part of a spar, yet equally in need of protecting, particularly from water absorption, is the inside of the sail groove. It cannot be reached with a brush and must be treated with a pull-through cloth. Much depends on the size of the groove, but a piece of absorbent cloth tied to line thin enough to pass along the edge of the slot may be all that is needed. For a rather larger groove it would be better to have a thin wood rod and put several layers of cloth around it (Fig. 9-12D). Saturate it with varnish and replenish the varnish through the slot as you slowly pull the device along. Go back and pull through again, with the cloth nearly dry, to remove any surplus varnish. Wipe along the slot with a flat folded cloth.

Lubricating inside the groove should be avoided, as any lubricant may soil the sail, but if there is a persistently awkward part when the sail is drawn along, beeswax or even soap could be used sparingly.

ATTACHMENTS TO HOLLOW WOOD SPARS

With a solid wood spar it is possible to take bolts through or to use quite long wood screws. For instance, a bolt through makes the strongest anchorage for tangs to take mast stays (Fig. 9-13A). That might be done on a hollow mast that has been made solid inside at that position, but if the mast is intended to have a halyard through it, a bolt would obviously be an obstruction.

Instead, it is more usual to rely on attachments that wrap around and either take longer screws into thicker wood or have a large number of shorter screws. On a box sectioned boom, a plate taking the boom vang may have its holes arranged so screws can go into the solid top and bottom of the spar (Fig. 9-13B). With the load coming sideways on the screws, there is little fear of them loosening.

On a mast section a metal strap cannot go around the sail groove. It is usual to have fittings that wrap around as far as possible, so plenty of screws can be used, of lengths that will not penetrate the hollow, carrying halyards (Fig. 9-13C).

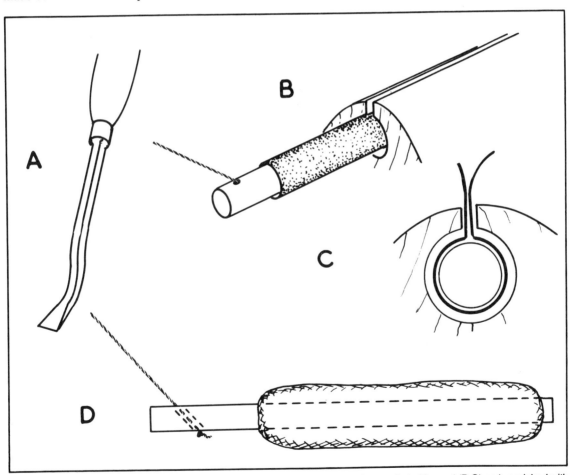

Fig. 9-12. A carving tool (A) will clean away glue inside a slot. The groove may be sanded with a rod (B,C) and varnished with cloth on a rod (D).

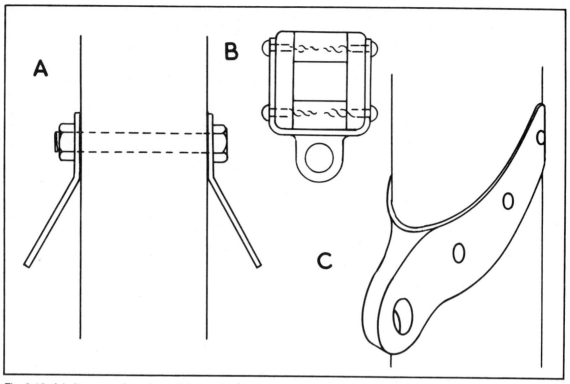

Fig. 9-13. A bolt may go through a solid mast, but the load has to be spread on a hollow mast.

TABERNACLES

Angling the fitting in the direction of pull and taking it more than halfway around, contributes to strength.

A mast supported directly inside the boat above its keel is getting the thrust in the right place. This is the best arrangement of a mast that can remain stepped throughout the season, at least. If it is a boat that is frequently hauled out and trailed behind a car, the mast must be easily lowered or removed. If it is a small open boat, there is no difficulty in lifting out the mast by hand so it may be laid along the boat and possibly allowed to project above the car. If it is a larger craft with a cabin, lifting such a mast out needs boatyard equipment, so some other way of arranging the mast to lower has to be planned. There is also the problem of a boat that has to pass under bridges too low for the mast to clear. Again, a simple method of lowering and raising is needed.

For these circumstances the mast is stepped in a *tabernacle*, so it can swing down aft. In effect a tabernacle is a hinge on deck. In a simple wooden form, the mast foot is square and it fits between two sides on a pivot bolt (Fig. 9-14A). When hauled up tight by the forestay, the mast foot comes against a stop and its beveled end fits on a matching support. The thrust should come on the support and not on the pivot bolt (Fig. 9-14B). In some tabernacles there is a retaining bar or other device to hold the mast foot in place, but it is the forestay and shroud assembly that should hold the mast up. The mast is wrongly rigged if there is any appreciable strain on the tabernacle when the boat is in use.

There is considerable downward thrust on a mast when sailing—much more than its dead-weight. This has to be dealt with. The best arrangement is to have the support part of a post going through to the keel (Fig. 9-14C). If the tabernacle is on the deck forward of a cabin top, the post can go through without causing much obstruction below,

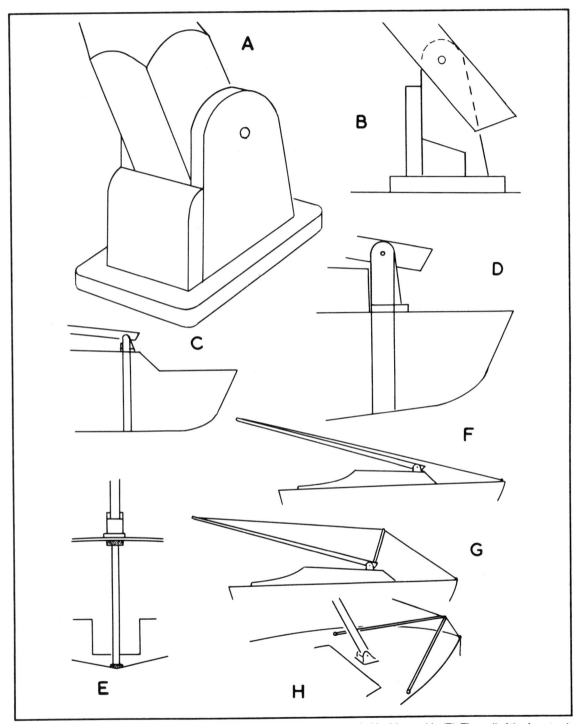

Fig. 9-14. A mast in a tabernacle may lower aft (A to D). A post may be needed inside a cabin (E). The pull of the forestay is better controlled by spars (F,G,H).

but the sides of the tabernacle have to be long (Fig. 9-14D).

If the tabernacle is wood or metal mounted on a cabin top, there must be some way of taking the mast thrust. A permanent post might come below in (Fig. 9-14E). If more space is wanted inside when the boat is moored, there could be a post to take out, but it must fit firmly in position. You have to remember to never start sailing without putting it in position, or you may have the cabin top cave in.

The boom position, plus any cleats and other fittings, should be arranged so they do not interfere with the mast being lowered. It should be possible, in an emergency, to lower the mast with the main sail still attached. That may not be advisable, but if it has to be done you should know that it is possible. As the shrouds lead slightly aft of the mast, they will slacken as the mast swings aft. Lowering is done by manhandling and by using the forestay.

You cannot use the forestay all the way. As the mast approaches horizontal the forestay reaches a point where it is in line and no longer having any effect, particularly if it comes from the stem at foredeck level and the tabernacle is on the cabin top (Fig. 9-14F). In a moderate sized cabin boat it is possible to do the final lowering by supporting the mast top by hand. You will have to handle the mast into its support, in any case.

There is a way of altering the run of the forestay to provide better control, but it involves arranging another one or two spars. If a single spar is attached to the foot of the mast, pointing forward, the forestay can be led over it, so it lifts the stay as the mast goes down (Fig. 9-14G). With a single spar there is a risk of the assembly collapsing sideways, which could do damage to the boat equipment or to helpers. It is better to use shear legs, but their feet need to be securely pivoted on deck (Fig. 9-14H). In both cases the stay should be firmly attached over the added spars, so they cannot slip. Their line in side view should be at about square to the line of the mast.

For small, open or partly decked boats with masts that are light enough to handle, there are arrangements something like tabernacles. The mast can mount on a step in the bottom of a boat, but it need not have a tenon if its lower part is square. A tenon would be needed to prevent twisting if the mast is round all the way. A three-sided box contains the mast up to deck level (Fig. 9-15A). There may be a retaining bar, but as with larger craft, it is the stays that should hold the mast up. The bar is useful during the preparations of the boat. Like a tabernacle on a larger boat, the mast can be lowered by using the forestay while manhandling the mast into the boat.

In an open boat without a foredeck, the mast might fit into a notch on the aft edge of a thwart (Fig. 9-15B). In that case the tenon and step should be fairly deep, so there is no risk of the mast jumping out accidentally during lowering. Round the forward edge of the tenon to give clearance during lowering.

In some partly-decked small boats the mast is mounted on the deck, with a tenon into a step there. With this arrangement the mast is entirely supported by the stays. If any of them fails, the mast and sails fall overboard, which is not as serious as it may seem. The parts are all attached to the boat, which does not capsize, and nothing, except for the failed stay, is likely to be damaged or broken.

A refinement in some small racing craft is to have a jack included in the deck-mounted mast step. By raising or lowering the step the tension in all stays can be adjusted at the same time. Whether this is included or not, there must be good support under the deck-mounted step to transfer the thrust to the keel.

METAL SPARS

Although there are still wooden spars and these are likely to continue, metal masts and other spars are increasingly used. Manufacture has reached the stage where metal spars and all that go with them, can do all that wooden rigging can and often much more. In many ways metal spars have taken over similar functions to wood spars, so all that has been said about wood masts, booms, and other spars, is applicable to metal, as far as a rigger is concerned.

Almost all metal spars and the parts that go with them are made of a sea-water resistant

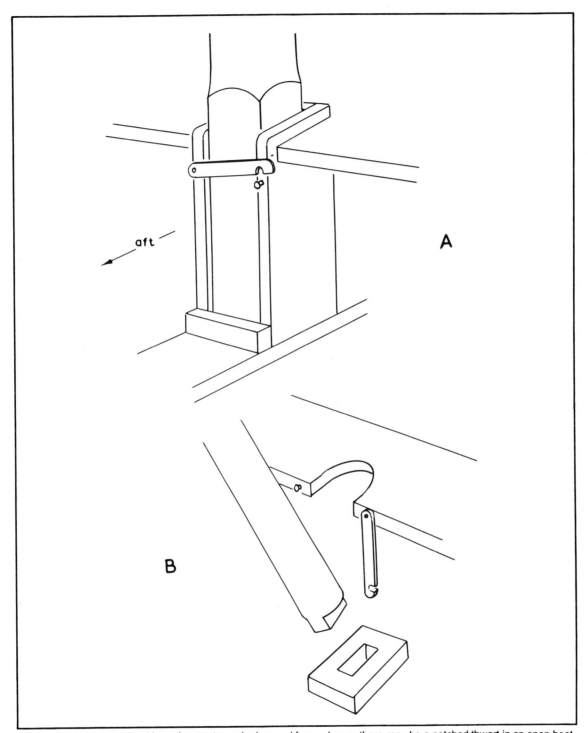

aft

A

B

Fig. 9-15. In a partly-decked boat the mast may be lowered from a box or there may be a notched thwart in an open boat.

aluminum alloy. To avoid the dangers of *electrolysis*, where two metals in the presence of salt water begin to function like an electric cell and one metal is eaten away, attachments should either be a similar alloy or stainless steel. Do not use brass, bronze, or plain steel with aluminum if the boat is to be used in a salt-laden atmosphere.

All aluminum alloy spars are hollow and are tapered for masts where required. A metal tube has much more room inside for halyards to pass without hindrance. Most mast sections have a groove for the mainsail luff rope (Fig. 9-16). As can be seen, not all rope grooves are round, but providing there is ample space inside and the gap suits the sail, the assembly will function easily.

Comparable sections are made with round and other shapes for booms and other spars. Some boom sections have a track underneath so fittings can be located at any position along it for sheet attachments, outhauls, and boom vangs (Fig. 9-17). Of course, intermediate arrangements of this sort cannot be included if the sail is intended to be reefed by rolling a round the boom.

Masts are made up during manufacture to suit particular boats. Adaptation by a rigger to another boat or use is not so easy as with wood spars. A typical mast assembly has end fittings and intermediate parts assembled to it, mostly with rivets (Fig. 9-18A). For a deck-mounted mast or a similar application, the halyards may lead out via sheaves in the mast base (Fig. 9-18B).

ALTERATIONS TO METAL SPARS

When alterations are to be made to aluminum spars, self-tapping sheet metal screws are useful, but they should be stainless steel. Plain self-tapping (self-threading) screws are unsuitable, even if plated. It is also possible to use *pop rivets*. They are hollow rivets that can be attached when there is no access to the far side of the metal, using a special tool. They are mounted on a *mandrel*, like a nail, and as the tool draws the mandrel back to form the far head (Fig. 9-19A), the head breaks off (Fig. 9-19B). These rivets should be aluminum alloy or stainless steel. The strength of one aluminum alloy rivet is

not very great, so there should be plenty to spread the load. It is better to use stainless steel, as all aluminum used is not necessarily salt-water resistant. A snag with the breaking mandrel is that you will have a collection of mandrel heads loose inside the spar, unless you can remove an end to get them out. The finished rivet has a hole through it. It is usual to make metal spars watertight so they would float, and any pop rivets should be plugged. Wood pegs are sometimes used, but it is better to use an epoxy filler paste.

Bolts through an aluminum spar should be used cautiously. Obviously, they should not be located where halyards pass through. Be careful not to overtighten and squeeze the section out of shape. When a nut is at a suitable position, lock it there.

There are places on an aluminum spar where plastic parts can be used. A round plastic fairlead could be put in a hole at the exit for a halyard on the smallest boat, but otherwise it is better to put in a sheave already mounted in a box for riveting on. Many masts include a track for a gooseneck fitting below the part with the sail groove. If the mast is being assembled, it is worthwhile putting the halyards through before closing the ends or, if not the actual halyards, pieces of line that can be used for hauling them through.

The parts made to fit into the ends of the spars are usually aluminum alloy castings and may be rough. The soft metal is easily filed and cleaned smooth with abrasive paper. Some end fittings, such as masthead assemblies may be fabricated by welding sheet metal parts, but aluminum welding is a specialized activity and should be left to the experts.

If a mast is being built up from a standard section, the sail rope groove will be the full length. For a small boat the makers will usually provide a gooseneck fitting to match the sail groove, but it is necessary to remove part of the rope groove in the position that the sail will have to be entered and the gooseneck can be put in at the same place. A coarse file cuts aluminum better than a fine one, but have a fine one and some abrasive paper ready to smooth the finished surface. File down to the bottom of the

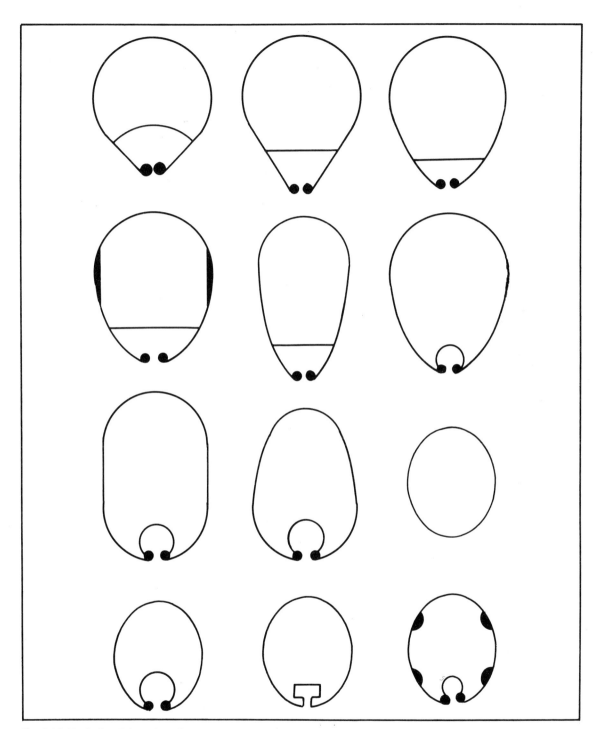

Fig. 9-16. Typical metal mast sections.

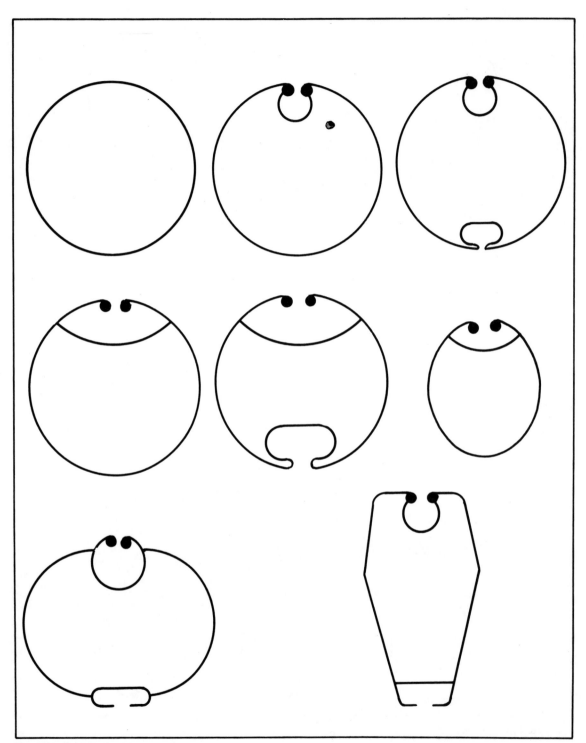

Fig. 9-17. Typical metal boom sections.

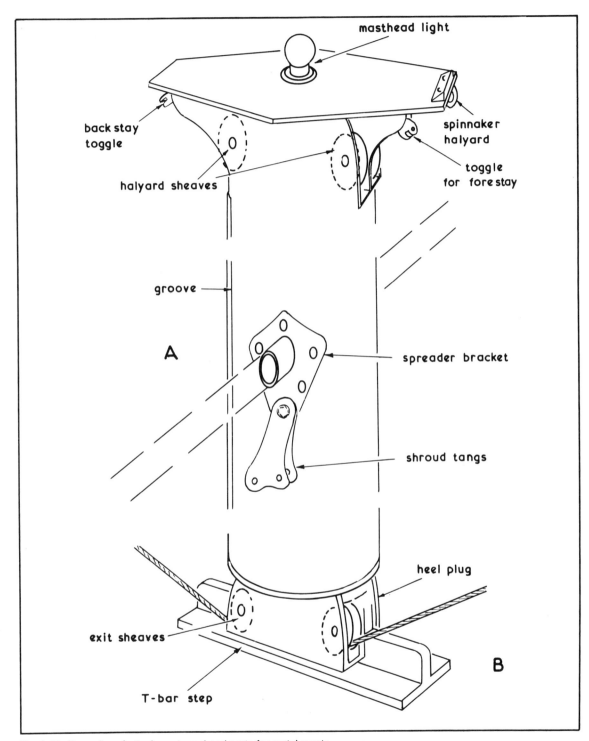

masthead light

back stay toggle

halyard sheaves

spinnaker halyard

toggle for fore stay

groove

A

spreader bracket

shroud tangs

heel plug

exit sheaves

T-bar step

B

Fig. 9-18. Examples of attachments and end parts for metal masts.

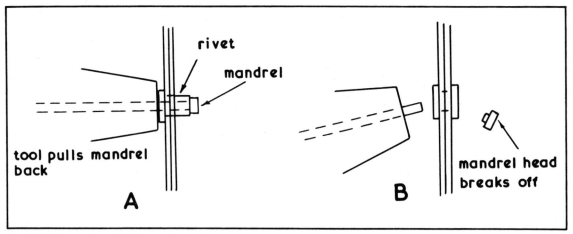

Fig. 9-19. The action of driving a pop rivet.

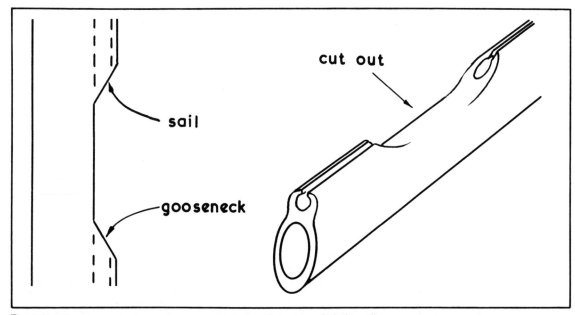

Fig. 9-20. The groove can be cut from a stock section of mast to admit the sail rope and a gooseneck.

groove and bevel the ends of the relieved section (Fig. 9-20). Use a round file inside the groove ends to remove any roughness.

Standard metal spars are made by specialist manufacturers. They all provide the parts to go with them and many of these are unsuitable for use with other makers' products, so if you are assembling or altering a spar, get what you need from the one maker.

Fortunately, aluminum alloy needs little maintenance. Some makers anodize their products. This is a chemical treatment that gives an effect that looks like plating and it can be in various colors. It is not a process that can be applied individually. Aluminum alloy can be painted if the surface is first cleaned of grease and a suitable paint used, but a painted finish on spars is unusual.

Chapter 10

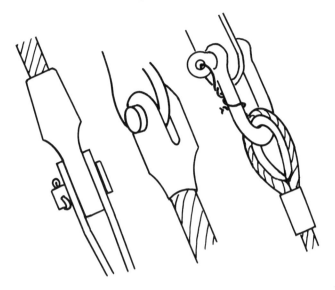

Mast Supports

IF A BOAT IS TO SAIL, THE SAILS HAVE TO BE HELD in position in relation to the hull. There have been schemes to use rigid sails, but so far none have been as successful as cloth sails supported by a mast and other spars. Therefore, a most important part of the rigging is the arrangements for keeping the mast in position. Masts have broken and will again, but the purpose of standing rigging is to keep the mast in position whatever the circumstances. At one time the rigging was also expected to keep the mast straight. In most cases that is still a requirement, but for some modern methods of sailing, particularly racing, a helmsman expects to be able to flex the mast to a controlled amount.

For the best aerodynamic results it would be better if the mast was not there. It serves no purpose in making the boat progress by using the wind. It obstructs airflow over the sail. Rigs have been arranged with a sail supported by a bipod mast, with the two supports rising from the gunwales and the sail hung from where they meet. But with two masts causing wind resistance, the effect negates

anything gained by improving the airflow over the mainsail.

Masts are made in shapes other than round, partly for structural reasons and partly to improve airflow around them. Making the sail better streamlined by enclosing the leading edge of the sail in a mast groove also helps. Any streamlining of the mast is only of advantage—in theory—if the sail is in line with the major axis of the mast section. This is not usually the case with a rigidly located mast. If the mast can rotate, the airflow should be improved. A properly rotating mast requires complicated rigging. It is sometimes done, but any improvement is probably marginal and it is more usual to have the mast non-rotating, with streamlining fore and aft.

The supporting rigging also has negative aerodynamic value. All stays and struts produce wind resistance. So the ideal, aerodynamically, is a mast of negligible section with no rigging. As that is clearly impossible, the rig of any sailing boat has to be a compromise. At one extreme is a mast with enough inherent stiffness that it does not need rigging. At the other extreme is a very thin mast, kept up with a cage of rigging. Thin, modern wire certainly does not produce much wind resistance, but too much of it can obstruct airflow enough to matter.

UNSTAYED MASTS

To get enough stiffness in an unsupported mast, it has to be relatively thick and usually solid, if of wood. This means weight aloft, which is undesirable, and a rather big section at the leading edge of the sail, causing poor airflow around it. However, there is a case for an unsupported mast in some circumstances.

If the sail plan has all of the area in one large sail aft of the mast, that mast has to be positioned far forward in the hull. The extreme example of this is the *cat boat* (Fig. 10-1). If the mast is right in the bows there is no base on which to spread worthwhile stays to help hold the mast up. Stays must spread outwards if they are to be effective. A cat boat mast must be stiff enough in itself, which means it has to be quite thick.

Unstayed masts have been used on other craft and some of them have been quite large. The usual unstayed mast is found in the smallest boats, such as canoes or short open dinghies. The mast then may be just a wooden pole, although it could be metal tube. Windsurfers or sailboards are in a slightly different class, where there is certainly no rigging and the mast is kept up only by the person standing on the board. In that case it is deliberately mounted so it will fall down in emergency or when the user wants to stop. In other craft the mast should be held rigidly upright in the boat.

The overall stiffness is helped by the distance between the foot of the mast over the keel and the support at deck level, or elsewhere. If the rigger has any choice in arranging supports, it is better to have the upper support at deck level or higher than to merely have a hole through a thwart lower in the hull. It also helps to have that support fairly tight on the mast. If there has to be a loose fit, for ease in putting the mast in and out, some tightening arrangement should be made. Wedges in the hole

around the mast are one method. The square foot part of the mast can fit closely into a box (Fig. 9-15A), but there should be a strong retaining bar as high as possible on the aft side.

One problem with an unstayed mast is the risk of the whole rig lifting out of the boat and blowing away. If the mast is held in position in some way, this does not arise. The rigger should try to use as many parts of the rig to secure the mast as well as to do another job.

With a simple one-sail boat there will not be more than two ropes to be secured at the mast, and there may be just the halyard. Cleats on the mast will take the ropes (Fig. 10-2A), but if the ropes can be taken to cleats or belaying pins on the deck beam or elsewhere, the tension will hold the mast down (Fig. 10-2B).

If the mast is not right in the bow, the halyard can be taken forward to near the stem head and aft to a cleat within reach of the helmsman, possibly on the side of a lifting keel case (Fig. 10-2C). Besides holding the mast down, the halyard also doubles as a forestay.

MAST LOCATION

At one time, particularly in the early part of the twentieth century, there was a fashion for spreading the sail plan. There was a feeling, without scientific proof, that something was to be gained by having a total area of sailcloth that extended well ahead of the hull and projected some way aft, without any of it going very high. This meant bowsprits of considerable length. Bumpkins extended aft of the transom, not as far as the bowsprits, but further extended with booms far beyond them and sheeted to the bumpkins. Coupled with this were two or more masts, with ketch or schooner rigs being most common.

The rigger was presented with the problem of making elaborate rigging to keep everything in place safely and with the most efficiency that could be obtained with the poorer quality ropes then available.

Such rigs generate a certain amount of nostalgia today. They certainly have an aura of traditional seamanship about them, so boats are still built and

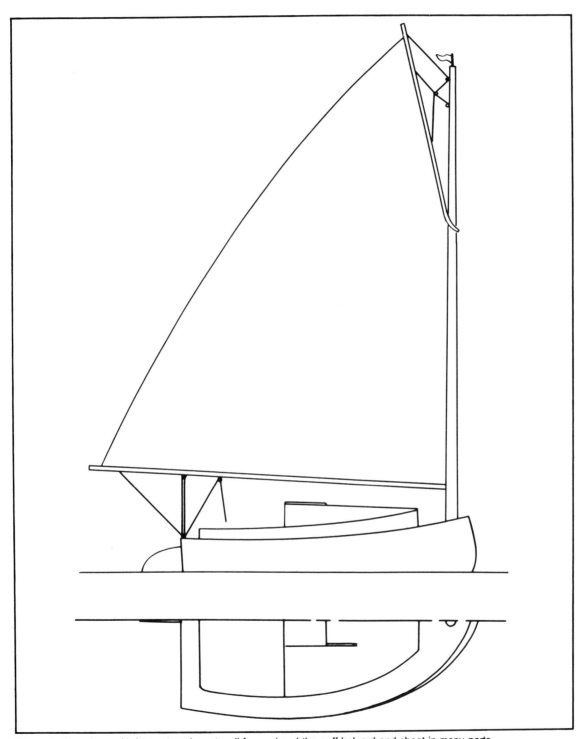

Fig. 10-1. A car boat with its unstayed mast well forward and the gaff halyard and sheet in many parts.

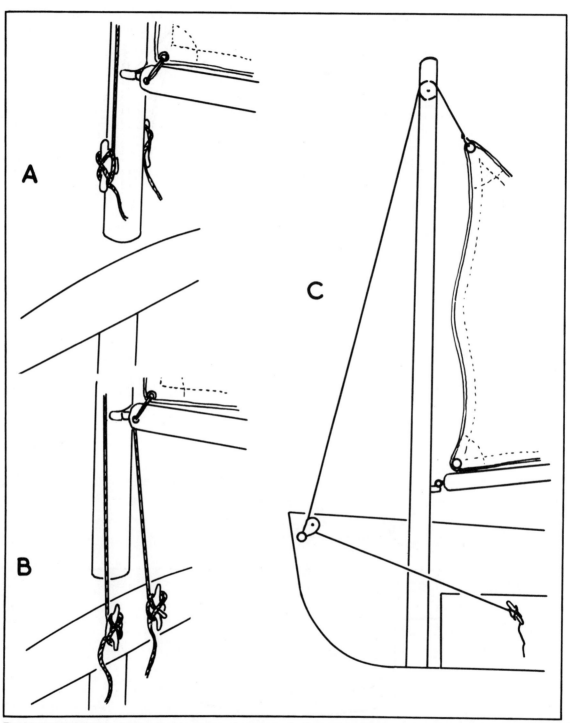

Fig. 10-2. Halyards for an unstayed mast may come to cleats on the mast (A) or will help to hold the mast down if taken to cleats elsewhere (B). A halyard taken forward also acts as a forestay (C).

158

rigged in that way. But if you want to sail fast, go closer to the wind, and have a more-easily handled and efficient rig, such boats are just about obsolete.

Aircraft research has caused revolutionary progress in sailboat design. A sail going to windward is similar in effect to an airplane wing being drawn through the air by an engine and propeller or jet. The research that was necessary to advance airplanes to the stage they are today has benefited sailboat design. A sail that performs best to windward will also be better than other sails on most other angles of sailing.

The research necessary to get early, low

powered airplanes when engines that would get an airplane off the ground contributed greatly to new sailcraft designs. Today, with the power available, there are other considerations in flight not so relevant to sail design.

At least two facts have emerged. One is that a high sail with a short horizontal dimension (Fig. 10-3A) is more efficient than one with the same area, but lower and wider (Fig. 10-3B). This emerged from wind tunnel tests with airplane wings, where longer and narrower wing were found to be more efficient.

Getting all the required sail area into one sail is

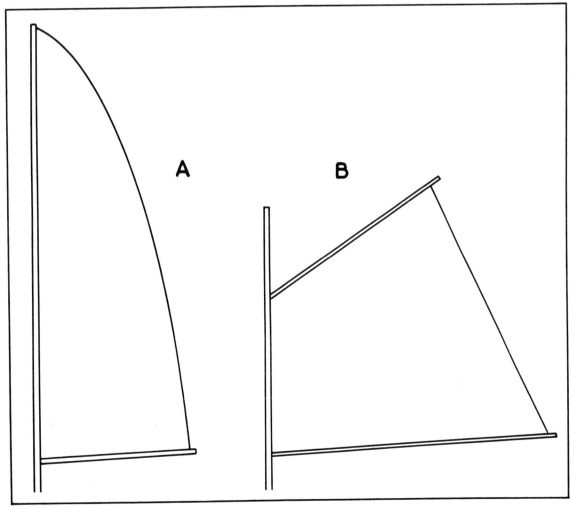

Fig. 10-3. A high sail is more effective to windward than one of the same area shorter and wider.

more efficient than dividing it into two or more. This is efficiency related only to driving force to windward. There are other considerations. A divided rig is easier to handle for a small crew. In a single-handed boat, the one man may only be able to raise and lower a part of the total sail area at one time. With two or more sails the boat is easier to keep on course and the sails can be worked independently to maneuver the boat, as when changing tack. In some boats it is possible to lower one sail in stronger winds, instead of reefing. However, the effect of research has been to reduce the number of sails generally. Two-masted new boats are fewer. Sloops, with only one sail forward of the mast, are commoner than cutters, with more forward sails.

Another change, due to wind tunnel research on sails and airplane wings, is a move to put more of the total sail area into the *fore triangle*—the area forward of the mast. Some of this has been due to the availability of non-stretch flexible wire rope of considerable strength in relation to a small section.

The interference of the mast section affects airflow over the mainsail, but with just a wire stay forward of a jib or other foresail, interference is negligible. This advantage is cancelled to a certain extent if the wire rope cannot be pulled bar taut. If it slackens and the sail blows it into a curve that sags away to leeward or even flays about, there is a considerable loss of windward efficiency. With modern wire stays that can be set up stiffly, sails mounted on them can make more use of the wind in relation to their area than can a mast-supported mainsail.

INCREASED FORE TRIANGLE

To get more sail area into the fore triangle there has been a tendency to design boats with the mast further aft. In older boats it was customary to position the mast between one-fourth and one-third of the boat length from the bow (Fig. 10-4A). Some modern boats have the mast in the center of the boat or aft of it (Fig. 10-4B). This has benefited the design of rigging. Fore and aft stays can take a more equal share of the load. Those shrouds and other stays to the gunwales can have the broadest base possible, because they go to points near the greatest beam (Fig. 10-4C), instead of a lesser width (Fig. 10-4D). Instead of the boom overhanging the transom, as it did in many older craft, the high aspect ratio mainsail only needs a short boom.

Besides aiding handling, this permits permanently set backstay, instead of the running back stays that, in older boats, had to be set up and released as the boat changed tack. There are still uses for running backstays, but the prime support can usually be in the permanent backstay.

Fortunately, with the knowledge that height was an advantage came improvements in mast design. Where earlier designers were restricted in the height they could provide, even if they realized there was an advantage in it, modern designers can produce rigs with very tall, still practical masts. Earlier masts had to compensate for their weaknesses by using very complex arrangements of rigging, not only to keep the mast up, but to keep it in shape. Much less supplementary rigging is needed to keep a modern mast straight so most rigging today is there to hold the mast up when under pressure from the sails.

There have been some very tall hollow wooden masts. Modern waterproof glues make their construction possible. Sections are not excessive and a tall wooden mast is feasible, but may be very expensive because of the long hours of skilled labor needed. The alternative is aluminum alloy. Modern manufacturing techniques allow for the production of accurately engineered, tapered hollow masts of almost any length. Design knowledge is also more attune with metal and its known characteristics than with wood. With wood, there has to be some allowances due to variations in its characteristics and because it is a natural product. Wood masts still have many uses, but for the largest sailing boats and increasingly in those of more modest size, the rigger will be dealing with metal masts.

SHROUDS

Of the many stays needed to support a mast, those that go athwartships (across the width of the boat) to, or near, the gunwales, need to be more complicated. Most masts have a greater dimension in

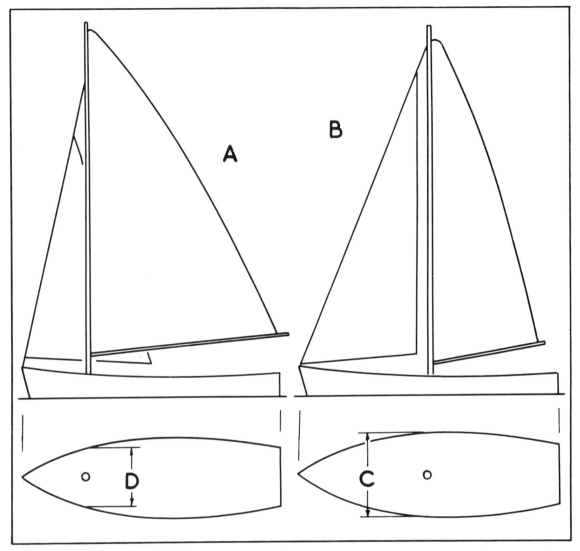

Fig. 10-4. A mast forward in the boat does not have as wide a spread for shrouds as one further aft in the boat.

section fore and aft than in their width, so they are stiffer in that direction. They do not need so much external support that way to keep them upright and straight.

The various parts of the rigging that support the mast may be collectively called *stays*, but it is usual to call those going to the side of the boat *shrouds* and only use the word *stays* specifically for those going fore and aft. In both instances another word may be added to define a particular rope.

If a mast is not very tall and has plenty of stiffness in itself, shrouds may go from the mast head to the gunwales (Fig. 10-5A). The shrouds then provide support, but do nothing to stiffen the mast. If the mast is not very stiff and the shrouds are tightened excessively, it is possible to buckle the mast. Because of the usual taper in the mast, the upper part is more likely to bend than the lower part (Fig. 10-5B).

Shrouds do not always go to the top of the mast

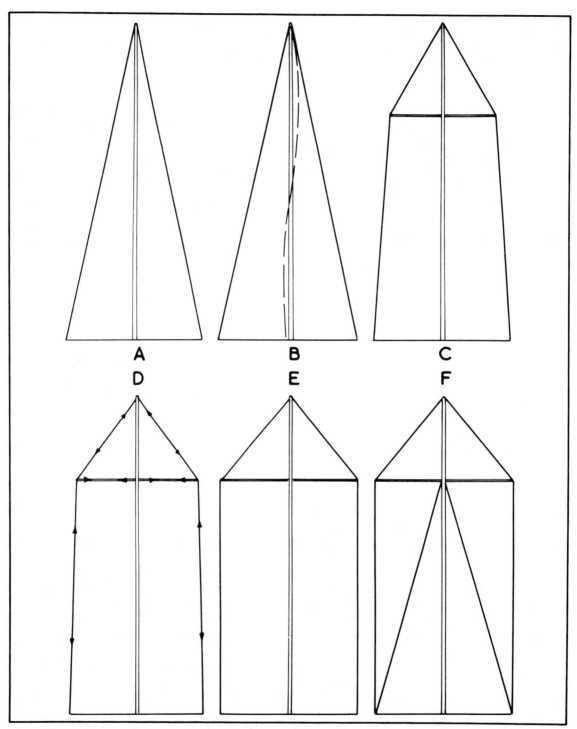

Fig. 10-5. Shrouds direct from a tall mast (A) do not stiffen the mast (B), but spreaders (C) both stiffen and give support (C,D). Further support comes from lower shrouds (F).

and they are sometimes attached lower down. A short length of mast above the shrouds will be stiff enough, but there are sometimes practical problems. The attachment points of the shrouds may interfere with the location of blocks and sheaves for running rigging or have to be kept to the sides to not interfere with a sail track or groove. There may be considerable strain on the shroud attachments. You can take the load with an eye in the shroud around the mast, but for halyards this could not be done below the sheaves in many rigs because of interference with sail hoisting. Having rope eyes around the mast is better engineering than using fittings that involve screws and bolts into the mast, because the mast is not weakened by drilling.

SPREADERS

If the beam of the boat is narrow, the angle of the shrouds to the mast is slight. Support would be better on a wider base, but that is impossible. To achieve a better, more effective spread and stiffen the upper part of the mast, use *spreaders* or *crosstrees*. Spreaders are light struts attached to the mast, over which the shrouds are taken (Fig. 10-5C). A shroud above and below the spreader is in tension, but the spreader is in compression (Fig. 10-5D). The thrust of the two parts of the spreader against opposite sides of the mast stiffens it.

The length of the spreader affects its stiffening properties. A short spreader is not as good as a long one. There are short spreaders on some small boat rigs, but it is usual today to have the spreader's overall length about the same as the beam of the boat at that point, so the shrouds lead down approximately vertically from it (Fig. 10-5E). It is unusual to see spreaders longer than that, but they have been used.

In moderate-sized boats, one set of spreaders is all that is required. As a further support there is usually a pair of lower shrouds from the mast below the spreader position (Fig. 10-5F). If more support is needed there may be a second pair of shrouds from the same point on the mast. At the gunwales the shrouds go to different points. This spreads the load on the hull and the different angles of the shrouds, when viewed from the side, give slightly

better support and stiffening than if they all led to one position.

For a taller mast there may be more spreaders, and in racing craft, where the mast is kept slender, the shroud arrangement becomes complicated. There may be two or three spreaders (Fig. 10-6). Sometimes shrouds may go from one spreader to another, but it is better if the shrouds over each spreader go separately to the gunwales. If parts are interconnected, a failure at one place might weaken the whole assembly, but if the systems are separate there would be less risk of the mast collapsing. If a stay goes over a spreader and back to the mast, it is a *diamond stay*.

Much use has been made of *jumper stays* to stiffen the top of the mast against the pull of the mainsail and the backstay. They were more common when it was usual for sails forward of the mast to be attached to the mast some way down from its top. In modern boats it is more usual for stays and sails to be attached to the top of the mast or very near it.

A single jumper stay might be directly forward of the mast (Fig. 10-7A), with the wire from the top of the mast to the spreader position and a strut to the mast near its midpoint. In fact, jumper stays are normally paired, with the strut coming near where the forestay is attached. They are angled to the mast so they stiffen the mast literally as well as fore and aft (Fig. 10-7B). The designer will have decided the angle, but the practical considerations of clearing sails and running rigging must be taken into account.

It might be considered that spreaders should bisect the angle made by the shroud (Fig. 10-7C). They have been arranged that way, but it is more usual and it looks better for both sides to be straight across. What is more important is for the spreader sides to match the angle the shroud makes when viewed from above. If the shrouds over the spreader go to points opposite the mast, the two sides can be in line with each other. If they lead to positions aft of the mast, there would be an unnatural strain on a straight spreader, so the two sides should be allowed to angle slightly aft (Fig. 10-7D). In some arrangements there is a hinge

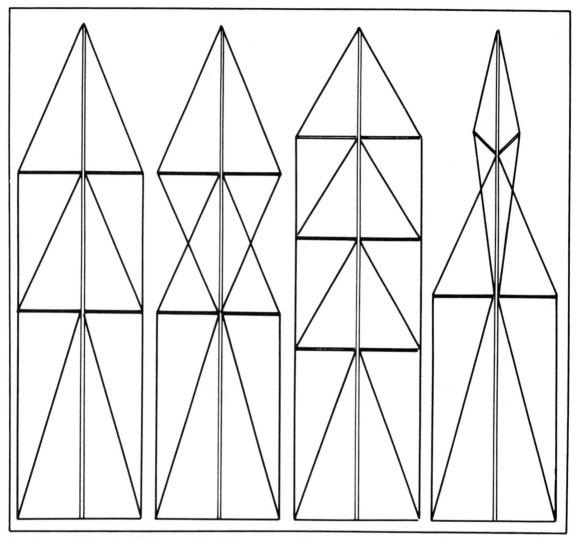

Fig. 10-6. Examples of the rigging needed with a tall slender mast.

fitting at the mast so the spreader can come to the best position automatically.

A shroud goes in one length from the mast to the gunwale. It is not in two parts joined at the spreader. Instead, the simplest arrangement has it going through a slot in the end of the spreader. There has to be an arrangement to prevent the shroud coming out of the slot when slack. With a wooden spreader there could be a screw (Fig. 10-8A) or a bolt through. With a tubular metal strut some sort of locking plug is usual (Fig. 10-8B). As

this position is well out of reach in use, there must be no doubt about the shroud staying in place.

It is important that the end of the spreader should be smooth and rounded because the mainsail may rub against it at some angles of sailing. It is common to add some sort of padding as anti-chafe gear to the end, particularly on a long voyage where the sails may be set at a particular angle for a long time. The padding of rope and canvas may seem large and unsightly, but preventing wear on the sail is important.

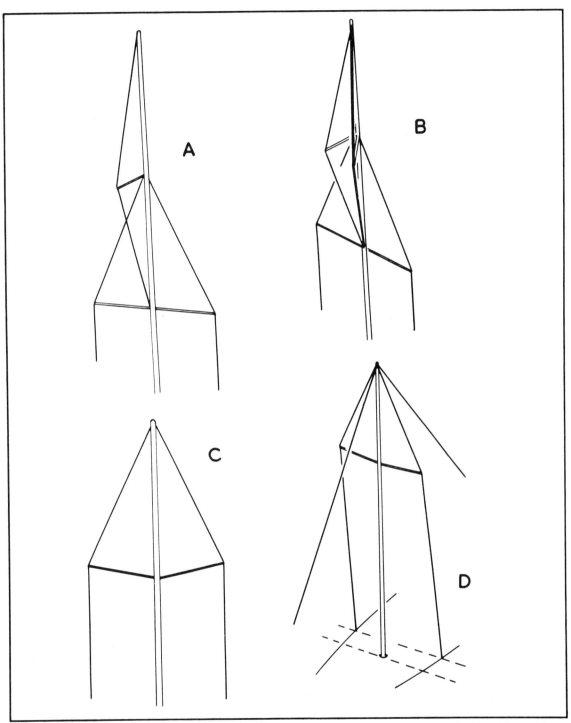

Fig. 10-7. Jumper stays (A,B) stiffen part of a mast. Spreaders may bisect the angles of the shrouds (C), which may also be angled aft (D).

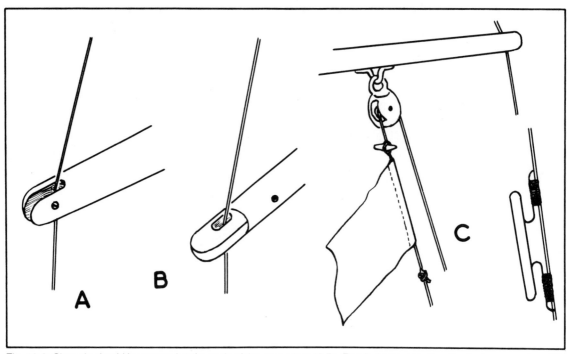

Fig. 10-8. Shrouds should be secured at the ends of the spreaders (A,B). Flag halyards may be attached to spreaders (C).

Spreaders may serve other purposes. Signal halyards are needed for hoisting flags on various occasions, as when entering a foreign port. A loop provided below the spreader allows the rigger to shackle on a small single block for a light rope halyard, which can be taken down to a convenient cleat. It will be kept out of the way if a small cleat is lashed to a shroud (Fig. 10-8C). The spreader is a good place for a light to illuminate the deck—not for a navigation light. It may be a lamp with a reflector below the spreader, but it cannot be very large or it may chafe the sail.

SHROUD ATTACHMENTS

On a wooden mast, the simplest and strongest way to attach shrouds at the masthead is with eyes around the mast—either resting on chocks or placed around a reduced part of the mast (Fig. 10-9A). The alternative is to use terminals directly or to shackle the shrouds to tangs held by a bolt through the mast (Fig. 10-9B).

There may be a metal top to a wood mast, designed to incorporate sheaves for halyards as well as attachment points for stays and shrouds. In this arrangement the shrouds, with terminals or eyes around thimbles, are attached to tangs that project from bolts going through the mast (Fig. 10-9C). A similar arrangement may be found for the lower shrouds, where one or two tangs project below the spreaders (Fig. 10-9D). With plain tangs the rigger has to use a terminal or a spliced end in the shroud with a matching shackle. With the shackle pin through the hole in the tang, the clevis must be locked (Fig. 10-9E) or the shackle wired (Fig. 10-9F) if it does not have any other locking arrangement.

Metal masts may be fitted with tangs similar to those on wooden masts. A pair of tangs can be spaced to suit the shroud end eye around a thimble. A clevis pin goes through the thimble and is secured with a split pin. This avoids the need for a shackle and makes a neater attachment, with less to chafe sails. With a single tang and a suitable open-ended terminal on the shroud there can be an equally neat joint.

In some metal masts there may be a top that includes all of the mast head equipment, including a

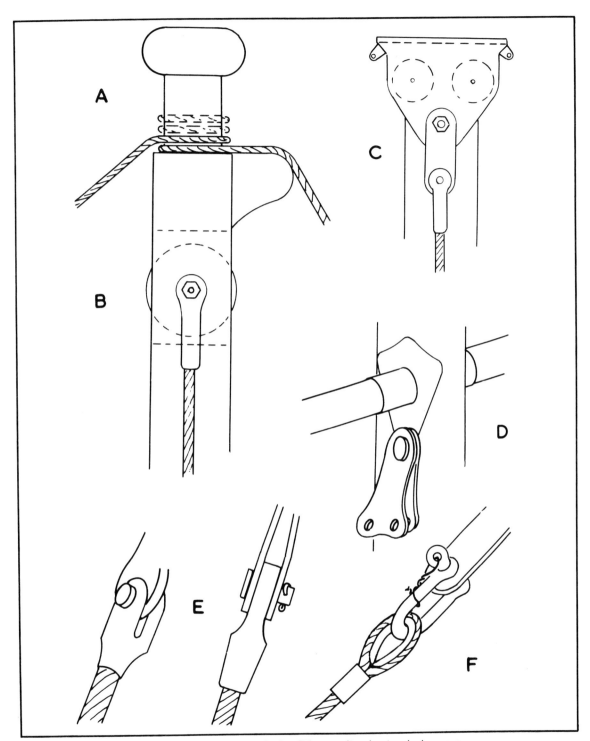

Fig. 10-9. Stays may be looped over a mast or attached to fittings on it, using terminals or eyes.

pin or tube on which the stays and shrouds can be put. The shrouds go through holes in the sides of the mast and the eyes at their ends go around the pin (Fig. 10-10A). This is the ultimate in keeping the ends out of the way and reducing wind resistance. Even if the shrouds do not go to the masthead fitting, there may be a very similar arrangement through the mast a short distance down. The rigger must put the shroud eyes on the pin, which is then locked to the mast tube.

In some spreader assemblies there is a tube that forms a spigot that goes through the mast and the tubular spreader parts fit on to it outside. There is plenty of room inside a hollow metal mast for a

tube to cross without obstructing halyards. The lower shrouds have eyes over the spigot inside the mast (Fig. 10-10B). Passing the spigot through the mast and the shroud eyes may be a little tedious, but it does not have to be done very often. While doing it, see that the halyards come at their correct sides of the spigot tube. If they are kept under tension while the tube is put through, there should be no trouble.

The lower ends of the shrouds go to the chain plates or other attachments inside or outside the gunwales. They are joined with lanyards, in a simple rig, or with rigging screws in most cases, as already described. If there is a masthead shroud

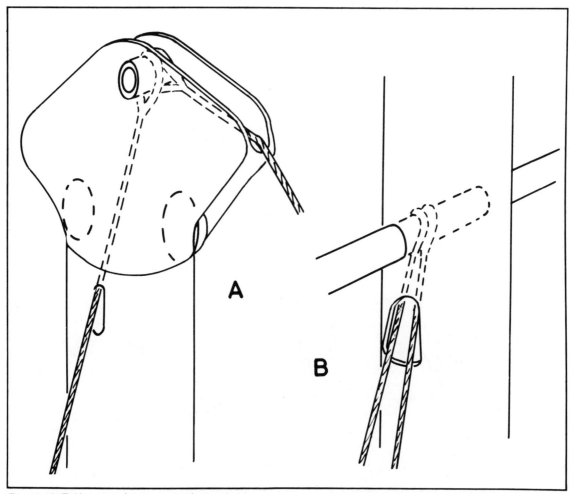

Fig. 10-10. Taking stays into a mast reduces windage.

coming from over a spreader and two lower shrouds, it is usual to bring the masthead shroud down to the center position. This is normally opposite the mast. Then lead the lower shrouds to the positions fore and aft of it.

FORESTAYS

Of the many mast supports, the simplest is the forestay. Besides holding the mast up, it provides a track for sail slides. In some rigs there are two forestays alongside each other, not so much for holding the mast up, but to provide two sail tracks. One sail can be clipped to the second wire before another sail is lowered on the first wire. This is a racing tactic rather than an arrangement necessary on a cruising boat.

With a sloop rig there is usually only one forestay, although if the foresail does not come to the masthead, there may be a forestay from the masthead and another from a lower position to suit the sail. This helps to stiffen the mast, but it puts on a pull without an opposite reaction. Care is needed in setting up the lower stay or the mast could be bent.

Attachment of the top of a forestay may be by any of the methods described for shrouds. With a wooden mast, an eye around the mast is traditional. In some rigs this may be found even when the shrouds have lower side attachments (Fig. 10-11A). The backstay would then be attached at the same place by the same method, so the two complement each other. The stay may go in to a head fitting (Fig. 10-10A) or it could have a terminal to a toggle (Fig. 10-11B).

At the lower end there will be an attachment to a secure point, usually not far in from the stem head. In some tall rigs the sail will be led to a point further back and the stay it is running on will go to a point there, with reinforcement below the deck.

Adjustment is with a rigging screw if it is a fixed mast. If the mast is intended to be lowered in a tabernacle, the forestay has to be used, usually with a tackle at deck level. It is unlikely that this can be just a whip, even if the end is led elsewhere to a winch or windlass. How much purchase to allow depends on the size and weight of the rig. In a typical example the tackle is made up of two single blocks (Fig. 10-11C). The length of the forestay should be made so the blocks are not very far apart when the rig is correctly set up (Fig. 10-11D). It would be wrong to bring them together (*chock-a-block*), as that would not leave any adjustment, and it is the tackle that has to take the place of a rigging screw in tensioning the forestay.

If you do not wish to rely on the tackle to set up the rigging, there can be a rigging screw with a quick-release attachment to the deck fitting and the tackle does not come into use until that is released (Fig. 10-11E). This is obviously more secure for a boat of appreciable size, and it allows more precise adjustment of the forestay tension.

Catamarans are rigged in a generally similar way to monohulls, but they present a problem in dealing with the bottom of the forestay. If there is a beam between the hulls, it may be taken to that. This is necessary if a foresail tack corner is to come reasonably low (Fig. 10-12A). If there are no foresails there may be a pair of stays (Fig. 10-12B). A forestay could go to a bridle between the hulls (Fig. 10-12C). The flatter the angles of the bridle, the longer the forestay and its sail. This increases the load on the bridle and hulls, but makes the forestay shorter and probably useless for sail carrying.

BACKSTAYS

If there is sufficient clearance for the sail to swing across, a simple backstay goes from the masthead to the transom. This is another assembly like a forestay (Fig. 10-13A). Even when there is a sail clearance, there may be complications at deck level. There could be interference with the rudder head or the movement of the tiller. When there are no obstructions, some designers and users prefer the backstay divided into a bridle at its lower part (Fig. 10-13B). This shares the load and directs the pull to near the corners of the transom, which should be better able to take it. The alternative of twin backstays going all the way to the top of the mast has been used, but is less common. This causes increased windage, although the two wires need not be as thick as a single one.

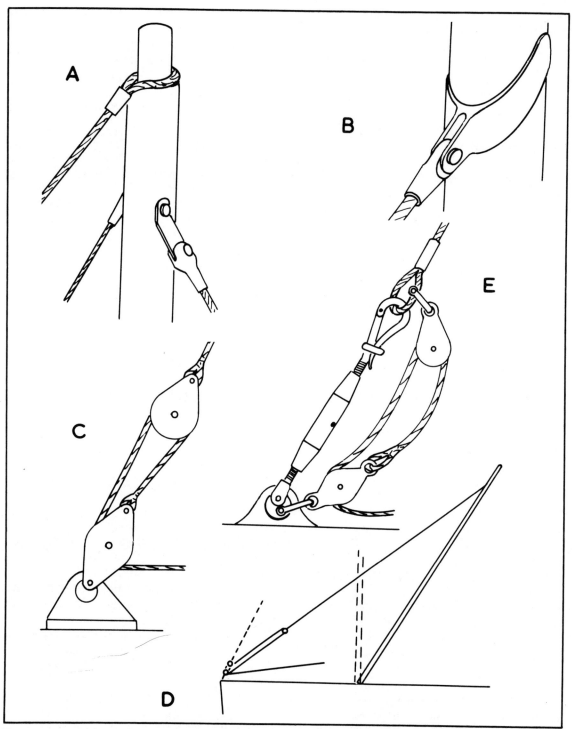

Fig. 10-11. Stays may join the mast in various ways (A,B). Tackle on the forestay can be used to lower the mast (C,D,E).

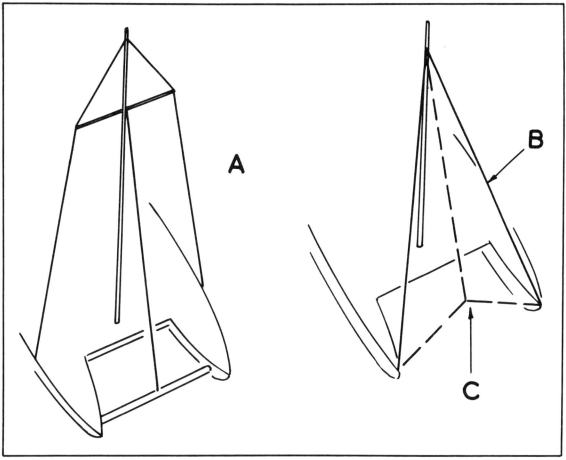

Fig. 10-12. The forestay of a catamaran can go to a beam, the ends of the hulls, or to a bridle between them.

The load on the two parts of the bridle should be equally shared. This can be balanced by making the bridle continuous through a block on the single part (Fig. 10-13C). Sometimes there is a plate with three holes in it (Fig. 10-13D). This also does something to balance the load by tilting slightly if necessary.

There are other uses for such a backstay. A life buoy or ring may hang from it, ready to be thrown astern to anyone going overboard. It is often possible to arrange a means of hanging the end of the boom from it when the boat is not sailing (Fig. 10-13E). This removes the need for a crutch or other support standing on the deck or in the cockpit.

There are many craft where the mainsail is of a shape that would not allow a backstay from the mast

to the transom. This was always so with a gaff-headed sail, but there are some Bermudan mainsails that come too far aft to clear the wire. Loads on the mast during most angles of sailing tend to push it forward, so there has to be some means of holding it back.

In a small open or half-decked boat it is possible to slope the shrouds aft of the mast. They then serve part of the purpose of backstays, but there is a limit to how far they can be taken, as they will prevent the boom going far enough forward (Fig. 10-14A). On a larger boat the shrouds may be brought slightly aft to get much the same benefit, but it is impossible to rely on them to support a high rig with large sails, so there has to be some other arrangement to support the mast from aft. Unfor-

171

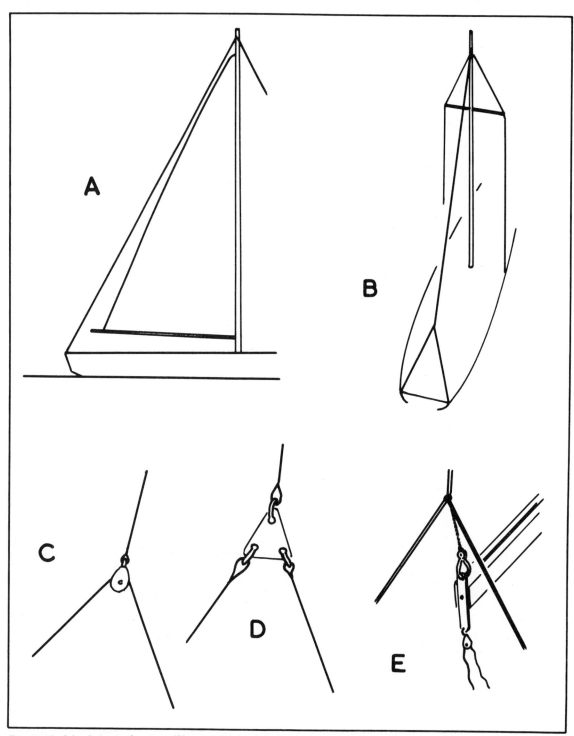

Fig. 10-13. A backstay to the stern (A) may be divided (B,C,D) and could support the boom when it is out of use (E).

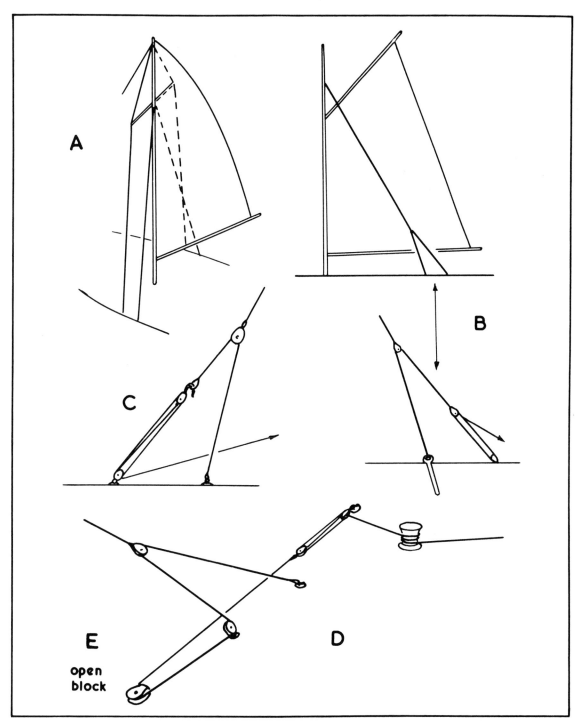

Fig. 10-14. Shrouds may limit the movement of a boom (A). Aft support of the mast may be by running backstays with tackle to release quickly when the boat changes tack (B to D).

tunately, there is no other way of providing permanent rearward support comparable to a permanent backstay to the stern. There have to be *runners* or *running backstays* to positions each side near the gunwales. Only the one on the windward side can be set up. Therefore it is necessary for there to be an easy and quick way of releasing one runner and setting up the other as the mainsail changes sides.

The practice in older boats was to bring the backstay down to a block. A runner attached to an anchorage similar to a shroud plate was run through the block and its other end hauled down by a tackle (Fig. 10-14B). This was repeated on the other side. A considerable length of line had to run through the blocks to slacken enough and this had to be taken up again on a change of tack. With the rather slow change of direction of long-keeled old cruising boats there was usually time to do this efficiently, but with modern craft that go about quickly, something more rapid and positive is needed. Having a hook on the tackle so it can be cast off avoids the need to run much rope from the tackle (Fig. 10-14C). There is then the need to retrieve the ring in the runner end each time you set up.

Another system on large boats leads the runner through a block on the deck and forward around a sheave in an open-ended block before going back to the horizontally arranged tackle (Fig. 10-14D). For the greatest tension the tail rope from the tackle can go to a winch. Sufficient slackness in the backstay can be obtained quickly by loosening the tackle and lifting the runner from around the open-ended block (Fig. 10-14E).

The backstay can run along a wire span (Fig. 10-15A) or a length of track on the side deck. This should be long enough to allow for hauling back and sliding forward far enough on release to slacken and not interfere with the sail. A rope tail may be used to haul the slide back and put tension into the backstay. If that can go to a winch, there is no need for a tackle to be included. In most boats the backstay would run forward of its own accord when released. If track is used, it should be of a stout type securely held down, to resist the strain the backstay will impose (Fig. 10-15B).

A lever action of tensioning is quick and positive. A type of backstay lever invented by J.S. Highfield is commonly used. In a *Highfield lever* the runner leads through a deck block to the lever, which is grooved. It is attached to one of several alternative positions in the lever. Considerable tension can be put on by the last bit of movement of the lever, yet swinging the lever the other way releases enough slackness (Fig. 10-15C). If more slackness is needed, there can be a hook on the runner to let more line run out. Variations on the Highfield lever have been made, but the principle is the same.

With any of these running backstay arrangements the rigger should remember that parts of the equipment on the lee side may swing about and could damage crew or sail. The backstay will be wire, so make sure there are no protruding wire ends from the eye splice. In all but the smallest craft the runner will also be wire. See that any blocks are without rough exteriors. A backstay takes a considerable load when the sail is full and pulling. Make sure attachments to the boat are adequate and mounted to structural parts able to take the load. If a backstay carries away, you might lose your mast.

TWO MASTS

If there are two or more masts, some of the rigging of each might conflict with the other. The designer might have arranged for rigging between the masts so they support each other or they may be stayed independently. A danger with combined rigging comes if there is a failure of any sort at one mast as that could affect both masts. In an extreme case both masts would be lost, where one might have been saved with independent supports.

This is a design consideration, but a rigger should be aware of the problems. If there is considerable difference between the sizes of masts and sails, as in a yawl or some ketches, the main mast can be treated as if it was the only mast. The permanent backstay may be divided to go each side of the mizzen mast without interfering with the movement of the sail on that mast (Fig. 10-16A). The mizzen mast cannot have the equivalent of a normal forestay, but it can have shrouds taken for-

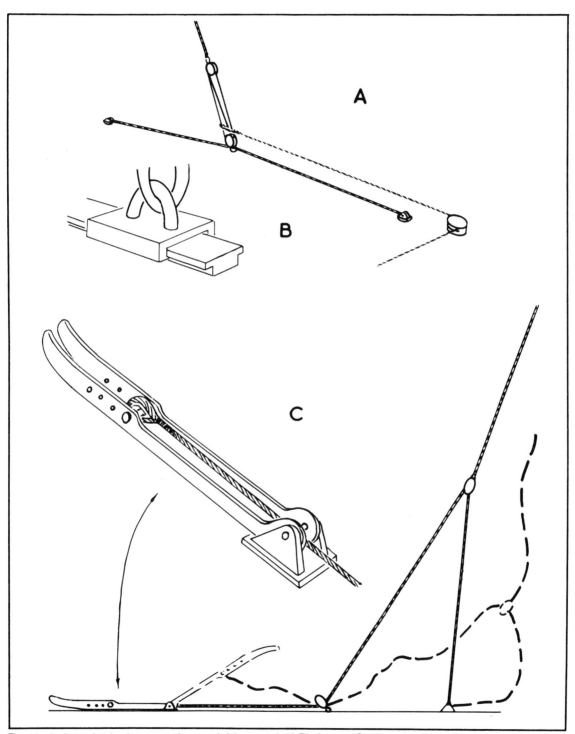

Fig. 10-15. A running backstay may be on a bridle or track (A,B). A lever (C) allows for quick release.

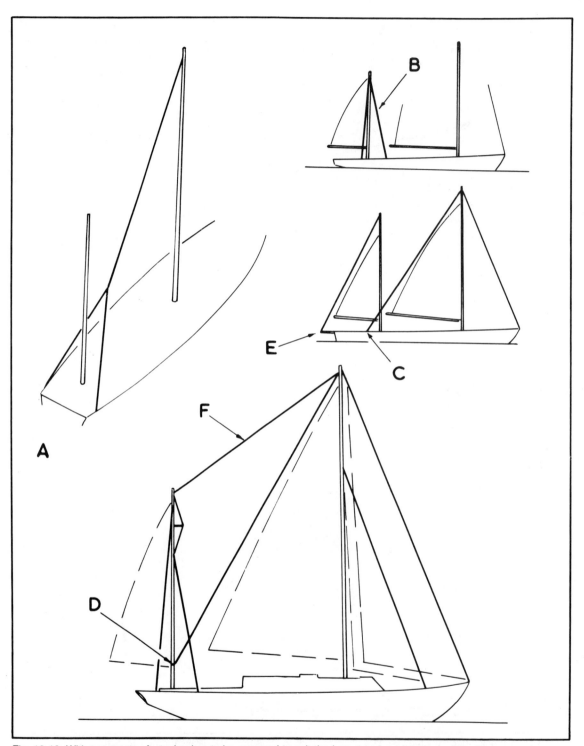

Fig. 10-16. With two masts aft staying has to be arranged to suit the layout and not interfere with sail movement.

ward enough to serve the same purpose (Fig. 10-16B). In some rigs the shrouds can go some way along the gunwales, so long as they do not interfere with the movement of the main boom and its sheet.

If the masts are not very different in height and the sail areas are closer to the same size, the forward mast may still be stayed in a similar way to a one-mast rig, with the backstay taken to points on the gunwale each side of the other mast (Fig. 10-16C). Sometimes a single backstay is taken to a point low on the second mast (Fig. 10-16D). If the sail on the second mast is all inboard, there can be a permanent backstay to that mast. Sometimes a short bumpkin has to be arranged to get the stay clear of the sail by bringing it a short distance outboard (Fig. 10-16E). Such a bumpkin needs to be stiff and have wire rope down from its ends to take a considerable strain. Shrouds forward, as far as the mainsail boom will permit, can take the opposite strain to the backstay.

Although the primary supports of two masts may be independent, there can also be a stay between their tops. This is called a *triatic stay* (Fig. 10-16F). It obviously serves an important function in the chain of load-taking from the stem, over the masts, and down to the stern. The designer has to consider what would happen if it failed; so other stays and shrouds are provided. The rigger needs to consider a triatic stay as a special case, because once it is in position, it is difficult to get at for inspection and servicing. Except for that it is a normal length of rigging wire with eyes or terminals at each end, that should be locked to the attachment points at the mast. Theoretically it should be possible to make the stay the right length, but there may have to be a rigging screw included. This screw needs safe locking and weather protection.

Some two-mast rigs have been designed so the aft mast needs more support than can be given by shrouds angled forward. There have to be running stays going forward to the gunwales, functioning like the more common running backstays. They have to be slackened and cleared from the path of the boom, every time the boat changes tack—not a very acceptable arrangement, but sometimes necessary.

If a rigger is left to devise standing rigging for an unusual or experimental craft, he should remember that support in one direction needs support to balance it the other way. Directly opposite may not be possible, but there can usually be a divided arrangement to share the reaction to the first load. The mast also has to resist the pull of the sails and the stays holding the mast up must do that as well.

Although the sails are driving the boat forward, the loads on them are not always trying to push the mast forward. That may happen when the boat is running before the wind, but as the sails are brought around to make the boat sail across or towards the wind, loads on the mast also move around until they can be almost the opposite way.

Chapter 11

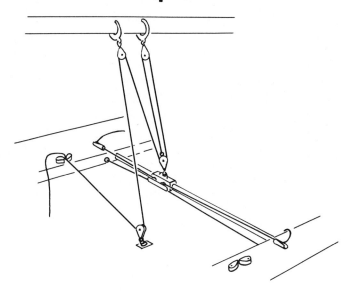

Main Running Rigging

SAILS MUST BE HOISTED FULLY AND WITHOUT trouble, and not always in ideal circumstances. When they are up they have to be controlled. If there is more than one sail, the main sail usually has the biggest area and usually the more important rigging. In some rigs the gear for lesser sails may be more complicated. When a boat is being sailed, the main sail does most work in driving the boat, so it is important that its running rigging should be efficient. If there are difficulties with a smaller sail it is not necessarily serious, but if the main sail will not hoist fully or resists lowering in a strong wind, it could be hazardous.

The main sail is hoisted with a halyard. If it is the usual modern Bermudan (Marconi or jib-headed) type, there is just the one halyard. If it is a gaff-headed sail there will be more than one halyard—with possible complications in hoisting. The sail is controlled by the *main sheet,* which can be complicated if the sail is large or the boat is raced. Unless it is quite a small boat, there will be a *topping lift,* which is a line from high on the mast to

near the end of the boom, which is used to take the weight of the boom when the sail is being hoisted or lowered. Additionally, most modern boats have a *boom vang* or *kicking strap,* which is used to prevent the boom rising while sailing. Other ropes may serve as an *outhaul* for sail along the boom or as a *downhaul* for the boom. Specialized rigging for traditional-type gaff-headed sails will be dealt with later. This chapter is concerned with Bermudan main sails and their running rigging.

HOISTING

At one time the luff of a sail was attached to hoops or ropes around a mast and it tended to sag away between them. The use of a *track* followed. Tracks are still used on some masts and booms, but in most cases they have given way to slots and grooves in the mast itself. A track may have internal slides (Fig. 11-1A) or external slides (Fig. 11-1B). In both cases the slide has to be lashed closely to the sail and a rigger may have to fit or replace slides. In the usual arrangement between the parts (Fig. 11-1C),

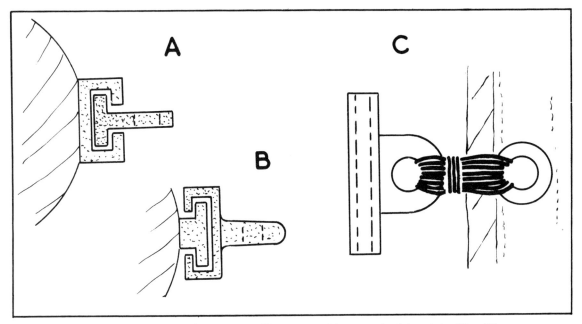

Fig. 11-1. Mast track may be internal (A) or external (B) and the sail is secured at intervals to slides (C).

use synthetic twine and wax it just before use so it stays as you want it. Knot the starting end into the slide, put on enough turns, then draw them as tight as possible with a few frapping turns around the middle. Securely knot the finishing end. At all stages see that the slide stays in line with the edge of the sail. Having it twisted may affect the set of the sail.

Loosening screw heads can cause trouble on a track, particularly because wood screws may not hold very well in soft wood. If necessary, countersink a deeper hole. If the thread has stripped in the wood try pushing a sliver of wood in to give the screw thread a grip. You may have to drill the track in a new place for another screw if the original one refuses to stay tight. An alternative is to drill for a wood plug and drive the screw into that, but that means removing the track first. Check the tightness of track screws frequently. If the track lifts at one screw, that could start loosening the next one and so on along the length.

You can provide for two sails with track. This is impossible with a grooved mast. Some craft are arranged to have a storm sail attached to its own track beside the working sail, ready for hoisting in emergency.

Even where the sail bolt rope slides in a groove there may be a length of track below it on smaller boats to take a slide attached to the boom *gooseneck*. (The name derives from the fact that a goose is supposed to be able to turn its neck in almost any direction.) There are a great many boom goosenecks, but all have the property of being universal joints that turn in almost any direction.

A common arrangement has two pivots mounted square to each other. If this goes on a track, there is a slide with a screw arrangement for tightening (Fig. 11-2A). In the smallest boats the boom is pushed down by hand after the sail has been hoisted, to tension the luff. In rather larger craft a downhaul is made up as a tackle, with the amount of purchase depending on the size of sail and boat. A basic type that is easily made up has a single block below the boom and a line from an eyebolt or plate, through it and down to a cleat (Fig. 11-2B). This gives a 2:1 purchase. The pull needed must get the luff of the sail straight, but not be so much that the cloth of the sail is distorted.

In dinghies and other small boats, reefing may be done by rolling the sail around the boom by hand. If the gooseneck has a pointed tang to go into the end of the boom, its square neck will engage with a square hole in the metal plate at the end of the boom (Fig. 11-2C), so the boom can be pulled aft from the gooseneck and a reef rolled in. The squares engage to prevent unrolling. The boom will stay on the tang while sailing without securing.

At the top of the sail there is usually a *head*

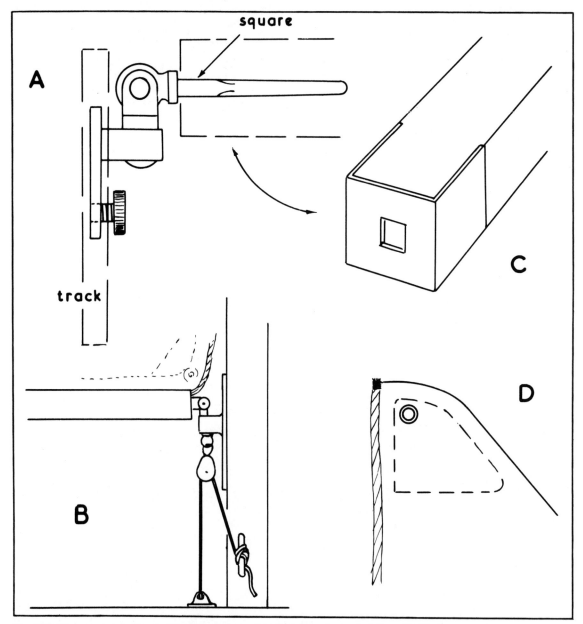

Fig. 11-2. The gooseneck of a small boat may be on a slide (A) that can be hauled down (B). The boom may have a square hole to allow roller reefing (C). The luff rope is cut to suit a grooved mast (D).

board, which may be metal, plywood, or plastic. This gives shape to the sail and avoids the acute angle of a narrow, useless part of the sail at the top. It also provides an attachment point for the halyard. If the sail goes in a mast groove, the board is clear of the bolt rope (Fig. 11-2D).

In most boats today there is a hollow mast and the main halyard passes down through it. Otherwise, there is a sheave through the mast and the halyard goes down the forward side of the mast. How to get a halyard through a hollow mast has already been described in Chapter 9. (Fig. 9-9 and 10). If the halyard is all fiber rope, the upper end will be spliced around a thimble for shackling to the grommet in the head board of the sail unless there is some other method of attachment used in the particular class of boat. In some utility sailing boats the halyard may be merely knotted to the head of the sail. In that case, be careful that the end is never allowed to run away through the sheave. Tie a knot in it when you remove it from the sail.

A wire halyard also needs an eye at its upper end, then a fiber rope tail has to be spliced on at the other end. If you are replacing a halyard, compare the new with the old, but allow for the fact that the old rope may have stretched slightly, particularly if the old tail is natural fiber rope. If you do not have an old halyard as a pattern, check the method of securing and tensioning the halyard in the particular boat. When the sail is up, the fiber rope tail should be free and not under any load. The wire rope should be taking the strain all the way between sail and cleat.

When a sail is lowered and disengaged from the halyard, always secure the upper end near the foot of the mast, usually to a cleat, and bring the hoisting part to it. Attach these parts as you would when the sail is hoisted—if you let an end go and it soars out of reach, the amount of trouble this causes may seem out of all proportion to the mishap!

SHEETS

The rope used to control the mainsail is often made up into a tackle that is the most complicated piece of running rigging on a boat. Much thought has been given to the design of sheet assemblies, but finality has not been reached. Most variations are due to the way suitable purchase is arranged, plus ingenious ways of locking the rope in various positions. Sheet arrangements are more complex on racing craft, but some of their ideas have found their way into cruising boats. If a boat is in a particular class, the rope, blocks, and cleats that make up the sheet will have to conform to the rules. Otherwise, it is probably wiser to start simple and try other methods if they seem worthwhile. Fortunately, it is possible to alter sheeting without much difficulty.

There are two general arrangements. The older and more common position for the sheet is at the end of the boom, either entirely (Fig. 11-3A) or with blocks leading the rope forward (Fig. 11-3B).

In a more recent arrangement the sheet pulls from near the center of the boom (Fig. 11-3C). In the first arrangement the sheet comes to you from the stern. In the other arrangement the sheet assembly is forward of the helmsman. A center sheet is claimed to keep the boom straighter. End sheeting is more out of the way of the crew. As there is more leverage at the end of the boom, the amount of purchase need not be as great, so there will be less rope and few blocks. Center sheeting is preferred for some smaller racing boats.

A main sheet is handled more than any other rope in a boat. Even in the smallest boat it should be thick enough for comfortable handling. That means about ½-inch diameter, even if a much thinner rope would be strong enough. Never have less than ⅜-inch rope. For large craft the rope may be thicker, but always consider ease of handling. For a very great load you have to rely on the parts of a purchase to reduce the actual load on the rope. Manufacturers now produce special ropes for sheets that are braided, soft, and flexible.

There is no easy way of selecting the sheet arrangement for a particular boat. There are too many variables for this to be reduced to a science. Choice has to be related to the size of the boat, the sail area, the location of the sheet, the conditions to be expected in the waters to be used, and the strength of the person pulling, either direct or with the aid of a windlass or other mechanical help. It really comes down to experience—probably

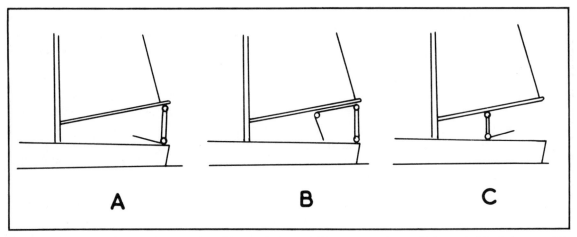

Fig. 11-3. A sheet may be entirely at the stern (A), brought forward (B), or arranged centrally forward of the helmsman (C).

someone else's. You can usually find sheeting known to be successful on another comparable boat. If you have to devise sheeting without other guidance, the above guidelines gives you a base on which to work.

The drive produced by the wind on a sail is transferred to forward motion of the boat through the attachments of the sail to the boat. Besides the mast, the sheet has to take its share of the load. In some very small boats the sheet is merely a rope from the boom to the hand of the helmsman. He must transfer drive to the hull through his body, which is unsatisfactory. Even in the most basic small boat it is better to lead the sheet through a block on the transom, probably beside the rudder head (Fig. 11-4A). The block does not provide a purchase, but it gets the pull to a point on the boat and alters the lead of the sheet to the helmsman's hand.

SHEET HORSES

It is an improvement to have the sheet on a *horse.* in many craft of all sizes this is a metal bar, above the rudder head (Fig. 11-4B). In a simple small boat it could be fiber rope, attached through holes in the deck or *knees* at the corners of the transom (Fig. 11-4C). In a more sophisticated boat there is a length of track across the boat, with the sheet block on a slide (Fig. 11-4D). The sheet then travels across to pull from the lee side. In the simplest

arrangement the block is on a shackle or ring that slides on the horse. A better arrangement has a combined or second block so movement is via a sheave.

If less effort than a direct pull is required, there can be a block on the boom. One end of the sheet may be attached to an eye plate near the center of the transom, then the rope goes through the block on the boom and down to the hand (Fig. 11-4E). This gives a purchase of 2:1, but it is considered better to bring the rope to the hand via the transom. There could be a single block at the lower end as well, to alter the direction of the rope without altering the purchase, and this might be on a horse (Fig. 11-4F).

This arrangement can be increased to give any degree of purchase according to the number of sheaves in the blocks and the parts of the rope involved. For a purchase of 3:1 a single block on the boom can be used with a double block on the transom (Fig. 11-4G). With two double blocks the purchase becomes 4:1 (Fig. 11-4H). The double blocks are shown with large and small sheaves, but they could be the type with similar-sized sheaves beside each other. Remember that it is the number of rope parts coming from the moving (boom) block that tells you the purchase ratio. If you turn these tackles around you can increase the purchase to 4:1 and 5:1, but the end is then coming from the boom. This may be acceptable, although the preference

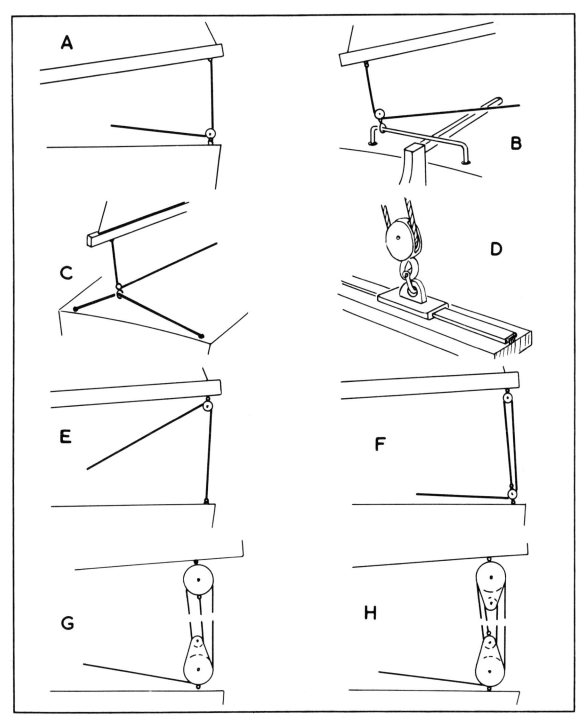

Fig. 11-4. A main sheet may have a simple pull (A) or be arranged on a horse (B,C) or track (D) across the boat. Purchase may be needed for a larger sail (E to H).

today is for the sheet to lead from the lower block. Remember, also, that when you increase the purchase you also increase the amount of rope that has to be pulled through. This may be necessary because of the load, but in a large boat the end of the boom may have to be pulled 10 feet between running and close-hauled. With a 5:1 ratio there is 50 feet of rope to be handled quickly and a tangle on the cockpit sole must be avoided.

There are a great many ways that the location of blocks and the lead of the sheet can be arranged. It is probably possible to devise any arrangement and find that it has been used on some boat. With the sheet pulling from aft the sheet can be led along the boom and down at any point. This may be convenient if there is a long aft deck and you want the sheet to come to the cockpit forward of the helmsman (Fig. 11-5A). It can be arranged with any degree of purchase as one or more blocks along the boom are merely guiding the rope.

An advantage of taking the sheet along the boom with two or more attachments is in spreading the load on the boom, so reducing any risk of it bending. The sail can put considerable bending strain on the boom. If the sheet is attached only at the end, a flexible boom may curve. If the sheet is attached only at a point some way in from the end, the outer unsupported part may bend. Dividing the pull of the sheet between several positions on the boom was carried to extremes in Victorian days. Today booms are stiffer, but the pull of the sheet and its effect on keeping the boom straight or not should be considered.

If there is to be more than one sheave involved on the boom, there can be two single blocks spaced along the boom instead of one double one (Fig. 11-5B). The effect on purchase is the same as if the sheaves were in the same block—in this case 4:1.

A horse or a central attachment can be avoided by taking the sheet to widely-spaced points on the aft deck or to the corners of the transom. In a simple arrangement for a small boat the sheet is knotted under a hole at one side, goes up to a block on the boom, down to a block at the other side of the stern, then forward to the hand (Fig. 11-5C). The end could be led to wherever is more convenient, but

additional blocks do not affect purchase (Fig. 11-5D). Purchase may be increased with additional sheaves working from one side (Fig. 11-5E).

An assembly with a rather similar effect suits the situation where the sheet is to be led along the boom. The end of the sheet is at the boom. It then leads across the stern deck and back to a block on the boom (Fig. 11-5F). The part across the deck may be a nuisance on some boat decks. The moving rope there could be fouled and if there is much curve to the deck the blocks would have to be raised. Having two lower blocks does not affect the purchase—they are merely two acting as one. The purchase is 3:1.

In small open or partly-decked boats where there is a risk of capsize (even if remote), it is the rule to never make fast the end of the sheet, but to always hold it in the hand so it can be allowed to run out without delay in an emergency. The rope may pass around something where the friction relieves the hand of some of the load. It could be just a half cleat or a belaying pin, but securing turns are never made around it. In a more sophisticated boat it could be a winch, but the end is still ready to throw off turns if quick action is necessary.

In a larger boat with cabin and ballast keel, where the risk of capsize is so remote as to be ignored in planning rigging arrangements, the main sheet can be secured. The helmsman then does not have to have one hand on the tiller or wheel and the other hand on the sheet. The end of the sheet may still be within his reach, but he or another member of the crew would have to go through the actions of casting it off. It is usual to use some form of jam cleat, rather than a plain cleat. It is then possible to let to without the need to release half hitches. It is possible to take up or let out the sheet to adjust the sail by jerking the rope to allow it to move. Clam, cam, and other cleats that grip the rope by compression are popular. They may be on the deck, cockpit coaming, or other convenient position (Fig. 11-6A) or it is possible to get them incorporated in a block, so jamming the rope can be done close to where it emerges from the sheave (Fig. 11-6B). Use of this type of cleating depends on having the particular block always within reach.

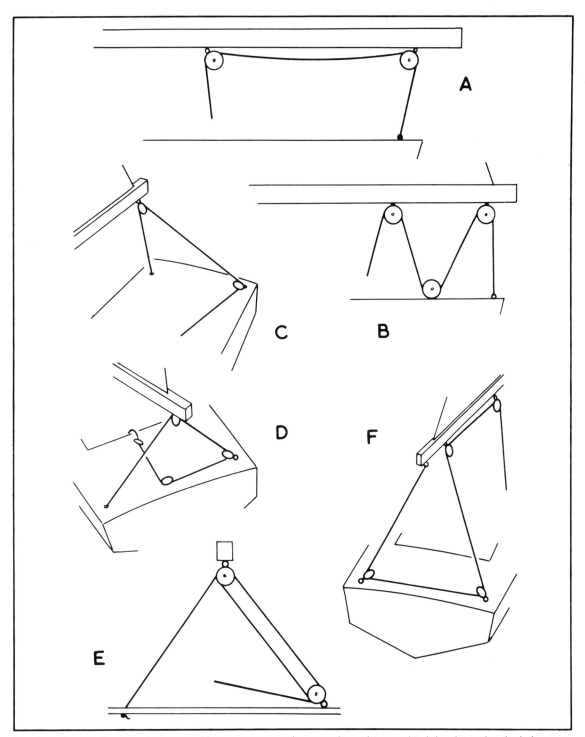

Fig. 11-5. A main sheet can be arranged in many ways to give enough purchase and to bring the end to the helmsman.

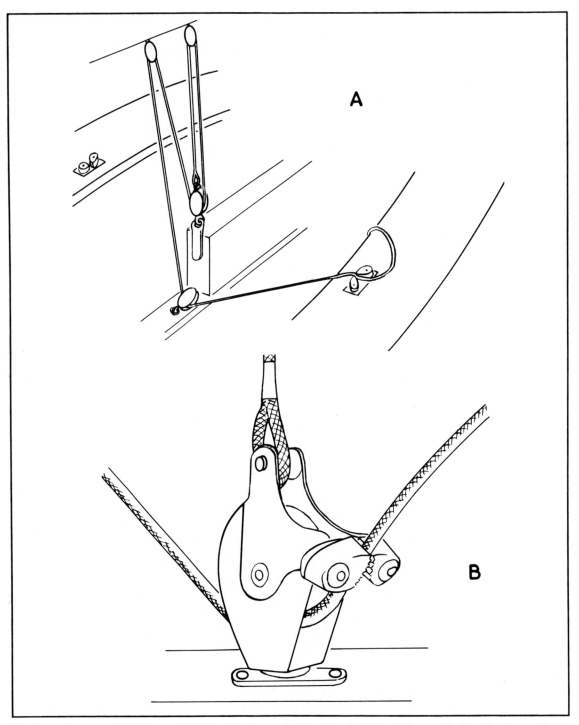

Fig. 11-6.   A center sheet may come to the drop keel case and be sheeted on the side decks or a cleat may be incorporated in the block.

186

Some of the arrangements described bring the end of the sheet from a block at one side of the boat, no matter which side the boom is on. This does not matter as much as might be expected in an open boat. In a larger ballasted boat, the position of the weight of the helmsman is not so critical. He may get a better view ahead and of the set of the sails by sitting to leeward. He may be central behind a wheel.

DOUBLE-ENDED SHEETS

In large craft there is an advantage in using a double-ended sheet. The sheeting arrangement has to be made symmetrical, but both ends of the sheet go to cleats, which should be of the quick-release type. Adjustment of the sheet can be made from either end. Besides this advantage, it is possible for two men to haul in at the same time, so the slack is taken up twice as fast. Wear can be allowed for by moving the rope.

Because neither end is made fast, this arrangement is suitable for even numbered ratios, such as 2:1, 4:1, and 6:1. For 2:1 there is a single block on the boom and the ends lead down to deck blocks and so to cleats (Fig. 11-7A). For 4:1 there has to be a single lower block and a double block on the boom, or two single blocks. The lower block may travel on a horse (Fig. 11-7B) or be central on the deck (Fig. 11-7C). For most cruisers a ratio of 4:1 is usually chosen. It would have to be an extremely large sail to require the extra sheaves to give a ratio of 6:1.

If the preferred arrangement has the ends of the sheets coming from a position forward on the boom, it is possible to use double-ended sheets. This may keep the men handling them out of the way of the helmsman and others who are handling foresail sheets.

For a 4:1 purchase there is then a single block on the deck, either on a horse or fastened centrally, with the rope taken through a double block on the boom. Instead of leading down the blocks at the side of the deck, the two parts go forward and over two sheaves further along the boom before being brought down (Fig. 11-7D). These two sheaves are better in two single blocks than in one double one,

as at different angles of the boom the lead of the ropes will vary and they might ride up or chafe on the sides of a double block. With separate blocks the sheaves will take up a natural angle to the lead of the ropes. The sheet ends then come down to winches or cleats arranged centrally in the boat.

In many cruising boats the block on the horse is allowed to run full width between stops that prevent it dropping around the curved ends (Fig. 11-8A). The length of the horse controls the amount of travel. In some small boats the horse is quite short and its main purpose is to keep the sheet clear of the tiller (Fig. 11-8B). Racing helmsmen prefer to have some control over the amount of movement along the horse. There are many ways of doing this, but a simple arrangement uses rope lanyards to jam cleats at each side (Fig. 11-8C). The rope on the windward side then stops the block going further along the horse, whether metal or rope, than intended.

CENTRAL SHEETING

With central sheeting most of the combinations of blocks that have been described to get different purchase ratios aft are used. The sheet may be attached to a central point on the deck or in the bottom of an open boat (Fig. 11-9A). It is more common to have a traveler on some form of slide across the boat. There could be a track mounted on a beam between the side decks (Fig. 11-9B) or there may be a tube across with the block on a part that slides on it (Fig. 11-9C).

Central sheeting is more often used on racing boats than on general-purpose or cruising boats, so manufacturers catering for racing needs have produced many more sophisticated fittings for those who welcome even very minor improvements that will enable them to go faster. As with larger cruisers a typical open partly-decked racing boat needs a purchase of 4:1, where sheeting at the end of the boom might have been sufficient at 3:1. The examples shown here are 4:1, but other ratios could be made using block arrangements similar to those described for use near the end of the boom. As the fall of the sheet comes from near the center of the boat there is no need for double-ended sheets.

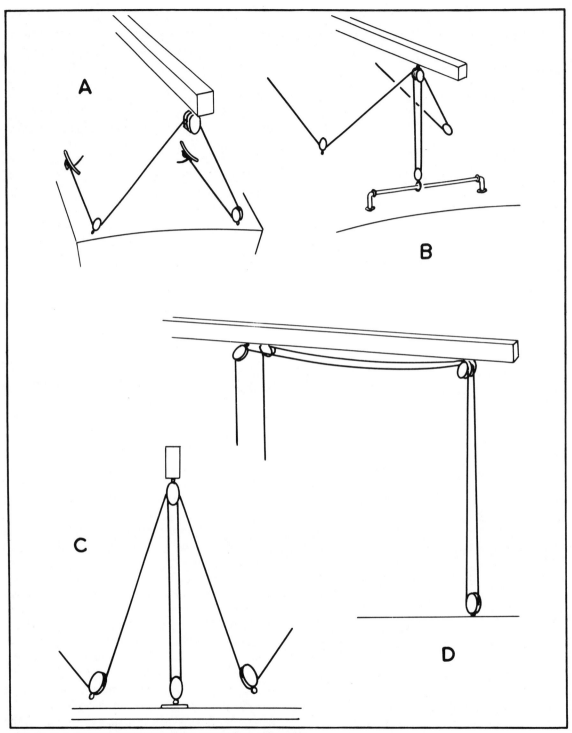

Fig. 11-7. A double-ended sheet allows control from either side.

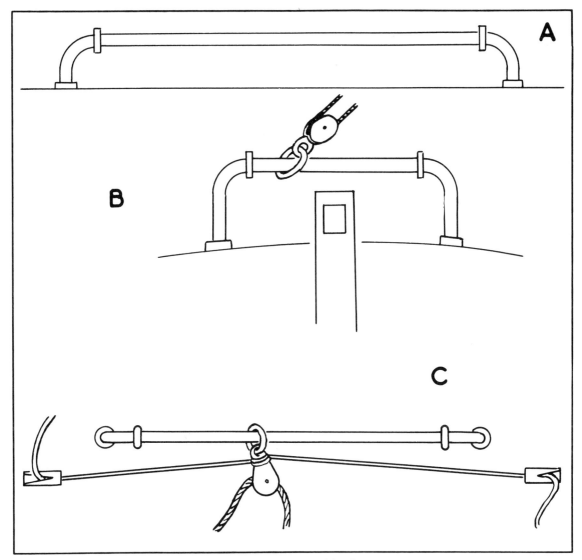

Fig. 11-8. A sheet on a horse may be limited with stops or a restraining line.

The range of movement of the traveler along its track is limited by the lanyards each side. They are given a 2:1 ratio, not because the load is exceptionally great, but because this allows the ends to come back to cam cleats, or other types, on the side decks (Fig. 11-9D). A plain slide can travel on a track, but the type that goes on a tube may contain rollers that minimize friction. Above the traveler is an eye for attaching the sheet block.

It may be a plain block, but it should be able to turn to take up the different angles experienced at differing boom angles (Fig. 11-9E). In that case the sheet goes from the second block on the boom to a block on the bottom of the boat. That block may be hinged in two directions so it swivels (Fig. 11-9F) and the rope passes through a cam cleat. From there it may go to the hand, although some boats have further cam cleats on the side decks to give more grip (Fig. 11-6B). In a lively racing dinghy the helmsman needs to be able to free the sheet in-

189

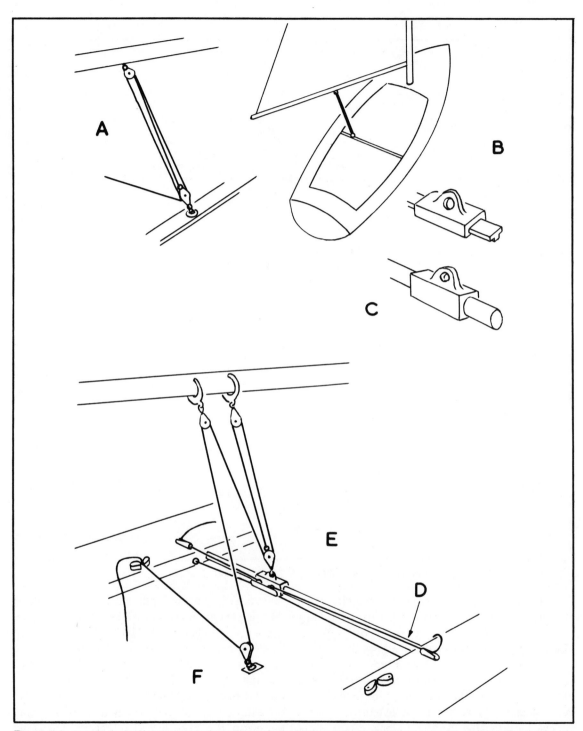

Fig. 11-9. In a partly-decked boat a center sheet may go to the bottom of the boat or be arranged on a slide between the side decks.

stantaneously, but these cleats give an occasional relief from the tiring hand grip. Instead of the block and cleat in the bottom of the boat, there may be a very similar swivel assembly on the slide.

REEFING

In a strong wind it becomes necessary to reduce the sail area and this is called *reefing*. The traditional method uses reef points. Design and construction of a mainsail with this method of reefing is not the concern of a rigger, but he may have to carry out repairs, so he should understand what is involved.

There are two or three rows of reef points across the bottom of the sail. At the end of each row are strong grommets or *cringles*. Then at intervals across the sail are *reef points,* which are lengths of light line hanging each side of the sail (Fig. 11-10A). To take in a reef the sail is lowered sufficiently for the grommet at the tack corner of the sail to be lashed or pegged down to the boom (Fig. 11-10B). The weight of the boom is taken temporarily with the topping lift, then the grommet at the outer end is hauled down and outwards, so the line of the reef is tensioned along the boom (Fig. 11-10C). This is important as the loads of sailing must be taken by the stretch of the new foot of the sail and not by the reef points. With the sail tensioned, the surplus canvas is gathered up and the reef points tied below it with a reef knot—it is this use that gives the knot its name. If the sail is in a grooved boom you will have to tie below the boom, but if it is laced or on a track, tie between the boom and the canvas (Fig. 11-10D).

Reef points tend to flap about when out of use and their whippings should be checked frequently. If an end becomes unlaid, it will soon unlay to the point where the rope is ruined. The method of hauling down and securing the reef grommets or cringles varies, but there are usually ropes, called *reef earings* either spliced on or ready to be attached. There may also be an outhaul for pulling the sail along the boom. In both cases replacement is a straightforward splicing and whipping job for a rigger.

It is more usual today to employ roller reefing for the mainsail. It is more suitable for the usual triangular sail than for the older gaff-headed sail. The principle is simple, but there are some practical problems.

In a small boat the boom comes away from the square neck of the gooseneck fitting (Fig. 11-10E) and a reef is taken in by rolling the sail around the boom by hand. In larger craft there have to be other arrangements for turning the boom without removing it. This is done at the mast end of the boom, where it can be rotated with a handle. How much gearing or leverage to include depends on the size of the boat and its sail. In one simple arrangement there is a pinion on the boom end and this can be levered around with a pawl engaging it (Fig. 11-10F). For a more powerful turn there may be worm gear (Fig. 11-10G).

The adoption of roller reefing brings limitations on the way the sheet and other items can be attached to the boom, as anything fixed where canvas has to wrap would be enclosed and of no use.

The simplest way to get over this problem is to only have attachments at the end of the boom. A plate on a central pivot has a projection downwards to take a block on the sheet (Fig. 11-11A). With this arrangement the boom does not have to be round as the sail will roll just as well on a square or rectangular section.

If the sheet arrangement needs to be attached elsewhere along the boom there are *claws* provided. They are metal shapes large enough to encompass the greatest diameter the rolled sail will make up, but with narrow openings carrying rollers (Fig. 11-11B). There may be a single block attached to one claw or a pair of sheaves can be in a special fitting (Fig. 11-11C).

A complication is the need to keep the claws in place along the length of the boom. They may not move much with some sheeting, but any movement is significant when racing. If the claws are not far from the end of the boom there may be a rigid rod pivoted on the end to hold the claw in the correct place (Fig. 11-11D).

For central sheeting this would mean a very long rod and it is more usual then to have a light line going each way to position the pull of the sheet (Fig. 11-11E).

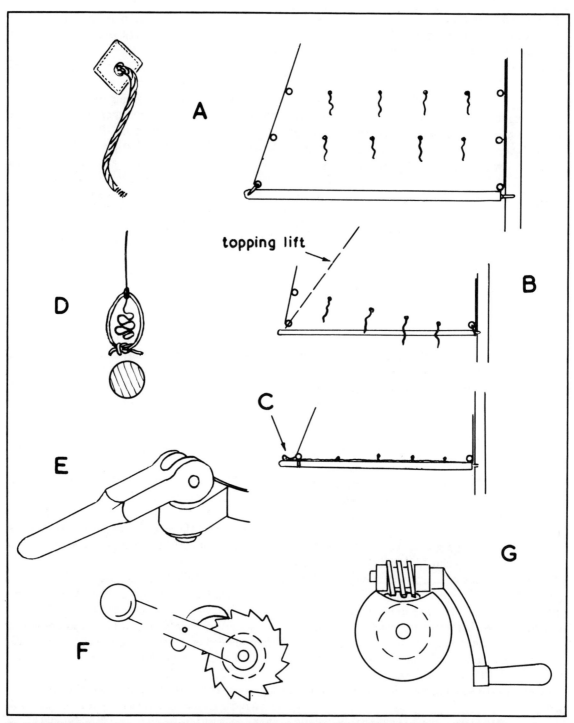

Fig. 11-10. Reef points allow canvas to be gathered on the boom (A to D). A square neck on the gooseneck allows the boom to be withdrawn and the sail rolled on it (E). On larger craft roller reefing is with a handle or lever (F,G).

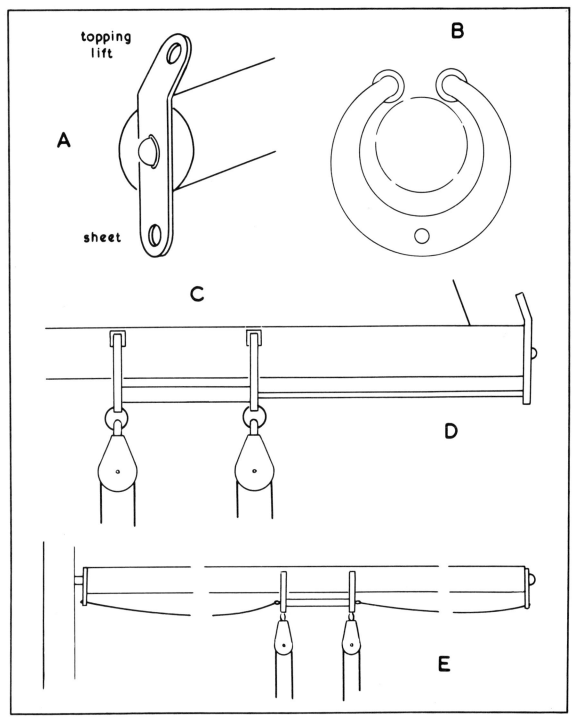

Fig. 11-11. When roller reefing is used attachments have to be arranged so they come outside the rolled sail and remain in position.

TOPPING LIFT

At times other than when the mainsail is fully set, the boom tends to sag and even when the boat is head to wind, it may swing from side to side with the rolling of the boat or the movements of the slack sail. In the smaller boats it is possible to restrain the boom by hand, but a heavier boom swinging freely can be hazardous. Its sagging extremity has to be pulled up by the hoisting sail, if nothing is done about it, and that puts an unnecessary load on the upper part of the sail, making it difficult to get the sail set properly.

If the boom cannot be manhandled easily, it should have a topping lift. Sometimes there are two, going each side of the sail, but one is now more usual. When the sail is being hoisted, the weight of boom is taken by the topping lift, which is adjusted to keep the boom at about its sailing angle to the mast. After the sail is up and its halyard secured,

the topping lift is slackened until it hangs clear and will not affect the shape of the sail when it bellies out under pressure of the wind.

The common arrangement of a topping lift is a light line taken from the end of the boom, over a sheave at the mast and down to a cleat. In boats rigged with gaff-headed sails it is led from a point on the mast that will not interfere with the gaff (Fig. 11-12A). With the modern jib-headed Bermudan sail it is better for it to pass through a block near the masthead (Fig. 11-12B). At the boom end the attachment should be clear of the claw of the sail. If there is roller reefing the usual place is opposite to the sheet attachment on a piece pivoting on the boom end. If there is a confusion of other sheaves and blocks at a masthead the topping lift block may come lower down, but not too far.

There are alternatives to that arrangement of topping lift, but they are not so common. There can

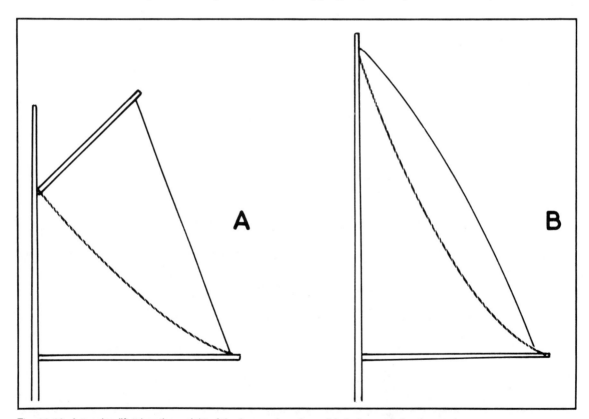

Fig. 11-12. A topping lift takes the weight of the boom when the sail is being reefed or lowered.

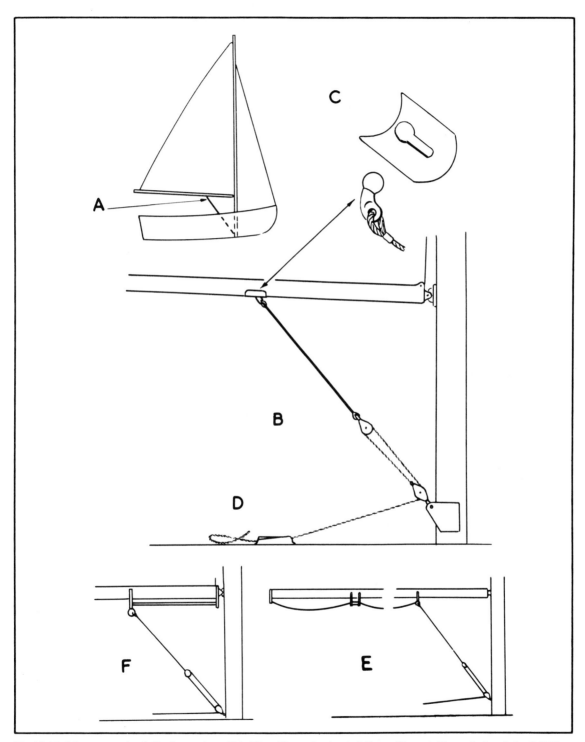

Fig. 11-13. A boom vang hauls the boom down (A to D) and it needs a jaw held in position outside a rolled reefed sail (E,F).

be a rope with a hook from the permanent backstay to engage a ring on the end of the boom. The topping lift may have one end attached to the mast at the top, then the other part goes over a sheave at the end of the boom to a cleat below the boom and some way forward. A snag with both of these arrangements is the effect of an unexpected gust of wind, although the boat is supposed to be head to wind. Limiting the movement of the sail by attaching the boom to the backstay could be dangerous if the wind fills the sail. If the boom swings out, a cleat below it may go out of reach.

BOOM VANGS

On some rigs there is a downhaul below the gooseneck. This serves as a tackle to draw the gooseneck down its slide after the sail has been hoisted, to get the sail luff tensioned, and the sail properly set. A comparatively recent addition has been a boom vang (kicking strap). Its purpose is to pull the boom down to take as much twist out of the sail as possible. (Center sheeting also does this and there may not be a boom vang then.)

When sheeting is at or near the end of the boom, the pull applied by the boom vang can make a difference in the windward sailing qualities of the boat. The system is used more with smaller craft, particularly those used for racing, than with cruising cabin craft, where there may not be enough clearance between the boom and the cabin top to make the fitting practical.

A boom vang is a tackle from the boom to as near the bottom of the mast as is possible (Fig. 11-13A). It is arranged at an angle usually slightly more upright than 45°. If a vang is doing its job properly there is considerable strain on it, so the two ends should be securely fastened.

There are several variations on boom vang assemblies, but the example shown uses wire for most of the length, and a 2:1 purchase is applied by a fiber rope (Fig. 11-13B). So the wire can be quickly disengaged there is a part engaging with a keyhole slot on the boom (Fig. 11-13C). The lower part may remain shackled to the mast foot. In some assemblies there is a cleat included in one of the blocks, so the rope may be secured there. Alternatively, it is led aft to a jam cleat (Fig. 11-13D).

A problem comes with roller reefing. There has to be a different arrangement at the boom and this may be a claw, similar to that described for the sheet. It has to be held at the correct distance from the mast.

There may be a line going to the sheet claws to prevent them from pulling towards the mast (Fig. 11-13E), or a compression strut can be attached to the mast (Fig. 11-13F). At times, the compression loads may be considerable, so the strut must be stiff.

Chapter 12

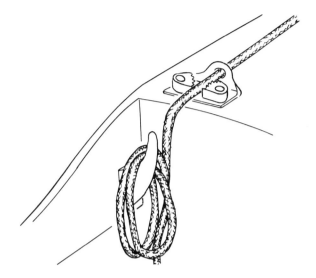

Foresail Running Rigging

IN MOST MODERN, SINGLE-MASTED BOATS THERE is only one sail forward of the mast at a time. There may be several alternatives for use in winds of different strengths and in varying conditions. Sometimes there are two or more sails set. In all cases these sails are triangular and they are controlled in basically the same way.

Sails are hoisted by halyards. The forward lower corner is held down by a tack line, a hook, a tackle, or some other short attachment to the stem or deck. Control is by a sheet in two parts attached to the clew of the sail and led aft each side of the mast. It is unusual to find a boom on a foresail, but older craft sometimes had one. There has also been a horse, similar to that across the stern, with the foresail sheet led to a slide on it.

With a better understanding of the aerodynamics of sailing has come an appreciation of the effect the foresail(s) can have on performance. Where a jib might once have been thought only to help the mainsail on some points of sailing, we now know that a properly set foresail can be more effi-

cient in relation to its size than the mainsail. Modern rigging methods allow for this and the gear used is more sophisticated than would once have been used.

HALYARDS

A halyard for a jib or other foresail is similar to that for the mainsail. It may pass over a masthead sheave and down the hollow mast. In that case it is made up in the same way with a wire main part and a fiber rope tail. If the rig uses a foresail that does not reach the top of the mast, there will be a wire stay at the appropriate height and the halyard will be rove through a block just below it, then led down externally to a cleat, with a winch as well for a large rig. For a new or replacement halyard the rigger has similar work to do to that involved in a main halyard.

Foresails have to be set up so their leading edges are taut. This requires a halyard that will not stretch when it is taking the load of the hoisted sail. It is better to have all of the load taken by wire than to have part of the fiber rope tail in tension after the sail has been hoisted.

One of the most precarious places to be is on the foredeck of a small, cabin sailing boat tossing in broken seas. Many of these craft have halyards, topping lifts, and other lines that in a larger vessel would require a member of the crew to go forward and bring them back to the cockpit. When rigging a boat with this scheme the rigger must watch that the ropes run fair and do not ride up the sides of sheaves or otherwise generate friction and chafe.

It may be possible for halyards to come directly back to fairleads that take them to cleats and a winch (Fig. 12-1A). Sliding hatches and other obstructions may require the ropes to be taken to the side of the cabin top, then led aft. In that case the sheaves may be flat on the cabin top in a series called a *turning block* (Fig. 12-1B). Mount this block so it approximately bisects the angles of the ropes. For wire ropes, have the sheaves as large as can conveniently be fitted (upwards of 1½ inches usually) to reduce internal friction in the wire.

If the halyards come to cleats on the cabin top, locate these where they are easily reached, but make provision for dealing with the long surplus tail after a sail has been hoisted, either with a further large cleat on the cabin bulkhead or a hook (Fig. 12-1C) on which the coiled end can be hung and easily cast off later.

SAIL LUFF

The luff, or leading edge of a foresail is usually made with wire enclosed, so it can be tensioned tightly. Attachments to both ends are to eyes in the wire. Whether there is wire or not, there are clips or hanks to engage with the stay ahead of the sail. Several patterns are used (Fig. 12-2A). For a small boat they may be plastic and sewn on, but for larger craft they are metal and sewn or lashed to eyes in the sail (Fig. 12-2B). Security is important and any sign of weakening should be dealt with, or failure at one place can spread along the line to other positions. Be careful to put each part on the same way as the others. A crew member may be depending on feel to attach a sail in the dark and the need for a

reverse action part way along the line would be disconcerting.

The pull at both ends of the luff should be as straight as possible. Perfection is not always possible, but if the halyard hauls parallel with the stay, the sail will set better than if it is angled downwards (Fig. 12-2C).

Similarly at the tack, the pull should be straight. A length of line on the sail may set the tack the right height (Fig. 12-2D). That could be shackled or hooked down, either with a plain hook or preferably one that closes. There is no need for adjustment in the line in most boats, so the tack line is usually a simple wire with eyes at the ends.

When rigging a boat, care is needed to set up the standing rigging correctly, with the forestay tensioned as required. This and the other stays for a modern rig should be fairly tight. Then when a foresail is set up there must be enough tension put on the halyard, but not so much that the sail is given more tension than the stay it is attached to and causes that to slacken. In correct sailing hoisting, there has to be a nice judgment of halyard tension, to get the sail tight without slackening its stay. The rigger should experiment with any sail he is newly rigging to get this right.

SHEETS

When a boat is sailing, the foresail will be to one side. Control of it is only by the part of the sheet on that side of the boat. The other part should be left slack enough for it not to have any effect or to get in the way. At the same time it has to be restrained, so that when you change tack you can also change sheets quickly.

Much more importance is now attached to the lead of the sheets than was given at one time. The method of using the double sheet can best be understood by taking a simple small cruising dinghy as an example.

The sheet is a continuous length on many boats. In a small boat it may go through a grommet in the clew of the sail and the two parts are seized (Fig. 12-3A). It would then remain with the sail when that was taken off the boat. Alternatively, it is

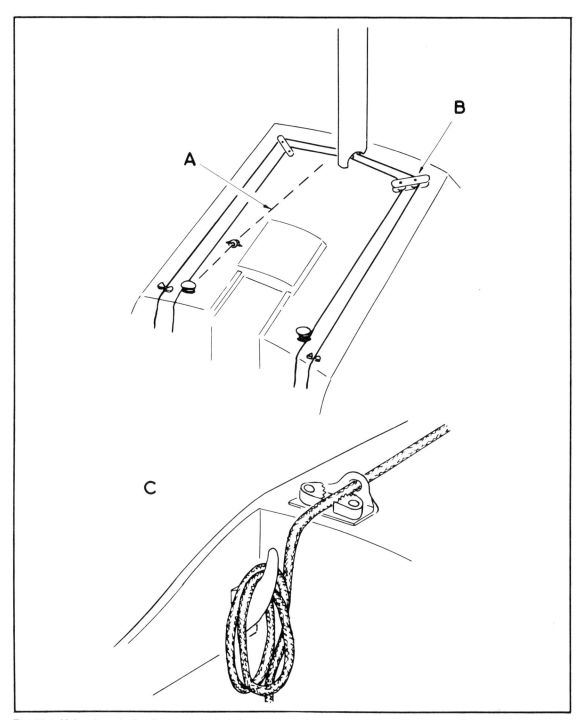

Fig. 12-1. Halyards and other lines may be led aft to the cockpit.

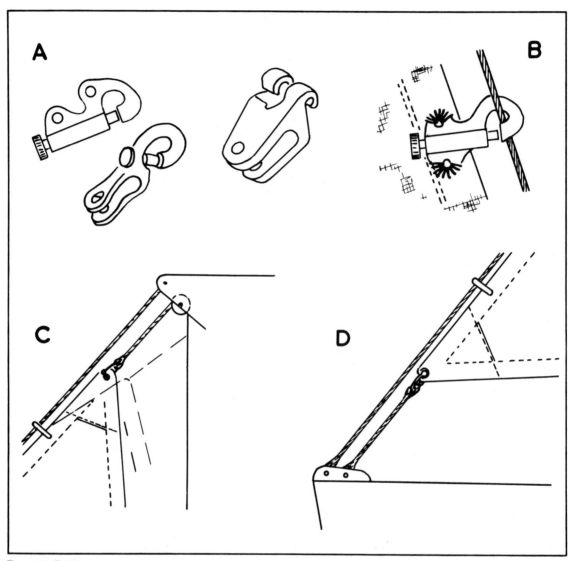

Fig. 12-2. Sail hanks attach a sail to a forestay (A,B). The pull at the ends should be straight (C,D).

attached with a shackle and the eye is made around a thimble (Fig. 12-3B). If it is in two parts, both eyes are on the same shackle or two shackles to through the grommet.

Each part of the sheet goes aft to a point on the gunwales. In this simple boat there could be a thimble spliced into a piece of rope through the gunwale (Fig. 12-3C). In a better-equipped boat there would be a proper fairlead, but the principle is the same. The end of the sheet then goes into the

boat and is knotted so it cannot pull out. There could be cleats on the centerboard case or elsewhere for making fast the end of the sheet in use (Fig. 12-3D). If there are two in the crew, the mate keeps one jib sheet in his hand and the helmsman holds the main sheet.

The position of the thimble or fairlead on the gunwale at each side affects the set of the sail. If it is too far forward, the pull on the sail is downwards (Fig. 12-3E) and the foot of the sail will not tighten.

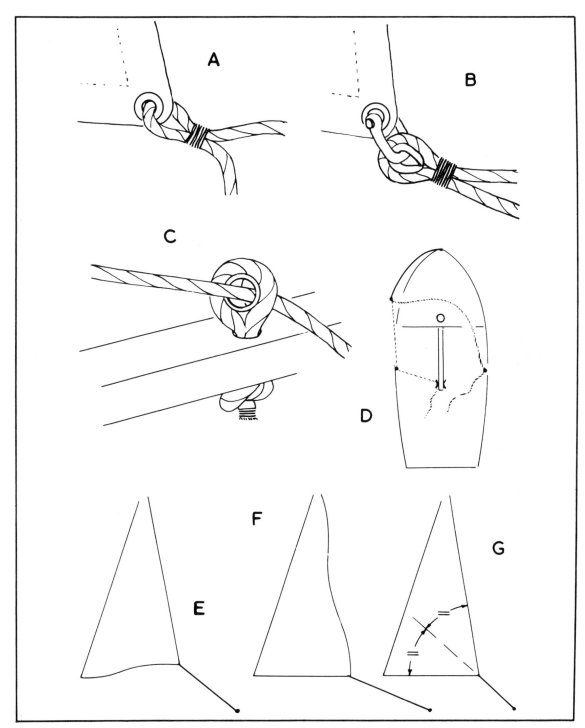

Fig. 12-3. A foresail sheet is divided (A,B) and leads to the gunwales (C,D). If the pull is untrue (E,F) the sail does not set as well as if it is correct (G).

If it is too far aft, the bottom will tighten and the leach will always be slack (Fig. 12-3F). The line of the sheet from the sail should bisect the sail angle at the clew corner, or be very close to that (Fig. 12-3G). Unfortunately, that angle may be drawn on paper and the fairlead positioned accordingly, but in sailing the cloth of the sail curves and the effective angle does not remain the same.

FAIRLEAD TRACK

For general purposes there can be immovable fairleads, but for racing craft the fairleads should be movable fore and aft. A complication comes with the use of other sails. Sails of different sizes do not necessarily need sheets leading to the same points on the gunwales. Sometimes there are fairlead locations at several points along the gunwales, but it is generally preferable to put the fairleads on tracks so they can be moved in use and locked wherever they set the sheet at the best angle.

A type of fairlead convenient on open and half-decked boats has a cam cleat attached (Fig. 12-4A). In another arrangement on a side deck the sheet comes through a fairlead to a cam cleat or other quick-release cleat near the inner edge of the deck (Fig. 12-4B). This arrangement suits a boat tacking in a limited space, where it goes about frequently and the crew needs to cast off one sheet and take up the other smartly while changing sides.

A rather similar idea is seen in a small cabin boat, where the sheet comes through a fairlead on the side deck and is then led through a hole in the cockpit coaming to a cleat on the cabin bulkhead (Fig. 12-4C). Such a cabin boat does not go about as quickly and is not so critical of the movements of the weight of the crew, so cleats may be plain, but there is still an advantage in using quick-release types.

The actual fairlead can take several forms. A bull's eye type may be mounted on a swivel (Fig. 12-4D). For small boats there are metal or plastic types that look something like handles (Fig. 12-4E). Particularly for larger craft with bigger loads, there may be rollers included on the sheets (Fig. 12-4F) to reduce friction, or a block on a swivel may take the place of a fairlead and allow the sheet to take up the correct angle in relation to the two directions of the sheet (Fig. 12-4G). Blocks are particularly used on a track for handling the sheet from the *genoa*, which is a foresail that considerably overlaps the mainsail. Its sheet has to go much further aft than that of the working jib (Fig. 12-4H).

The track is drilled for screws, either wood screws or, where the other side of the deck can be reached, bolts taken through and washers used to spread the load under nuts. In either case the heads should be countersunk below the surfaces so they cannot catch on the fairlead slide. There are several ways of securing the slide to the track. There may be a compression arrangement to grip the track at any place, but it is more usual to have holes in the track and a spring-loaded or other type of plunger to fit into them (Fig. 12-4J). Holes about 3 inches apart give sufficient precision.

Foresail sheets should be of fiber rope similar to that used for the main sheet, but usually not as thick. The rope should be flexible and as free from stretch as possible. In the layout of most boats with shrouds, the foresail sheets go outside the shrouds. Soft fiber rope rubbing over hard wire will chafe and it is usual to put something over the wire to protect the sheets. A neat arrangement is a piece of plastic tube (Fig. 12-5A), which can be a loose fit so it rotates and long enough to come higher than the sheet of any sail hoisted in the fore triangle. Ideally, this tube is threaded on the wire whole, usually before the second end of the shroud is made into an eye or a terminal fitted. If a tube has to be put on afterwards or a worn one replaced in position, a tube can be cut along the length with a knife, then sprung on. Bands of adhesive tape at intervals will hold it, as the cut edges usually remain closed. Transparent plastic tube is less obvious than darkly colored types.

There is sometimes the problem of getting a foresail down in a hurry, without the need to go forward, possibly in hazardous conditions. Slackening the halyard may not be enough as there is not much weight in a small sail to make it slide down. This can be taken care of by a downhaul. It can be a thin line as it does not have to take much load and for most sails a piece of ⅛-inch braided cord will do. Pass it through the sail slides and attach it to the

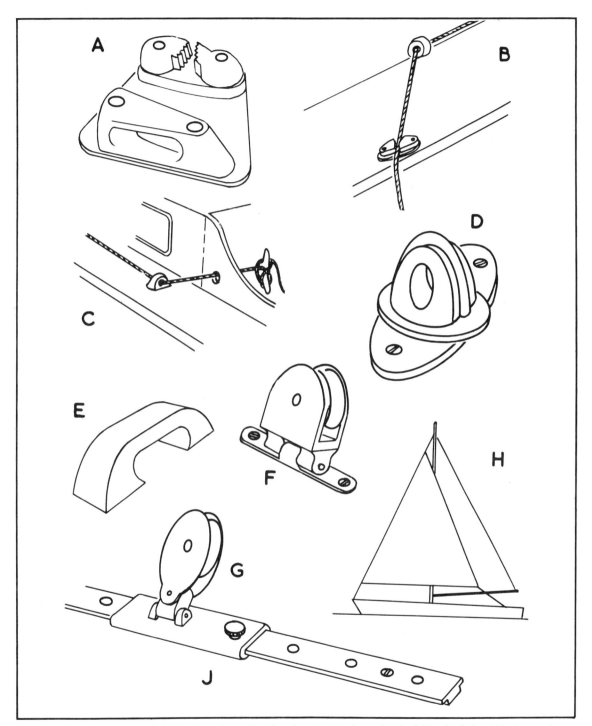

Fig. 12-4. Sheets pass through fairleads to cleats. To allow for changing foresails, the fairleads of sheet blocks may be on slides.

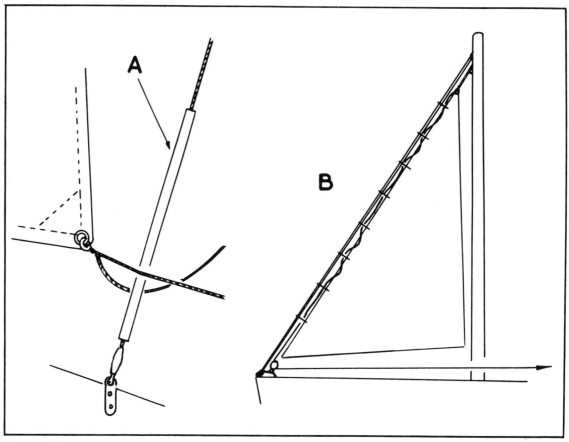

Fig. 12-5. Plastic tube on a shroud will protect from chafe (A). A downhaul can come from the top of a sail for ease in lowering (B).

grommet at the head of the sail. Mount a small block near the lower corner of the sail, so the downhaul pulls through it to get the sail down (Fig. 12-5B). The other end of the line goes to a small cleat in or within reach of the cockpit.

FORESAIL HORSE

It is unusual for a foresail to have a boom and a horse, but some traditional craft have them. The boom is there to provide weight and does not have anything like the mainsail gooseneck. Tension should be taken by lashings along the boom (Fig. 12-6A) to keep the foot of the sail in shape. In some cases the sail may be loose-footed, without the lacing along the boom.

With or without the boom there may be a horse across the foredeck and a sheet to it. The object is to make the foresail self-acting, so there are no sheets back to the cockpit. Some efficiency is lost, but for a boat tacking in narrow waters, such a foresail that goes across automatically without any attention from the crew may be of more use than one that has to be set on each tack at frequent intervals.

The horse is usually as far aft on the foredeck as conditions allow, so the sheet can come to it approximately bisecting the corner of the sail. The sheet is arranged as a tackle, the number of its parts depending on the size of the sail (Fig. 12-6B). The rope end must be locked to the tackle so there is no restraint on sail movement and the slide along the horse. Usually the sheet is adjusted for average conditions and left at that setting, particularly on rental boats, where the crew are assumed to not be concerned about maximum efficiency.

Older foresails were provided with reef points. It is more usual today to replace a large sail with a smaller one, rather than reef the large one. Such a sail performs more efficiently than a large one with a roll of cloth along its foot. If there are reef points (Fig. 12-6C), they are arranged similarly to those on a mainsail, with grommets to use at the ends of the lines before gathering up the surplus cloth as closely as possible.

JIB FURLING GEAR

The area of a foresail can be reduced by rolling around its leading edge, to the point where it is completely rolled and there is no area exposed to the wind. On many craft, there is just the one working foresail that is kept rolled in this way when the boat is not sailing. It is unrolled for use, either completely or partly, if the strength of the wind makes a smaller area advisable. This may be described as reefing the jib or foresail, but dealing with it in this way is more correctly called *furling*.

Such an arrangement is convenient. No one has to go forward to change sails and all of the control can be from the cockpit. Adversely, the sail does not set properly at all positions and it may get distorted and become baggy and less efficient in use.

There are several makes of equipment for jib furling, but the basic type is called *Wykeham-Martin gear* after the name of its inventor. The edge of the sail is tensioned and rolling takes place around it. That means the sail cannot be hanked to a forestay, but must rely on the tension of a wire edge

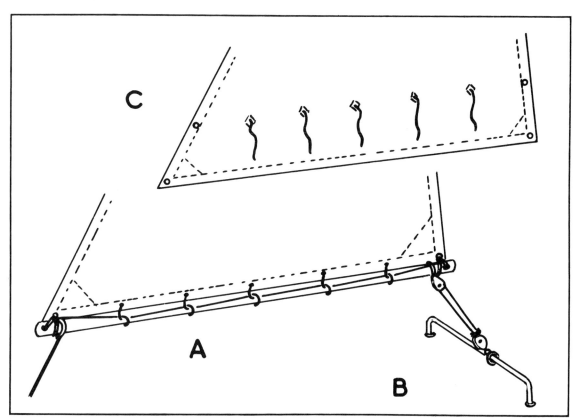

Fig. 12-6. If a foresail is arranged to reef it can have reef points. If it has a boom it can be arranged for automatic sheeting on a horse.

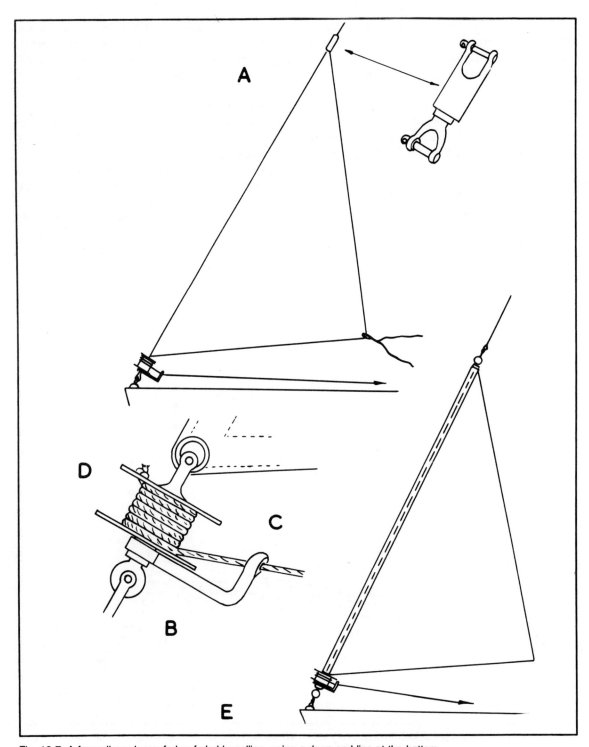

Fig. 12-7. A foresail can be reefed or furled by rolling, using a drum and line at the bottom.

to keep it straight and prevent the sail from sagging away so it performs less efficiently to windward.

The halyard is attached to the head of the sail via a swivel (Fig. 12-7A). Modern equipment has friction reduced to a minimum by the use of taper, thrust, and ball bearings. At the tack the main part is a drum to take a line that wraps around. The drum is another swivel with a means of attaching to a deck plate, the stem head or the bowsprit (Fig. 12-7B). The line from around the drum usually passes through an eye (Fig. 12-7C), then via blocks or fairleads along the deck to a cockpit cleat.

The end of the line is attached to the drum, probably through a hole in its flange, then enough turns are put on to be rather more than needed to fully roll the sail when the line is pulled (Fig. 12-7D). If this line has to be replaced, use a flexible synthetic cord—braided rope will run better than three-strand rope.

A problem with this basic type of furling gear is the flexibility of the luff of the sail. The roll imparted by the turning drum may not be transmitted all the way up, so the upper part of the sail has less roll in it. After a time this affects the set of the sail.

There have been several designs with the sail attached to a roller or tube on the forestay. At one time the roller was wood and comparatively thick, but with modern metal or plastic tubes the luff of the sail can be much thinner. Besides giving a smooth roll to the sail, this keeps the leading edge straight, as tension is applied to the stay through the roller and not to the sail. The drum turns the roller and there is no need for a bearing at the top, although there should be a spacer (Fig. 12-7E). Except for the tube, the arrangement of this furling gear is the same as the other type.

If jib furling gear is new or has been serviced, try its action several times. Jerking one end of the sheet should fully open a furled sail. At the same time, the furling line should coil smoothly on its drum. The reverse action should go equally smoothly and all of the sail be rolled. In use, the wind may help to open the sail but it may make full furling difficult.

Chapter 13

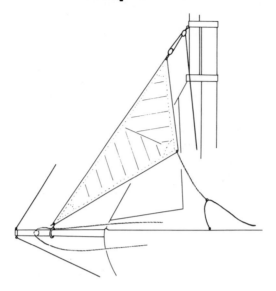

Gaff-Headed Rig

NOT MANY MODERN CRAFT ARE DESIGNED WITH gaff-headed sails. There is still interest in such mainsails, however, and some owners may claim advantages for them over the more usual jib-headed Bermudan mainsails. Older boats that used this traditional rig may have to be repaired and serviced, so a rigger should be familiar with the differences. Traditional gaff-rigged craft had many peculiarities of rigging that are of interest. Results were achieved with much simpler and less expensive equipment then, and may show you that there is not always the need for some of the complications seen on many modern sailing boats. Besides this there is always the nostalgic interest that makes traditional rigging appealing.

In older boats there were professional crew members to handle the gaff-rigging. Working boats obviously had professionals, but pleasure craft also carried paid hands as well as amateurs. There were always enough helpers to deal with complicated rigging and sail handling, even to the extent of going aloft in unpleasant, sometimes dangerous condi-

tions, to deal with some parts of the rigging. The less pleasant tasks went to the paid hands.

Not every gaff-rigged boat was complicated, but if a more complicated rig is considered, then dealing with a simpler example can be more easily understood. In a typical rig the main mast was in two parts, described as lower and top masts (Fig. 13-1). The gaff and its supporting halyards came from the lower mast, which was supported by several shrouds with ratlines for climbing aloft. The forestay came from the top of the lower mast to the stem head and there were running backstays from the same point. The topmast could be lowered, so its supports were not so permanent, but there was a stay to the end of the bowsprit and its own pair of running backstays. Above the gaff came a topsail that was laced to the topmast, in some cases, and projected beyond the end of the gaff with a jack yard. Although this sail moved with the mainsail, it also had its own sheet.

The staysail was hanked to the forestay and this is the equivalent of the single foresail in most

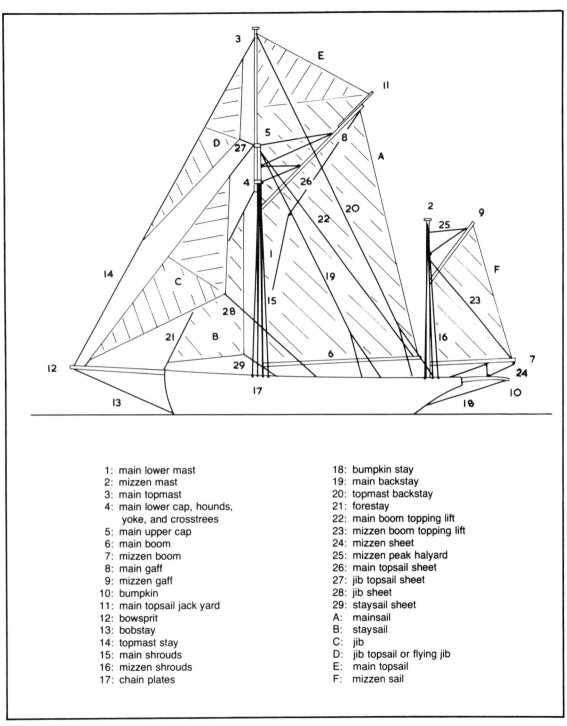

Fig. 13-1. Parts of a traditionally rigged yawl.

1: main lower mast
2: mizzen mast
3: main topmast
4: main lower cap, hounds,
    yoke, and crosstrees
5: main upper cap
6: main boom
7: mizzen boom
8: main gaff
9: mizzen gaff
10: bumpkin
11: main topsail jack yard
12: bowsprit
13: bobstay
14: topmast stay
15: main shrouds
16: mizzen shrouds
17: chain plates

18: bumpkin stay
19: main backstay
20: topmast backstay
21: forestay
22: main boom topping lift
23: mizzen boom topping lift
24: mizzen sheet
25: mizzen peak halyard
26: main topsail sheet
27: jib topsail sheet
28: jib sheet
29: staysail sheet
A: mainsail
B: staysail
C: jib
D: jib topsail or flying jib
E: main topsail
F: mizzen sail

modern rigs. Above it the jib was not accompanied by a stay, but its halyard led from the highest attachment point on the lower mast. From the top of the topmast came the jib topsail or flying jib, with its tack line taken to the end of the bowsprit and hanks on the sail to the topmast stay.

There was often a mizzen mast and sail, making the whole rig into a yawl or ketch. Except for the mizzen mast being in one piece its sail and rigging were arranged as a smaller version of the mainsail, but usually without a topsail. This serves as a guide for dealing with a gaff-headed sail on a boat with a single pole mast. In a yawl there would have to be a bumpkin (bumkin or boomkin) to provide an outboard position for the mizzen sheet.

MASTS

The two parts of the mast are solid pieces of wood. It was possible that some older ones were laminated, but older glues were unsatisfactory in damp conditions. Because of the weight of solid spars, the topmast was arranged to be *sent down* when it was not needed. Lowering it was not a simple task, but it was considered necessary when conditions were too bad for using the topsail and flying jib. In the lowered position the topmast is said to be *housed.*

The topmast passes through an iron cap on the extreme top of the lower mast and another support lower down. This may be another iron yoke above a supporting *bolster or trestle tree* (Fig. 13-2A). A short length of the heel of the topmast projects below its support, but the pole is held up by a topmast *fid*, which is a strong metal wedge through a slot (Fig. 13-2B). In the heel of the topmast is a sheave.

There will almost certainly be a spreader or crosstree and this may cross between or forward of the two parts of the mast (Fig. 13-2C). When the topmast is to be lowered there has to be a halyard rove through the sheave in the heel of the topmast, probably with one end to a point provided close in on the spreader or on the bolster at one side. Another block at the opposite side leads the fall of the halyard to deck level (Fig. 13-2D).

Before lowering a topmast, consider what will

happen to the rigging. Shrouds from below the bolster will not be affected. Shrouds from the cap of the lower mast lead over the spreader and they will not be affected. Shrouds from the topmast will also lead over the ends of the spreader (Fig. 13-2E), but as the topmast comes down, so do they. It is probable that second attachment points will be provided on them to take the lowered position (Fig. 13-2F) and these will be found part way up the vertical parts. Note how to disengage and couple them to the lowered mast positions. The stay going forward should be slackened and any load taken off the topmast running backstays. There may be a signal halyard or other ropes to be eased as well.

The topmast fid is taking the weight of the topmast and this load must be reduced. Take up a little on the heel rope, so that takes the weight and lifts the fid a little off the bolster. Knock it out. Its large end ought to be on a lanyard, but that is not always so. Take care not to lose the fid overboard.

There is not usually any stop provided for the lowered topmast and it may not always be sent down the same amount. Control lowering with the heel rope. Let the rope run out via a winch or give it several turns around a samson post or bitts, so friction helps in restricting movement. Obviously, the topmast must not be allowed to fall rapidly. Having the shroud parts approximately parallel gives a clue to the intended position of the topmast (Fig. 13-2G). In any case, do not try to bring the end of the topmast below the level of the cap of the lower mast. If there are no marked positions or stops, lash the bottom of the topmast to the main mast and put another lashing above the crosstrees (Fig. 13-2H).

Secure the heel rope so it is still tensioned. Make fast the ends of the shrouds that have come down with the topmast and lightly tension its forestay. Deal with the flag halyards or other ropes that have slackened. To send the topmast aloft again, the procedure has to be reversed.

MAST MAINTENANCE

Maintenance is mainly the replacement of worn ropes with new ones made up to the same sizes. If it is an old boat, the rigging may be of natural fiber and

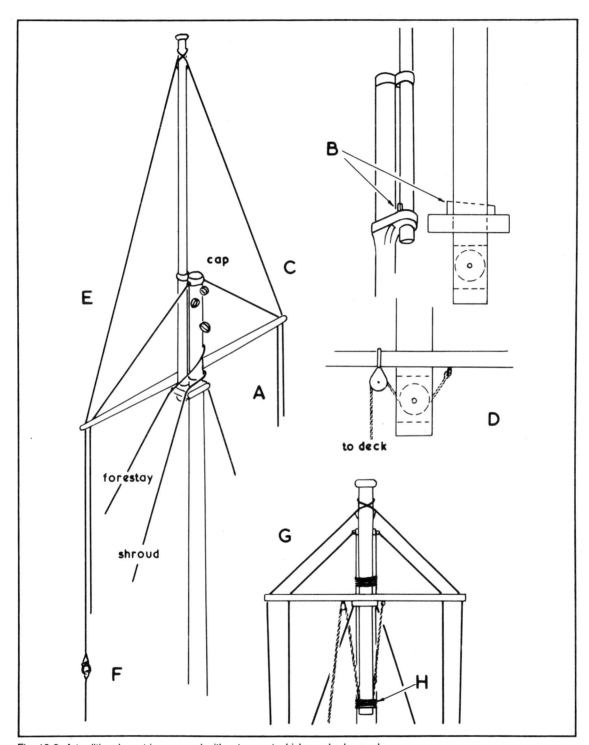

Fig. 13-2. A traditional mast is arranged with a topmast which can be lowered.

211

galvanized steel ropes. For authenticity it would be necessary to use similar materials, but for serious sailing the boat will have a stronger and more easily controlled rig if synthetic fiber and stainless steel ropes are used. Their end attachments also may be modernized. Iron parts should be examined. Bolts through a mast should be withdrawn. Sometimes a bolt will rust and become thinner in the part hidden within the wood. Wrought iron fittings will usually be in good condition. Slight surface rusting is better left, although it could be treated with a rust inhibitor and painted over for the sake of appearance.

If there is a wood *truck* or cap on one or both parts of the mast, check the condition of the wood in its vicinity. This is where rot may start. If that part is sound, its unlikely that rot will be found else-where, except at the main mast foot, if that is supported in a way that may trap moisture.

The wood used for these masts is likely to be one of the more resinous softwoods, rather than the more recent Sitka spruce. Resin protects the wood from the entry of much water, although it adds to weight, but no part of the masts should be left bare to absorb water. Touch up varnish where necessary and revarnish all over whenever possible.

MAINSAIL RIGGING

The boom of a gaff-headed sail is basically similar to that of a Bermudan mainsail, except that in a traditional boat it would be a solid round spar with the sail laced to it, instead of being grooved or fitted with a track. Reefing would be by the use of points and not by rolling, although that could be used in a modern version of the sail. Attachment to the mast is by a gooseneck similar to that of any other boomed sail.

The gaff of a traditionally rigged boat is solid and round, but in a modern version it could be grooved for the sail bolt rope. The gaff may rest along the boom when the sail is lowered, then it has to be raised by halyards and must be free to swing with the sail in use. To permit this movement, the usual gaff has jaws. In a small boat they can be quite simple (Fig. 13-3A). For a large sail there will be considerable pressure on the jaws against the mast and something more complicated is required (Fig.

13-3B). Lining with leather is common, to give a good smooth bearing surface against the mast.

If there is a leather lining, it should be kept in condition. Stitches tend to pull and wear away. The saying, "A stitch in time saves nine" comes from this sort of situation. If broken stitches are left, there will soon be more break and the whole thing may fail. Use stout sail twine with plenty of wax. Sew with double thread, if possible and knot at start and finish of repair stitching. Follow where the old stitching was and keep stitches away from wear surfaces. If you have to make new stitches, pierce holes with a fine awl, to give clearance for the needle, then push the needle with a palm.

The action of sailing pushes the jaws against the mast almost all the time, but there have to be precautions against the jaws coming off the mast. The traditional method, which is still used, is a *parrel line*. Parrels are small hardwood balls with holes through them. Today they might be plastic. Sizes vary, but for an average-sized boat, they can be about 1 inch in diameter. They are threaded on a line and spaced by knots, then one end of the line is spliced or knotted to one side of the jaws and tied to the other side when the jaws are coupled to the mast (Fig. 13-3C). The parrel line must be slack enough to go around the mast without strain when the gaff is resting on the boom. The line is slacker when the gaff is in position, but all it has to do is prevent the jaws coming off the mast. When the gaff is hoisted, the parrel balls revolve on the mast.

The luff of a four-sided mainsail cannot be attached to the mast with slides on a track or be fitted into a groove, because of the need for the gaff jaws to slide up the mast. It is still necessary to hold the sail to the mast for if it was left free there would be a gap between the sail and the mast, air would pass through, and the sail would lose efficiency.

In a smaller boat, where it is possible to reach up the mast almost to the gaff jaws when the sail has been hoisted, there may be a lacing line attached to the highest grommet. That is then taken around the mast (Fig. 13-3D) and secured at the bottom. If the sail has to be lowered in an emergency, the lacing will slide down the mast. It should not be half-hitched, as recommended earlier for lacing to a

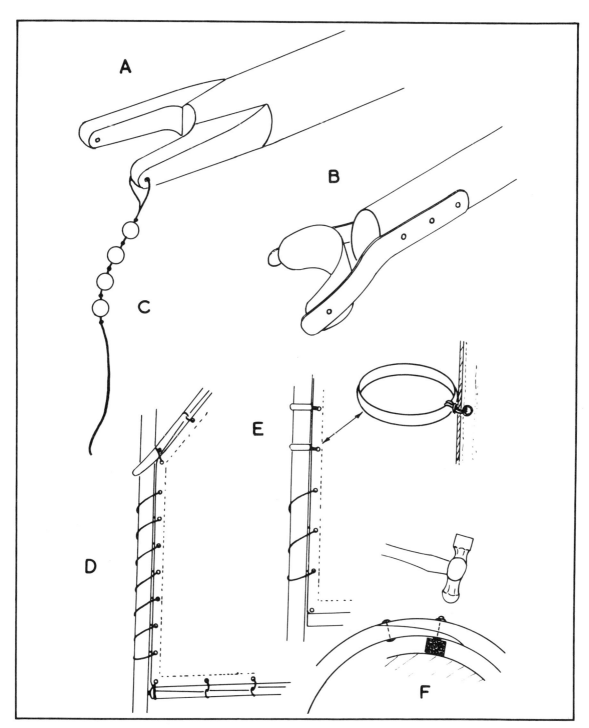

Fig. 13-3. Gaff jaws (A,B) fit against the mast and may be held with a parrel line (C). The sail is held to the mast with lacing (D) or hoops (E), which are riveted (F).

boom, as that might not slide as easily, if quick lowering was called for.

In larger craft lacing to the main mast ceases to be practical as the height of the luff is too far to reach. It may still be possible on a mizzen sail. Instead there are hoops (Fig. 13-3E), which are wood rings on the mast. Grommets on the sail are lashed or clipped to them and they are drawn up the mast as the sail is hoisted. They hold the sail reasonably closely to the mast when sailing. Even if there are hoops the bottom few grommets, which will be within reach, may still be laced with a line spliced to the highest of them.

Wood hoops are preferred, but there are metal ones. Hoops are bent wood with the ends spliced and riveted. On some masts it may be possible to put new ones in place before the mast is stepped, but a rigger will have to replace a broken one. The wood chosen is springy and a ring may be supplied with the end splice already cut but not joined. It should be possible to spring the hoop on the mast. If it resists springing open and there is a risk of it breaking, soak it in hot water to make it pliable. Rivet in position. The rivets may be copper nails closed over copper washers. Arrange the heads inside and put a strip of iron between the hoop and the mast to act as an anvil. Drive the washer over its nail and cut off the end of the nail with enough projecting to allow hammering a head (Fig. 13-3F). Two rivets are usual. If there is any roughness, file the rivet ends.

There have to be two halyards to hoist a gaff. The *throat halyard* lifts at the jaw end (Fig. 13-4A). The other is the *peak halyard* and lifts further along the spar (Fig. 13-4B). The throat halyard gives a simple lift, in the same way as the sail halyards already described, even if it needs tackle or a winch to get the sail tightly raised. Both halyards are used at the same time, but the throat halyard should be leading slightly, so the luff is tensioned before the peak of the sail is pulled up.

How the peak halyard does its work depends on the size of the sail. In a small boat it may be satisfactory to have a direct pull, providing the mast is high enough to bring the rope to a good angle

(Fig. 13-4C). It is more usual to arrange the halyard through several blocks spread on the mast and on the gaff (Fig. 13-4D). Besides providing a purchase, which is valuable with a heavy spar, this also spreads the support along the spar and reduces any risk of it bending.

If a gaff-headed sail is to be used without another sail above it there is a gain in windward ability when the angle of the gaff is brought nearer upright (Fig. 13-5A). Carried to its logical conclusion, the gaff is brought straight up, so it continues the line of the mast, to make a *gunter mainsail* (Fig. 13-5B). The sail shape is then almost the same as a Bermudan sail, but the rig suffers in efficiency by movement between the mast and gaff, which the one-piece Bermudan mast obviates. However, there is an attraction in the gunter rig when it would be an advantage to have all spars shorter than the boat, for convenience in storage or ease of trailing.

In practice there is a limit to the size of boat that can be safely given a gunter mainsail. For a large rig, the overlap of mast and gaff puts too heavy a load high up. However, it is used for open boats and decked boats up to about 25 feet long.

The main problem is getting the gaff close to the mast. The jaws have to be angled, so they will embrace the mast when the gaff is horizontal and when it is raised (Fig. 13-5C). There is no need for a throat halyard and the sail is hoisted by a single halyard that brings the gaff to the correct amount of overlap. In some older boats there was a wire span on the gaff, but that allowed the gaff angle to fall away from the mast. To get the most out of the rig, the gaff must be drawn tight. There may be a strop on the gaff (Fig. 13-5D) or the halyard may be knotted to bring the gaff closer (Fig. 13-5E). The closest joint comes from taking the halyard through the gaff (Fig. 13-5F), angling the hole if it is a slotted gaff (Fig. 13-5G).

Another problem with a gunter sail is reefing. If sail area is reduced by gathering up cloth at the boom, the gaff has to be lower. If it is to stay tight against the mast, there has to be a new attachment point (Fig. 13-5H), otherwise the gaff will sag away and the sail lose its shape.

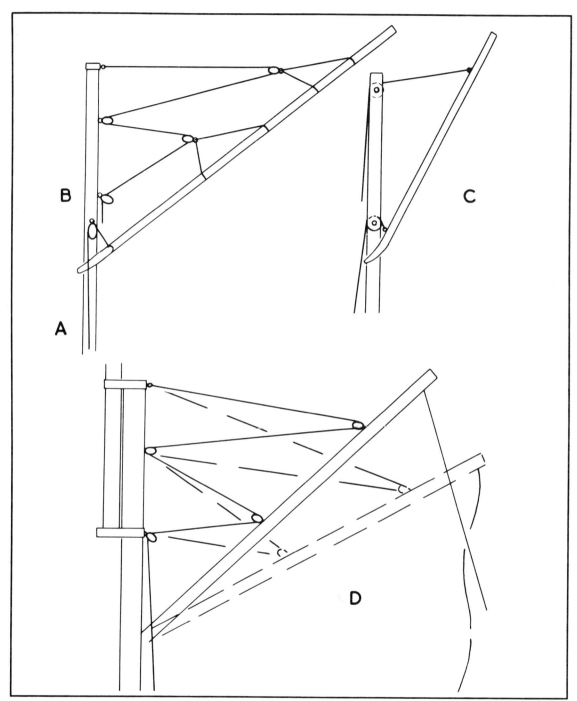

Fig. 13-4. A gaff is raised by a throat halyard (A) and a peak halyard (B), which is attached to several points along the gaff. A small, more upright gaff may have a direct pull (C). The gaff is raised by both halyards, then the peak tightened (D).

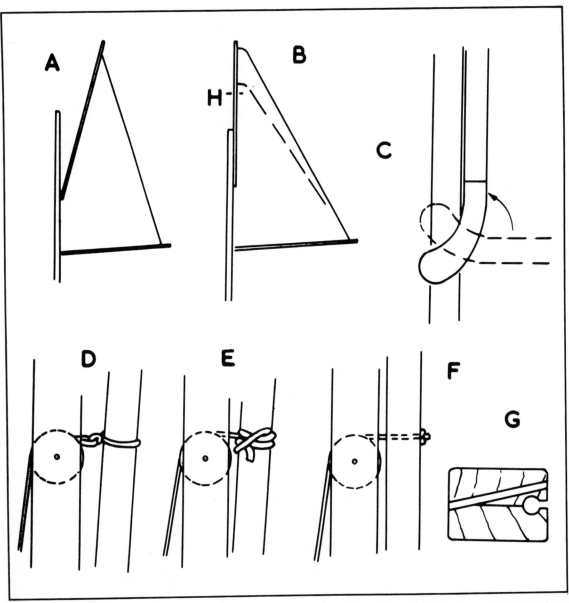

Fig. 13-5. From a high-peaked gaff (A) comes the upright spar of a gunter sail (B), with jaws to allow movement (C). The halyard must draw the gaff close (D,E,F). A diagonal hole clears a slotted spar (G). A second hoisting position is needed when reefing (H).

FORWARD SAILS

Of the three sails forward of the mast, the staysail is similar to the single sail on a modern sloop rig. The forestay goes from the lower cap of the main lower mast to the stem head and is permanently ten-sioned. The staysail is hanked to it, so its luff is kept straight, then its tack is secured near the stem and a halyard goes over a sheave near the upper end of the stay. In a traditional rig the sheave was in a block on the forward side of the mast. The double sheet goes back to fairleads on the gunwales in the usual way. The other two sails are dependent on the bowsprit for keeping them extended.

BOWSPRIT

In some older craft the bowsprit was of considerable length in relation to the size of the boat. This meant that it had to be stayed in a very similar way to a mast. Even with a shorter spar there needs to be supports because the load taken by the pull of mast stays and sails has to be resisted. Although most of the pull is upwards on the end of the bowsprit, sailing in a beam wind puts sideways loads on the spar. With a very short bowsprit there may be enough inherent stiffness to resist this, but usually there are bowsprit shrouds, while the downward stay is the *bobstay* (Fig. 13-6A).

In a boat rigged with top and lower main mast, it is usual for the bowsprit to be arranged so that it can be hauled in and stowed on deck when conditions are such that the topmast is sent down. In rough conditions the boat then sails with the staysail and mainsail only and may come down to storm sails of quite small areas.

If the bowsprit is arranged so it can be stowed, there has to be enough space on the foredeck to take it. At the stem it passes through a substantial iron eye, which may carry attachments for the forestay and staysail tack. At the inner end is a substantial bolster to take the inward thrust, where there is a fid, similar to that on the topmast. The bolster needs to be strongly mounted and it may form part of the bitts.

The bobstay goes from the end of the bowsprit

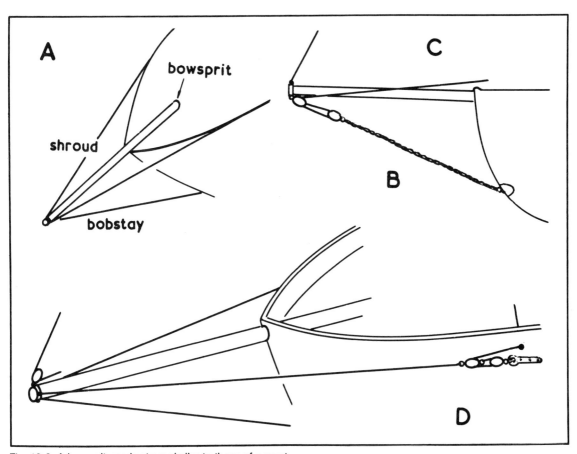

Fig. 13-6. A bowsprit needs stays similar to those of a mast.

to near the waterline on the stem. Much of its length is usually chain, although it could be wire rope. This is because of the risk of chafe when the anchor cable is down (Fig. 13-6B). Rubbing between the two cannot be avoided as the boat swings at anchor. If the bowsprit is not to be stowed, the outer end of the bobstay could be tensioned with a rigging screw, but if the spar can be moved there has to be a means of tensioning the bobstay from the deck. In that case there is a tackle, its number of parts depending on the size of boat, with the rope end taken back to a cleat or other strong point on deck (Fig. 13-6C).

The bowsprit shrouds also lead from the end of the bowsprit, where there is usually a band with four eyes for shackling on stays. As with the bobstay, the shrouds of a bowsprit that stays in place can be tensioned with rigging screws, but if it can be drawn back they are better controlled with tackles. The shrouds should be wire rope. The amount of movement required of the tackle is not much, so the blocks can be arranged fairly close together (Fig. 13-6D). The shrouds are brought inboard when the bowsprit is stowed and the bobstay may then be pulled and held up with a temporary lashing.

Maintenance is much the same as for the mast and its stays. Pay particular attention to the stem plate, which is a key point in the security of the outer and upper parts of the rig. It is "between wind and water," which is a crucial place for corrosion. The chain bobstay is also liable to suffer wear and rust, so it should be replaced if there is any doubt about it.

OUTER SAILS

The topmast goes to the band at the end of the bowsprit. In a permanent assembly on a short bowsprit it could be tensioned with a rigging screw, but it is more usual for there to be a block and the rope end led aft to the deck (Fig. 13-7A). The wire tack line from the flying jib comes down to an eye on the block (Fig. 13-7B) or it may come to another block for its end to be brought to the deck.

The flying jib can be hanked to the topmast stay and hoisted by the usual halyard from the topmast,

with its fall brought down to a belaying pin or a cleat near the deck.

The sheet of the flying jib is too high for the normal jib sheet arrangement. Instead, there is a single sheet led back to the upper cap of the main mast. It may lead directly down, or be arranged with a purchase (Fig. 13-7C). At deck level there may be a belaying pin or cleat on the mast, or the end can go via a block to the cockpit or within reach of the crew member handling the other foresail sheets.

The jib needs special treatment. It does not have a stay to hank to and straightness of the luff depends on tension in the sail. In traditional sails the leading edge is fiber rope and liable to stretch, but in a more recent sail it should be wire. The halyard hooks to the sail and may be a simple pull, or there can be a purchase arranged at the lower mast-head (Fig. 13-7D). In modern usage it would be better to provide any purchase at deck level, either with a tackle or a winch.

The tack of the jib goes to a traveler on the bowsprit, so the sail can be attached near the stem and hauled out. The traveler is an iron ring with a hook and eye (Fig. 13-7E). The outhaul is a rope going over a sheave set in the bowsprit (Fig. 13-7F). Although it may be possible to pull the traveler back with the sail, it is better to bring a part of the outhaul back. It may be arranged as a continuous rope. It is only the outhaul that keeps the jib extended, so it should be strong.

The jib sheet is in the usual two parts, but because of the overlap of the sail on the forestay, care is needed to keep it from becoming caught as the sail changes sides. There may be simple lines each side, with any purchase provided at their ends, but another arrangement on some traditional rigs has a whip from the sail at each side, long enough not to be pulled completely over the forestay. A sheet then goes through a bullseye fairlead or a small block (Fig. 13-7G).

TOPSAIL

Topsails have taken many forms. There have been four-sided sails with supporting yards, but those found today are three-sided. The luff follows up the line of the topmast, the clew is sheeted to the end of

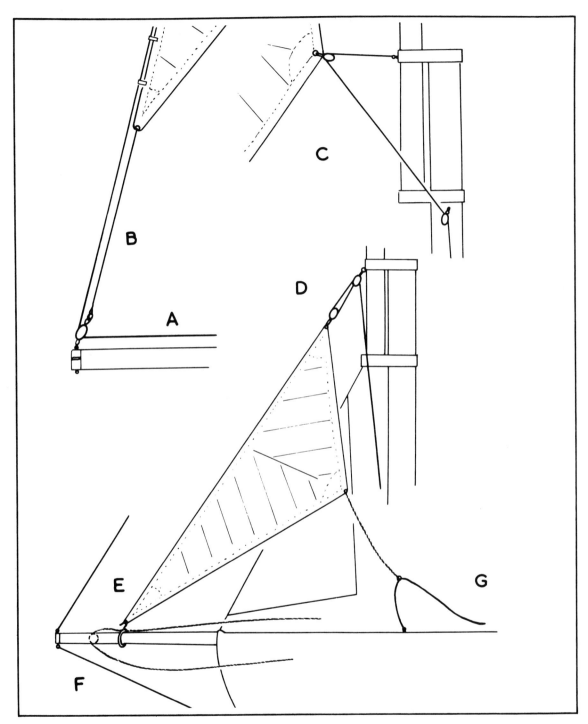

Fig. 13-7. A flying jib has a long tack line and is hanked to the forestay (A,B). Its sheet goes to the mast (C). The jib hoists from the lower masthead (D). Its tack goes to a traveler (E,F) and there may be whips each side to sheets (G).

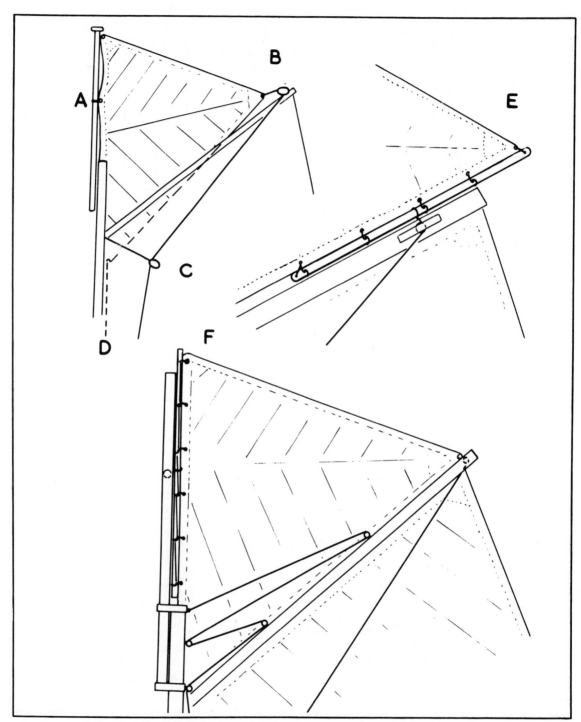

Fig. 13-8. A topsail goes above the gaff and may be secured to the topmast, with a sheet from the end of the gaff (A to D). It can be extended past the end of the gaff (E) or be laced to a spar against the topmast (F).

the gaff, and the tack may be attached to the jaw end of the gaff or have its own line hauling downwards. The sail may be almost wholly above the gaff or there may be a foot going below the gaff. In any case, the topsail provides useful extra high sail area where it is effective, but there are difficulties in hoisting a topsail whatever its pattern.

A basic topsail is hoisted by its head with a halyard to near the limit of the topmast. There may be lacing to grommets along the length of the mast or just one or two lashings (Fig. 13-8A). The clew is pulled out to the end of the gaff by a sheet (Fig. 13-8B), then the fall of this is led clear of the main-sail by a block on a short whip (Fig. 13-8C). A downhaul or tack line keeps the leading edge of the sail tensioned (Fig. 13-8D). It would be possible to have a two-part tack line, so the corner of the sail could be pulled over the boom when sailing with the wind from the other side, but there are many obstructions, so the sail is normally kept at one side. Traditionally the sail is on the starboard side of the gaff and the sheet on the port side.

To get a little more spread of canvas there may be a short *jack yard*, which is a sort of small boom lace to part of the sail (Fig. 13-8E). The sheet leads from near the balance point of this and may go

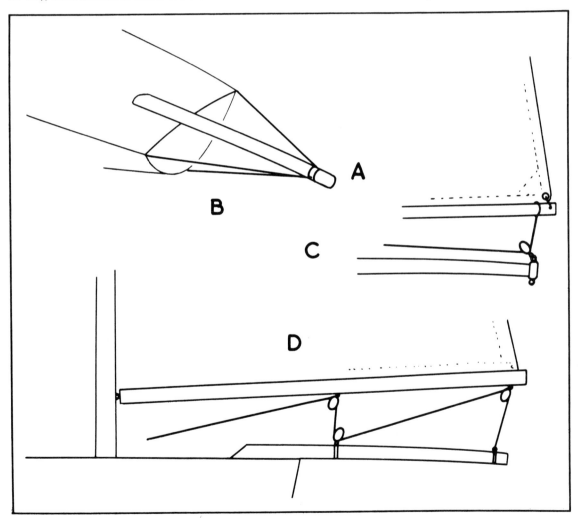

Fig. 13-9. A bumpkin extends over the stern to take the sheet from a mizzen sail.

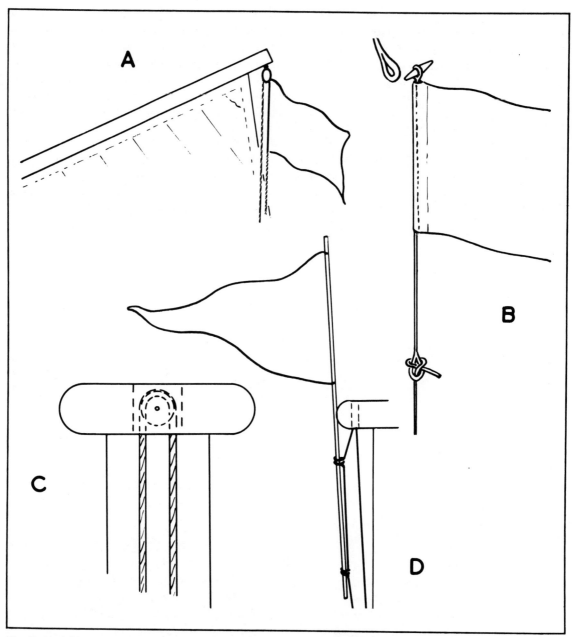

Fig. 13-10. A flag may be at a block at the end of the gaft (A,B) and a burgee goes at the masthead (C,D).

through a cheek block on the gaff, so it can be pulled close.

The name *jack yard* has also been applied to a spar attached to the luff of the topsail (Fig. 13-8F). This light spar is hoisted with the sail and ensures a straighter luff. Its effectiveness depends on how close and steady it can be held by the halyard attached near its balance point.

In maintenance work the rigger needs to see that any replacements still function correctly.

There ought to be practice hoistings to check that it is possible to get the topsail up without snagging on other parts of the rigging.

MIZZEN SAIL

On some boats with two masts the mizzen sail may be jib-headed, even when the mainsail is gaff-headed. If the mizzen has a gaff, the mast is in one piece and tall enough to allow for the run of the parts of the peak halyard. In schooners and other rigs with large sails aft, the mast and sail details are generally similar on both masts. For the smaller mizzen sail of a yawl or ketch, most details are similar to those for the mainsail, except for the arrangement of the sheet.

If the boom does not extend far over the stern, it is possible to arrange the sheet in a similar way to that of the mainsail. If the boom extends some way aft, as it will in a yawl rig, there has to be a bumpkin, which is the equivalent of a bowsprit over the stern. It is not arranged to be hauled in, so it is an almost permanent installation. It does not have to be very long. On some craft it is given a curve down towards its end (Fig. 13-9A). The loads on the bumpkin are not as great as on the bowsprit, but it needs a stay downwards and a pair of shrouds (Fig. 13-9B). How far the stay can be taken downwards depends on the shape of the stern, but the lower it comes on the hull, the less acute will be the angle to the bumpkin and the more effective the pull. The stay and the shrouds can be adjusted with rigging screws.

How the mizzen sheet is arranged depends on the size of the sail to be controlled and the purchase needed. A small sail might have the sheet through a block on the end of the bumpkin and the end brought back to a cleat on deck (Fig. 13-9C). If some purchase is needed it is convenient to divide this along the boom and bumpkin, with bands on the bumpkin for the blocks (Fig. 13-9D).

FLAG HALYARDS

The national ensign is *worn* on a short staff at the transom on a power boat or a sailing boat under power, but traditionally it is worn at the end of the gaff of a sailing craft. This means providing a halyard through a block there (Fig. 13-10A). Where the halyard leads has not been agreed. If the flag is to fly free of the edge of the sail, the halyard might go down to the end of the boom. It might be taken into the mast near the gooseneck, but will not then keep the flag so clear of the sail. The flag has been sewn to the edge of the sail, but that is not considered seamanlike.

A modern flag may be attached to its halyard with brummel hooks, but in the traditional way a wood toggle on the top of the flag engages with an eye spliced in the halyard. Below the flag is a length of line about equal to the depth of the flag and that finishes in an eye. There may be a toggle in the halyard or it can be joined to the flag eye with a sheet bend (Fig. 13-10B). When there is no flag on the halyard, the ends of the halyard are joined together.

At the highest point on the main mast there should be a pennant or *burgee*. Usually it is the flag of a club or association to which the owner belongs. It has a secondary purpose of showing the direction of the apparent wind. When a boat is moving through the water, the burgee does not indicate true wind, but a result of the true wind and the movement of the boat.

There may be a block at the masthead or there could be a sheave in the mast truck or cap for a light flag halyard (Fig. 13-10C). The burgee is usually mounted on a *flag stick*. In its simplest form it is a straight piece of wood, then the halyard attaches to it with two clove hitches (Fig. 13-10D). There are many more elaborate arrangements, some have easy-running bearings so the flag turns smoothly and the stick may be cranked to bring the flag upright, as well as have different attachments to the halyard. These and more advanced wind vanes are used when racing.

Some similar halyards may be provided to blocks on the crosstrees for hoisting signal flags.

Chapter 14

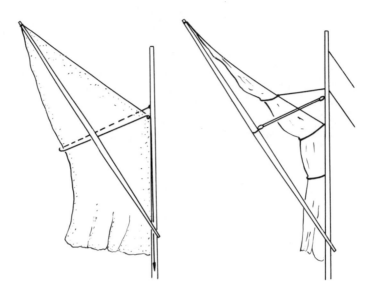

Other Sails

NEARLY ALL MODERN SAILING BOATS ARE rigged as sloops, with a mainsail (usually jib-headed) aft of the mast and one triangular sail forward of it. Some have more than one mast and a few have more than one sail forward of the mast, but the basic methods of rigging are the same. Although a sloop may only use one sail at a time forward of the mast, there may be many headsails of different sizes to choose from, depending on wind strength from light airs to storm conditions. The common names are shown in Fig. 14-1. The rigger is not concerned with these changes in sizes, except to see that the sheets lead correctly. To take care of this there is usually a very long track at each side for positioning fairleads.

The exception is the addition of a spinnaker in light airs. It is not intended for general sailing, but it can make the most of what air is available when a light wind is coming abeam or aft of it. The spinnaker probably causes more bother to the enthusiastic sailor, particularly if he is racing, than any other part of this rig.

SPINNAKER RIGGING

Spinnakers have been known for a long time, but they have only been developed to their present form in comparatively recent times. This has largely been due to the availability of nylon cloth, which is particularly suitable for spinnakers and much more effective than the older natural fiber cloths. Some early spinnakers had little more curve than other headsails, but later ones have been made to very deeply curved shapes. Early versions of the very curved sail were called *parachute spinnakers* to distinguish them from the flatter ones, but now that all spinnakers are this shape, the word parachute is rarely used.

A spinnaker is hoisted outside all stays. It can be hoisted and used with another headsail, or put into position before the other headsail is lowered. The mainsail is normally set at the same time as a spinnaker.

A spinnaker sail has a central head and its cloths are cut so it opens to an extremely rounded shape. The usual form is symmetrical, with a

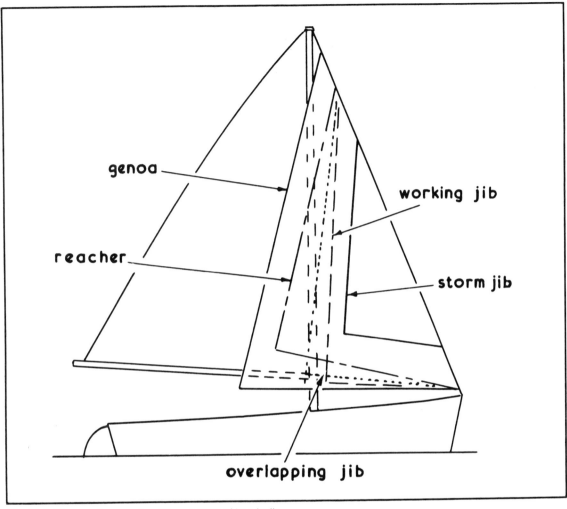

Fig. 14-1. The usual names for different sizes of headsails.

straight foot when the sail is set. The lower corners are obvious angles and may both be called clews, but if the practice with other sails is followed, one is a clew, while the other is tack, although they may change functions when the sail changes sides. The head may not be very angular, but it is marked by a clip or other attachment for the halyard.

The tack of the spinnaker is held out by a pole from the mast and this is kept at the intended angle by an uphaul (topping lift) and a downhaul (Fig. 14-2A). From its end goes a *guy* to a position aft on the gunwale or side deck. In a similar position comes the sheet at the other side. That is the general principle (Fig. 14-2B). There are variations and the parts available for connections and detail work are plentiful, but the setting of a spinnaker is as follows.

The spinnaker may hoist with a halyard from the masthead or from lower on the forward side. There may be a block or it could be an internal halyard. If the halyard has to be identified, it is usually thinner than those for other sails. As the spinnaker moves from side to side and the pull may come across the mast, there is a risk of chafe at the outlet if it is an internal halyard (Fig. 14-3A). It may be possible to get more use from the chafed rope by

225

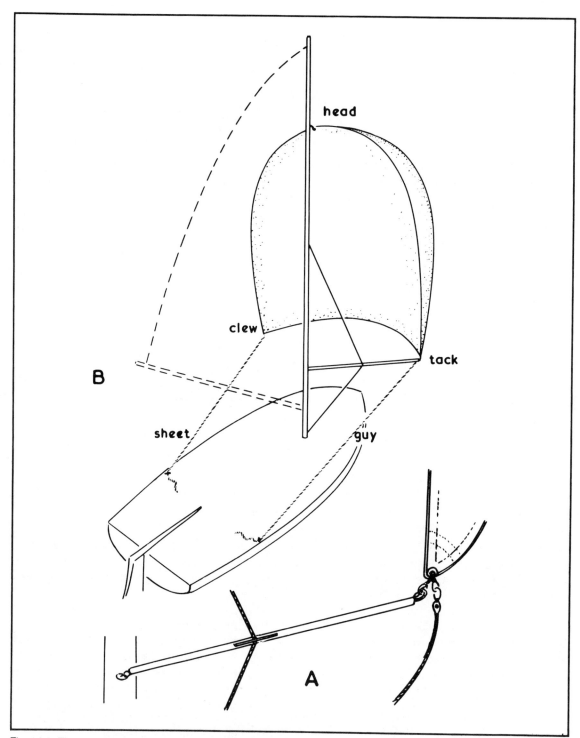

Fig. 14-2. The main parts of a spinnaker and its rigging.

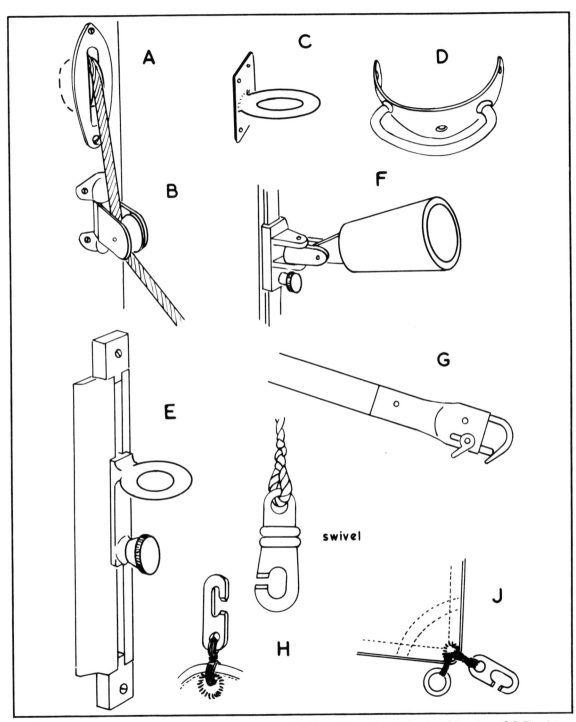

Fig. 14-3. Spinnaker halyard and lift may be from the mast (A,B). The pole attaches to fixed or sliding rings (C,D,E) or into a socket (F). The pole end may have a quick-release clip (G). Attachments can be with brummel hooks.

shortening it so a different part takes the wear. A better arrangement uses a swiveling fairlead below the outlet (Fig. 14-3B).

The spinnaker pole attaches to the mast at an eye (Fig. 14-3C), which may spread around the mast (Fig. 14-3D). In the simplest form the ring is in one position, but it may be on a track to give a choice of positions (Fig. 14-3E). On a large boat there may be tackle for moving the rig.

The uphaul and downhaul go to points on the mast. The uphaul may be through a block or be taken into the mast. In that case it should have a swiveling fairlead (Fig. 14-3B). The downhaul will probably go to a cleat low on the mast. The loads on these ropes are not great, so they need not be very thick.

The spinnaker pole or boom is usually an aluminum alloy tube today. When out of use it stows on the deck. In an older version, the pole was wood and at the mast end it tapered into a sleeve fitting (Fig. 14-3F), where it was held by a pin. In some traditional craft it was stowed up the mast. The uphaul was then more of a topping lift and included a tackle to suit the weight of the spar.

A modern pole has a clip at the inboard end. There are several variations, but basically it is a hook to engage with the ring on the mast and a spring arrangement to keep it in place (Fig. 14-3G). A similar arrangement at the other end links with the tack of the sail. This makes the pole double-ended, which is convenient when changing sides. The uphaul and downhaul join at the midpoint on the pole. There may be separate attachments, or for a small boat the uphaul and downhaul can be a continuous piece of rope that fits into a clip like a long fairlead. Height control is then by stops on the rope. This part of the equipment is unlikely to need much maintenance. Rope may have to be replaced. The spring clips on the pole may need lubricating.

For quick attachment the spinnaker head and its halyard may have brummel clips (Fig. 14-3H). At the two lower corners there have to be rings or eyes to take the clip on the spinnaker pole, but at both positions there should also be brummel clips lashed on, so whatever the function is at that setting, whether tack or clew, the means of joining on are

there (Fig. 14-3J). Other attachments are also used, but whatever they are, the rigger should check security and wear on the lashings. Replace doubtful lashings, because wear becomes progressive and broken lashing line can soon unwind and give way.

The spinnaker sheet and guy are identical, with brummel hooks for attaching to the sail and the other end sealed and whipped. Wear is unlikely but if a part has been worn or damaged, it may be possible to give the rope further life by changing it end for end.

If a rigger gets an opportunity to sail a few times with a spinnaker, he will realize that there are many problems that can arise in handling the considerable expanse of light cloth. One help in smaller craft is to stow the spinnaker in a chute below the foredeck. There is a large opening to the chute on the foredeck close to the stem and usually to one side of the forestay. In one arrangement the halyard also hauls the spinnaker into its chute (Fig. 14-4A). The hauling point is at the center of the sail, just below its geometric balance. By taking the rope back to cleats on the centerboard case, control in both directions is within reach (Fig. 14-4B).

Hauling down can be commenced with the guy and sheet pulling the sail back against the forestay, while the retrieving end of the halyard pulls the sail down and into the chute. Then the clew and tack are disengaged and allowed to follow and finally the head. Hoisting is straight forward with the pole, guy, and sheet attached as soon as the corners emerge.

Experience will show what modifications might be made to spinnaker gear, but otherwise it is advisable to make any replacements or repairs match existing practice.

SPRITSAILS

The idea of supporting a four-sided sail with a diagonal spar instead of a spar at the top and usually another at the bottom, has never been very popular, yet it is found in craft ranging from the tiny Optimist dinghy to some large commercial craft. The word *sprit* is of Saxon origin and means "to sprout," as the bowsprit might be considered to do from the bow.

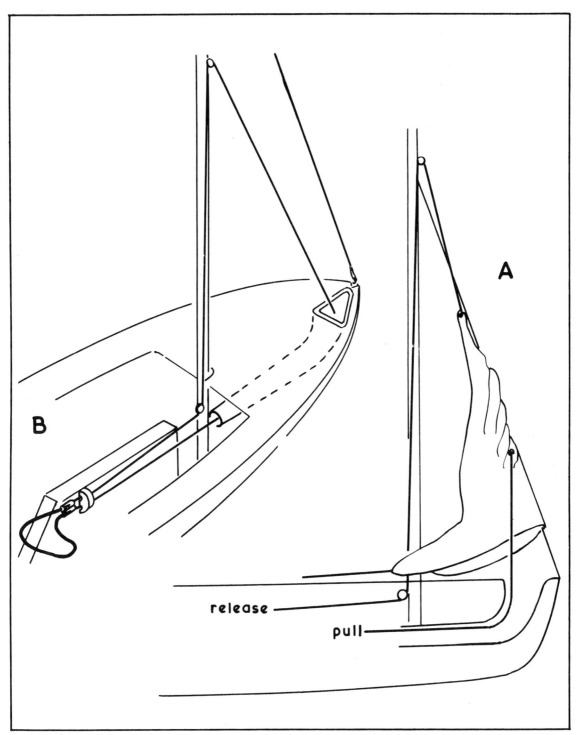

Fig. 14-4. In a small boat the spinnaker can be stowed ready for use in a chute through the foredeck.

In smaller craft, the sprit and sail are taken down when out of use, but in commercial craft the sprit is always in position. The sail is *brailed* when not needed, by drawing it into a bundle close to the mast. Many of the points of rigging are the same as other boats, but the rigger will be concerned with the means of attaching the sprit and the brailing arrangements.

For a small boat the sprit is a plain round spar and its end is pushed into a pocket at the corner of the sail (Fig. 14-5A). Its lower end has to be held to the mast so as to thrust the sail into shape. A simple way is with a short halyard, either on a sheave let into the mast or through a block (Fig. 14-5B). In that case there may be no need of any attachment to the mast. If there is, a metal or rope ring might travel on the mast to keep the end of the sprit close in.

A large spritsail has a substantial spar across it. It may be lightened by tapering towards the end and weight may be partly taken by a tackle from near its center to near the masthead (Fig. 14-5C). The head of the sprit may be tapered to fit into a stout rope cringle attached to the sail (Fig. 14-5D). The sail will have plenty of strengthening and may also be lashed to the sprit.

If the sprit slipped, the weight in it would cause its heel to do considerable damage to the boat, so the support there has to be strong. In a boat of moderate size there may be a loop of rope (Fig. 14-5E), with the tapered end of the sprit in one part and the friction of the rope around the mast being enough to prevent slipping down. However, there is a risk of movement and it would be better dealt with as in a larger boat.

The support in a large rig is called a *snotter*. There is a halyard from a point higher on the mast, attached to an iron band on the reduced end of the sprit, which in turn is joined to a slide on the mast (Fig. 14-5F). The halyard allows the sprit to force the sail as flat as possible, or to relax and allow it to curve.

Brails are ropes which encircle the sail. They have to be long enough to rest slackly on the sail when the boat is sailing, yet pulling them will gather in all the canvas. The main one is at the throat, but others come above and below. One end of the brailing rope is attached to the mast, then a loop of the rope goes around the sail and back to a block on the mast and down to a point where it can be pulled (Fig. 14-6A).

A brailed sail may look rather untidy (Fig. 14-6B), but it is effectively put out of action and it can be brought into use again quite quickly by the efforts of one man, where a sail of this area in any other form would require many crew members.

A spritsail is loose-footed. There have been spritsails with booms, but this cancels much of the simplicity of the rig. Control is by a sheet from the clew of the sail in the usual way. There is no boom to spread blocks along, so any purchase has to be by a tackle between the clew and the horse. On a large sail there may also be guys to the corners of the transom from the top of the sprit. They prevent the sprit going too far forward when running and they become supplementary sheets.

Apart from the peculiarities of the rig, maintenance is very similar to other boat rigs, as the equipment employs standard parts, except for the ends of the sprit. The rope forming the lift for the snotter should be in good condition, because of the possible serious consequences of failure. Other parts around the heel of the sprit should be checked over.

Because the head of the sprit is normally out of reach, its condition is rarely checked. Failure there could bring the sail down, even if the tackle from the masthead prevented the sprit falling. The sprit and sail should be lowered periodically for inspection. The condition of the sail at the throat should also be inspected. Any weak points may need reinforcing canvas sewn on. On a traditional sail the grommet over the head of the sprit will be of tarred natural fiber rope. A replacement would be more durable if made of synthetic fiber rope.

WISHBONE RIG

In the usual ketch rig there is a largely unused area high up between the masts, as the mainsail has its greater area near the boom (Fig. 14-7A). In an attempt to make use of this area effectively a rig was devised with a sail controlled by a sort of boom with its sides shaped enough to clear the curve of

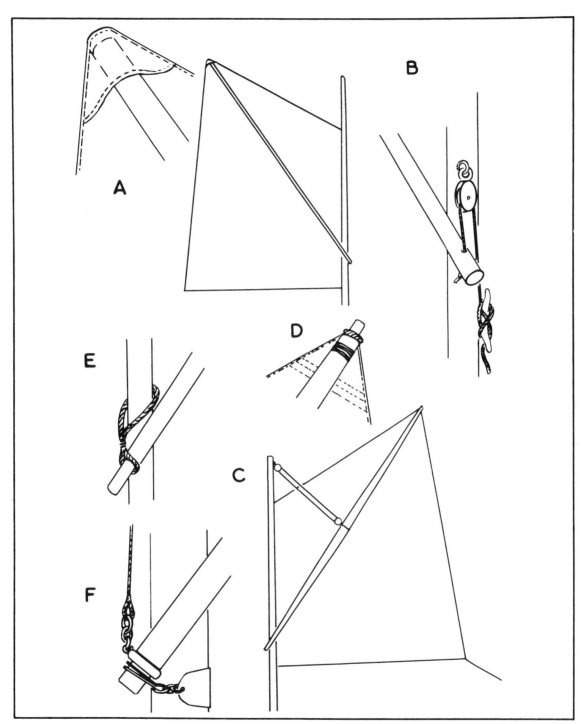

Fig. 14-5. A small sprit goes into a pocket in the sail (A) and its foot is hauled up by a halyard (B). In a large spritsail rig the heavy spar has a tackle from the mast (C), its top fits a grommet on the sail (D), and its foot is held to the mast (E,F).

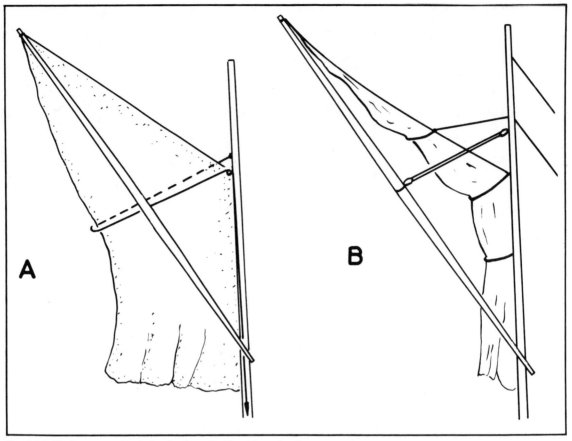

Fig. 14-6. Brails are used to furl or reef a sail without lowering it.

the sail and aptly named a *wishbone* rig (Fig. 14-7B). The wishbone was attached to the mast with a form of gooseneck and the sheet was taken from the end of the wishbone to near the top of the mizzen mast. Within the wishbone an outhaul from the corner of the sail could be adjusted to pull the sail flat or allow it to curve.

Many large ketches were built that way in the 1930s. It is unlikely that there are many in use now, but the wishbone has been revived for sailboards. There is not much on a sailboard for a rigger to attend to and what there is, is obvious. The origin of the wishbone is included here as a bit of nostalgic ships' lore.

HEAVY WEATHER SAILS

With modern synthetic cloth it is fairly safe to as-sume that sails capable of standing up to heavy weather at least as well as any special sails, are part of the normal equipment of a boat—assuming they are reefed adequately. At one time the working sails made of natural fibers were not considered strong enough for use in extreme conditions. They were taken in and small storm sails, made of very heavy canvas, were set in their place. These con-sisted of a tiny jib as the only sail forward of the mast and a mainsail with parrel lines to the mast. The foot was sheeted loose, while the working mainsail was removed and its boom was supported on the deck out of the way.

If such gear has to be serviced, details are very similar to other sails, but all materials are heavier. Obviously, any repairs or replacements should be on a similarly heavy scale. However, if the boat is

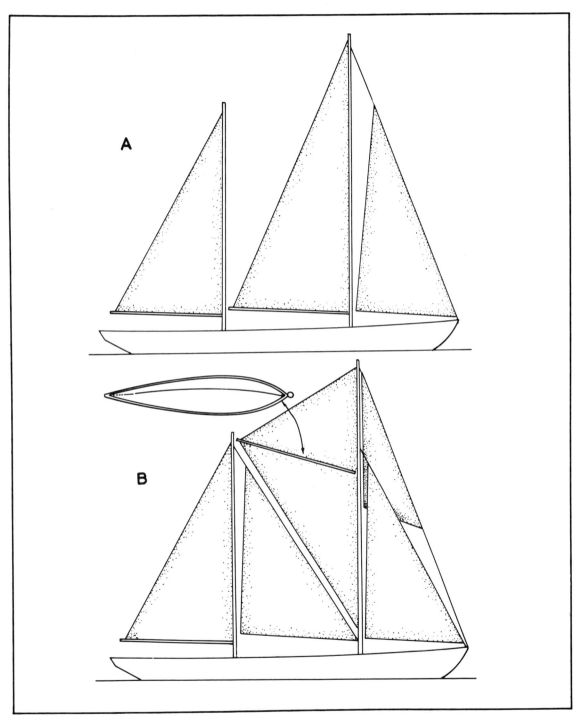

Fig. 14-7. In a normal ketch rig there is unused space high between the masts (A). One way of getting useful sail area into this space uses a wishbone (B).

equipped with good synthetic sails it is unlikely that the storm sails will be required.

AUXILIARY SAILS

Sail may be added to a powerboat for several reasons. If the boat has been built for sail as well as power, the hull will be shaped so it will have a grip on the water to prevent excessive leeway when the wind is on the beam or forward of it. The boat is then described as a *motor-sailor* a *fifty-fifty* or something similar. In that case the rig may be very similar to any of those described for purely sailing craft. If the emphasis is on sail, it will really be a sailing boat with an auxiliary motor, or it could be anything between that and a powerboat with auxiliary sails. Whatever the ratio of sail to power, rigging problems and servicing are similar to normal sailing craft.

Another category includes boats not primarily designed to carry sail. If a hull was designed purely for power there is a limit to what use sails may be. With that shape of hull there is no way that the boat can be rigged to sail at all the usual angles to the wind because it will make too much leeway. Modification to add a keel or leeboards would help, but such an adaptation is unlikely to be satisfactory.

Sail may be added to a powerboat for steadying purposes. A small amount of sail area can make the motion much less and the boat more comfortable, although the sails add little, if any, propulsion. Rather more sail area may be added so it is possible to sail the boat, in the event of engine failure, although the only possible directions will not be very much either side of downwind. A small sail may be provided right aft. It is there to give a weathervane effect by turning the hull bow to wind if it is stopped. That is done as a safety measure—the boat will *heave-to* with its bow to wind and sea in heavy weather. The sail is also of value when fishing as it keeps the boat in the most comfortable and convenient attitude to the wind.

If a steadying sail of sufficient area for downwind sailing is to be added to a motorboat there will probably have to be a new mast. The small signal mast that carries flags and lights will not usually be high enough or strong enough to be any use. Where the mast is put will depend on the cabin top layout.

If the mast can be located forward, the sail plan may be something like that of a pure sailing boat (Fig. 14-8A), but a boom can be a nuisance when not sailing and the mainsail may be loose-footed. For running it could be boomed out by a boathook. It might be possible to devise a combined boathook and boom. It may be better to have the mast aft of center, in which the steadying sails will not follow the conventional layout.

It is important to approach aerodynamic balance with the center of the combined sail area about vertically above the center of the sail area is well aft, there will be a tendency for the boat to want to turn into the wind. If the center is well forward there will be the opposite tendency to turn away from the wind. In both cases, the rather small area of a motorboat rudder may not be able to correct the course.

The sail area may have to go into a long jib and a smaller sail aft of it (Fig. 14-8B). Keeping the mast reasonably low simplifies rigging, but these sails cannot be expected to contribute much towards progress. The high sides of the usual motorboat cabins can be regarded as unalterable sails that will try to push the boat sideways in a beam wind. Added canvas would have to be of such a size that the boat would be in danger of capsizing if the working area was enough to counteract the sail effect of the cabin sides.

A small sail aft to turn the boat into the wind can be quite simple. The mast goes through the deck and will not need shrouds or other stays if it can be rigidly held at the deck and some way below. The boom may have a gooseneck or there could be jaws (Fig. 14-9A) with a downhaul to a ring on the deck. That serves a secondary purpose of holding an unstayed mast down to prevent it lifting out of its step in a freak gust.

The foot of the sail need not be laced along the boom. The luff hoists with a halyard in the usual way, but may then be laced to the mast (Fig. 14-9B). Unless it is a very large boat with proportionately large sail that needs purchase in the sheet, the rope can come down to a block and forward to a cleat near the foot of the mast (Fig. 14-9C). For its weathervane purpose the sheet will be kept hauled in to

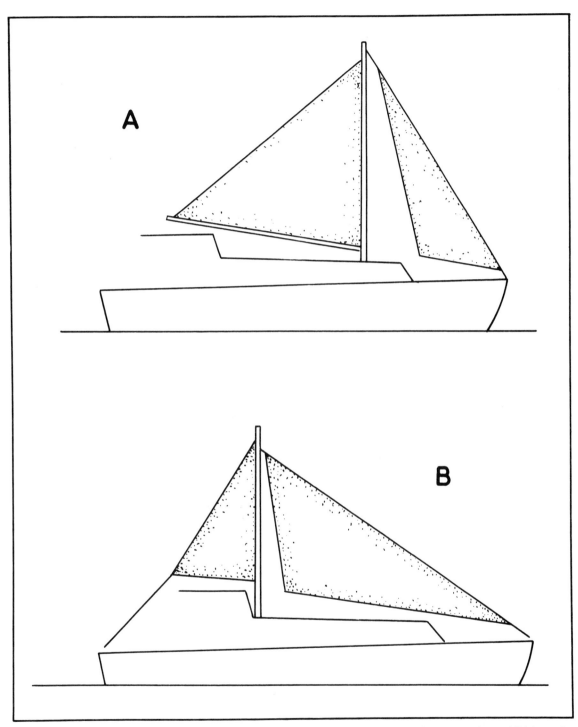

Fig. 14-8. Auxiliary sail on a motorboat has to be arranged to suit the cabin layout and may have a mast forward (A). It may be more convenient aft with a long foresail (B).

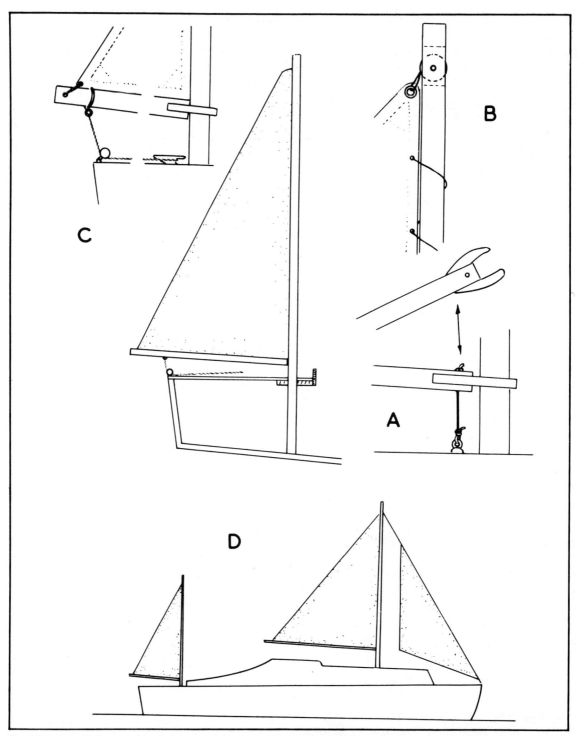

Fig. 14-9. A small mizzen sail can be arranged simply over the aft deck (A,B,C) and it may be part of a larger auxiliary rig (D).

bring the sail tight and central.

This aft mast and sail will be too small to have much effect on the boat when under way. It might affect steering of a boat at low speed under power, if left set in a crosswind. Leaving the sail set when the boat is traveling at high speed may not affect steering, but it could damage the sail and would be unseamanlike.

The small sail right aft could be combined with other sail area on another mast forward to provide steadying in a crosswind or alternative propulsion if the total area is enough (Fig. 14-9D). Using the second mast allows the design of sails of more usual shapes.

Chapter 15

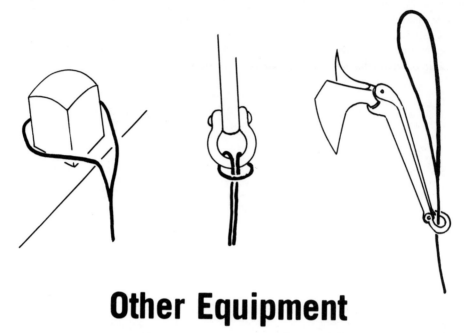

Other Equipment

BESIDES STANDING AND RUNNING RIG-
ging and other gear associated with sail, there
are many other areas of a boat that are the concern
of a rigger. A carpenter may deal with woodwork
and a sailmaker may be the expert on sails, but a
rigger is expected to know something about their
work. He has to know something about most crafts
and trades connected with boating. Boatmen tend to
regard a rigger as the man who can tackle most
work about a boat.

Much of the gear is the same whether the boat
is powered by the wind, an internal combustion
engine, oars, or steam.

ANCHOR CABLES

At one time all but the smallest boats had chain
anchor cables. With the coming of strong synthetic
ropes most of the cable length may be made up of
fiber rope with only chain near the anchor. The
weight of a length of chain there helps to keep the
anchor pulling along the bottom to get maximum
grip (Fig. 15-1A). With rope all the way the pull is
angled more upwards and this is not as strong (Fig.
15-1B). The whole length may be called a *cable* or
warp, whether chain or rope or both. Much depends
on the anchor. By the nature of its work, it cannot be
inspected in use, so all joints must be as good as
possible.

There should be a shackle or ring on the anchor. If it is a shackle, the end of the screw may be
hammered over to prevent it loosening (Fig.
15-2A). Another shackle joins this to the end of the
chain. Lock that shackle by wiring (Fig. 15-2B). If it
was riveted, there would be difficulty in disas-
sembling later.

The rope part of a cable must be protected
from chafing where it joins the chain. A shackle
there must have its pin through the chain, so a
thimble must be large enough to pass the body of
the shackle. At both ends of the chain the shackle
pins should be at least as thick as the metal of the
chain links. Splice the rope tightly around the
thimble and tuck the strands five times. Seal the cut
ends. It may also be advisable to serve over them.
Lock the shackle with wire (Fig. 15-2C).

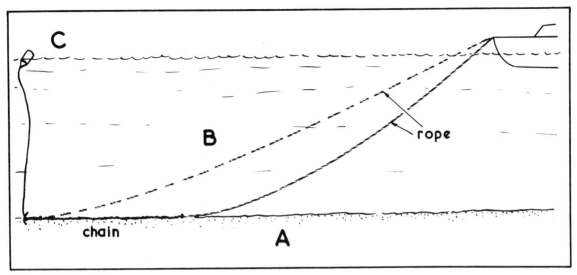

Fig. 15-1. Anchor cables.

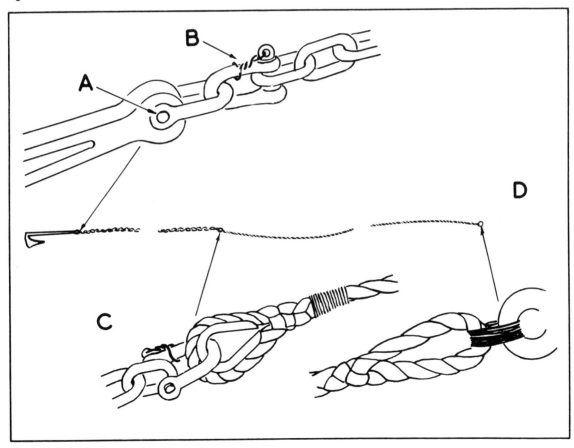

Fig. 15-2. Shackles.

At the *bitter end* splice an eye. It need not include a thimble. This is for securing to an eyebolt in the cable locker or on deck. It is not intended to take the strain of anchoring—that should always be at a samson post or other strong point on the fore-deck. It is to prevent the whole cable being lost overboard, yet it must be capable of quick release if it is necessary to slip the anchor in an emergency. Secure it with light line that is strong enough, but which can be cut (Fig. 15-2D).

An anchor buoy may have to be provided. It could be a proper buoy, but a sealed plastic container would serve. This goes on a light line attached to the crown of the anchor. It serves two purposes: it shows you and others in a crowded anchorage where your anchor is and it gives you a means of pulling the anchor out backwards if it becomes fouled and will not retrieve normally (Fig. 15-1C). This need not be a permanent installation, but a line could be made up with spring hanks at the ends for attachment to anchor and buoy.

A rigger may have to select an anchor for a boat. There are a large number of variable factors and there is no positive way of deciding on an anchor that will be right under all circumstances. One guide is to allow one pound weight of anchor for every one foot of length of boat. That refers to the traditional fisherman's anchor. A plow anchor and most of the other special types are claimed to be twice as efficient, so half that weight should be satisfactory. Seven pounds is about the minimum practical size for a small open boat and for a decked boat, ten pounds would be the smallest advisable.

MOORING ROPES

All boats need ropes available for mooring or tow-ing and do not have any other function on board. They may be plain lengths of rope adequately sealed and whipped at both ends. There would be an advantage in splicing an eye to one end, particularly if the rope is used regularly at a permanent dock mooring. The eye may suit a bollard or post ashore (Fig. 15-3A). If it is a samson post or cleat, make sure the eye cannot come away accidentally by making it small enough (Fig. 15-3B) or by always taking turns as well (Fig. 15-3C).

When coming alongside a dock, a large eye is worth having to put over a bollard or post, particu-larly if you are passing the line to someone ashore without knowledge of knotting (Fig. 15-3D).

It is worthwhile having one long line that can be used for towing, but which also has a long eye spliced in it, so it can be used with a second anchor. Make the eye long enough to pass through the ring of the anchor, over the whole anchor (Fig. 15-3E), and back to the ring (Fig. 15-3F). The same loop is useful if the boat has to be towed from shore. A pole through the loop (Fig. 15-3G) can be used by two people to pull against.

The mooring rope or *painter* for a small open boat or dinghy is usually kept attached. Use an eye splice doubled back on itself (Fig. 15-3H), rather than splice directly to the ring or use a knot. If you have to knot there, use a round turn and two half hitches. If a dinghy has to be towed astern of a larger craft, it is better done with double painters to the corners of the transom (Fig. 15-3J), attached low on the dinghy stem and adjusted so the boat rides on the top of the first stern wave.

TILLER LINE

It is convenient to be able to secure the tiller in any position, if only for a brief period while a single-handed sailor goes forward to attend to something else. The simplest arrangement is a rope with an eye to go over the tiller and jam cleats for the rope ends at each side, either inside the cockpit coaming or over the side decks (Fig. 15-4A). It is then possible to slip the rope over the tiller and jam the ends at the exact position to keep the rudder on course. Some other systems of locating the tiller stop it in stages, so the ideal position will often be between two positions.

Join two pieces of rope or cut one and join its ends with a cut splice (Fig. 4-7B) just big enough to go over the tiller. There will be more leverage, and therefore a better hold, if the line is near the end of the tiller, rather than pushed far back.

The jam cleats can be cam, clam, or the wooden wedge type (Fig. 15-4B) where there is no need to pass the rope through anything to secure it.

Locate the cleats opposite or slightly aft of

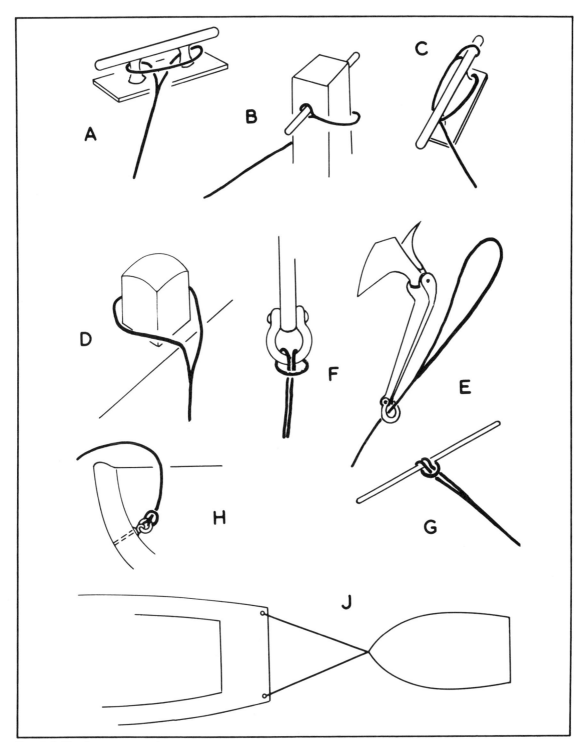

Fig. 15-3. Mooring ropes.

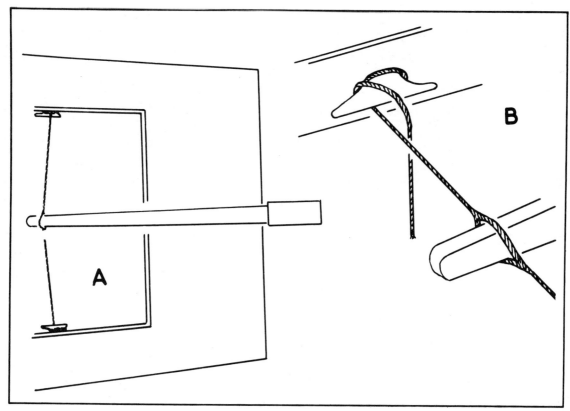

Fig. 15-4. Tiller line.

where the cut splice will come on the tiller to allow for its sweep. An eye spliced in one end will allow the line to be hung on a cleat when out of use, so there is less risk of it being mislaid or used for some other purpose.

There is one bit of decorative ropework to mark the end of the tiller by feel when you slide your hand along it. This is a *Turk's head knot* worked in light line tightly on the wood. It may also have uses elsewhere about the boat and will give the craft a cared-for, traditional look. Specialist knotting books may show a great variety of Turk's heads, but the basic one is all you need.

Allow enough line to go around the tiller at least five times. All of the work is done with one end, so keep the standing part out of the way. Put on a round turn, with the working end over the standing part (Fig. 15-5A). Continue around the same way, so the working end goes over itself the next

time around and under the first turn (Fig. 15-5B). Leave all this fairly slack so further turns can be made easily. Lift the second turn over the first and hold it there (Fig. 15-5C). Take the working end over the second turn and under the first (Fig. 15-5D). All the parts now go over and under each other, one at a time. Check that no part is going over or under two anywhere. If so, go back and try again.

Spread the crossings evenly around the tiller. You will see that what you have done is make a continuous three-part *sennit* or plait, with the two parts of projecting line alongside each other (Fig. 15-5E). This is not substantial enough nor very decorative and the next step is to double or treble it. Take the working end around the knot from where it has just entered, alongside the other part, making exactly the same crossings, until it has gone around to the same point again. Keep the parts parallel. That makes a double Turk's head knot and

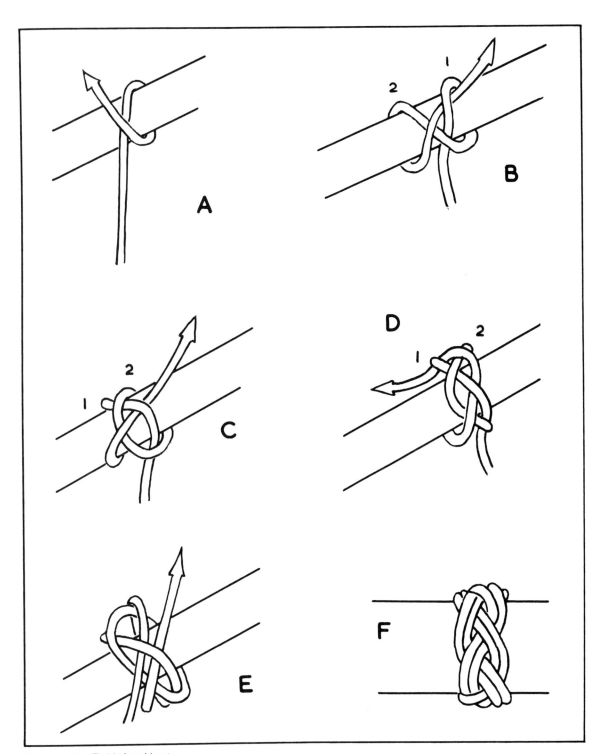

Fig. 15-5. The Turk's head knot.

it may be all you need, but if the line is rather thin in relation to the size of the tiller you can go around again so the line is trebled.

You may have had to use the point of a spike up to this stage to lift parts of the line for tucking and the next job is to go around the knot a tuck at a time using the spike to tighten the turns on to the tiller, progressively working around until any slack can be taken up at an end. When you have the knot tight, cut off the ends so they are jammed under the turns that cross them (Fig. 15-5F).

That may be all you need do, but it is worthwhile varnishing the line to harden the knot and prevent movement.

HEAVING LINE

A properly equipped boat should carry a *heaving line*, which is a light flexible line of ample length, suitable for throwing ashore or to another boat, usually to haul a larger line across. The rope itself only needs the ends sealed and whipped, but one end has to be weighted to help it to fly and straighten the coils that follow it. There have been canvas or leather pouches filled with sand and attached to the line with a splice through a grommet, but it is satisfactory to provide the weight with a large knot in the rope itself. The finished knot should be symmetrical and the working end should come out pointing back along the standing part.

One *heaving line knot* is based on the *hangman's knot*. Bend enough of the end into a long S-shape (Fig. 15-6A). Pass the end through the bight and around it (Fig. 15-6B). Continue wrapping around all parts (Fig. 15-6C) and finally through its own bight. If the top loop is first pulled and then the standing part, the turns tighten and the knot closes to a symmetrical cylinder (Fig. 15-6D). For hanging it was the bight opposite the standing part that was opened to a loop around the victim's neck!

A knot that is more of a knob than a cylinder is the *monkey's fist*. The knot itself may have sufficient weight, but it is possible to make it around a ball or pebble to get extra weight. The knot is formed of several turns taken around each other in three directions. For clarity, it is shown with two turns

each way, but there could be more to hold a large stone or to provide more weight in itself.

Experiment with the amount of slackness needed in making the knot. There has to be some freedom to allow the turns to be made, but an excessive amount makes tightening tedious. With the usual size of heaving line, turns can be looped around one hand while working with the other. Put on two complete around turns, then change direction and put two turns around them (Fig. 15-7A). Hold these turns in place and put two more turns around them, but inside the first turns (Fig. 15-7B). If a more bulky version is being made, work the same greater number of turns each way to get a balanced knot. Work through the slack until the knot is tight and a foot or so of the end is alongside the standing part.

The knot can be tightened on itself or you can press the ball or pebble in before final tightening. Use the end of a spike to force the turns really tight. It is usual to seize under the knot and splice the end into the standing part (Fig. 15-7C), but they could be joined with a bowline if the knot is only for temporary use.

There may be a loop spliced in the other end of a heaving line to put your hand in, so the whole rope is not lost if you let it slip when throwing.

FENDERS AND FEND-OFFS

There has to be plenty of cushioning available to prevent boats chafing each other or against a dock, either with loose *fend-offs* put where needed or all-around, permanent *fendering*. At one time most of this was done with rope, but today rubber and plastic are cleaner and more effective. Rope fend-offs have a traditional appearance and older knotting books show how to make them. However, they were dependent on a plentiful supply of older thick, natural fiber rope. Synthetic rope does not make such good fend-offs and it is expensive.

A plastic or rubber fend-off may have any eye, into which a lanyard should be spliced (Fig. 15-8A). A more secure type has the lanyard going through and that needs a figure-eight knot below and an overhand knot above (Fig. 15-8B). Usually the lanyard has to be adjusted in length and positioned to suit the particular circumstances, so its length should be enough to allow it to be knotted anywhere convenient. If it has a regular setting, possibly at the home dock, there can be a clip or eye in its end. There is a form of brummel hook on a plate to screw on for this purpose.

All-around fendering is mostly of a screw-on type and its attachment is obvious. Another rubber or plastic type is available for going around the stem and the corners of the transom. This fits with screws through holes, but it is a good idea to put quite large washers under the screw heads. When any fender becomes trapped between two hard surfaces the strain on it can be considerable, so screw heads might pull through.

A rigger may be asked to fit or tighten an all-around rope fender on a small open boat. This is

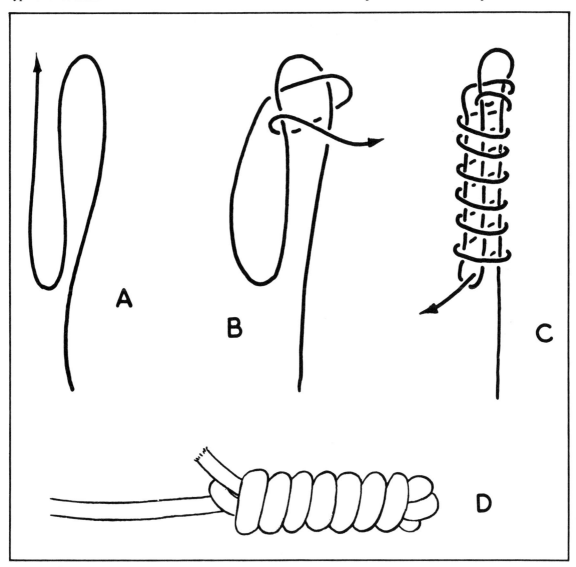

Fig. 15-6. The heaving line knot.

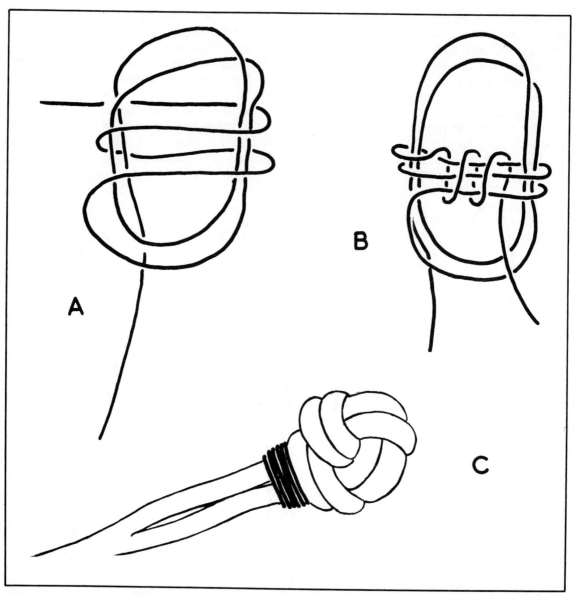

Fig. 15-7. The monkey's fist knot.

usually one piece around the stem and taken a short distance on to the transom (Fig. 15-8C). It looks bad if it becomes slack and sags between its attachment points. Usually it is held by copper wire through the rope and through holes in the gunwales (Fig. 15-8D). To get the rope tight, put its center around the stem and stretch it straight to the transom corners. There may be a metal clip as well as wire

through to the transom (Fig. 15-8E). With a good stretch in this way, the maximum tension will be put on when the rope is forced out to the gunwales (Fig. 15-8F).

BATTENS

The sails may not be the prime concern of a rigger, but there are repairs detailed elsewhere. One thing

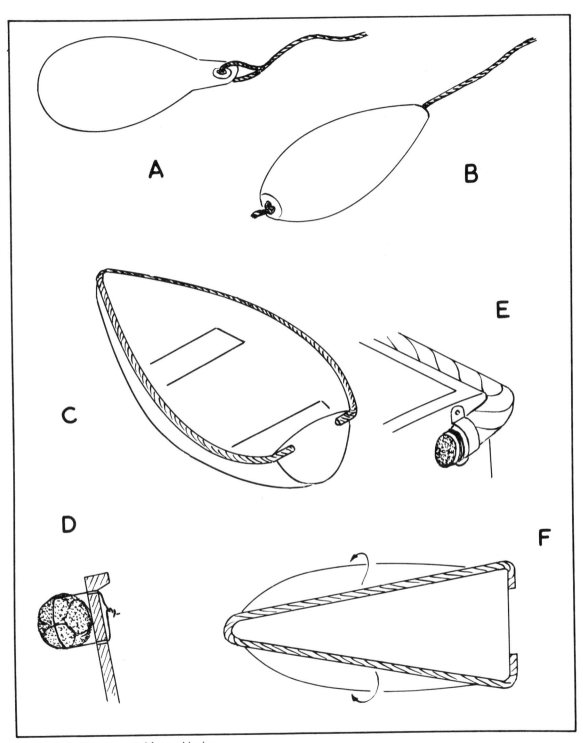

Fig. 15-8. Fenders are used for cushioning.

a rigger may be asked to see to are the *mainsail battens*, which are used to hold out the roach of a very curved sail. They fit into pockets and are easily lost or broken. At one time they were always of wood, but they may now be fiberglass or other plastic. They have to be a compromise between flexibility and stiffness. Replacements made of wood should preferably be ash or hickory which are sufficiently springy.

An existing batten will serve as a pattern. For

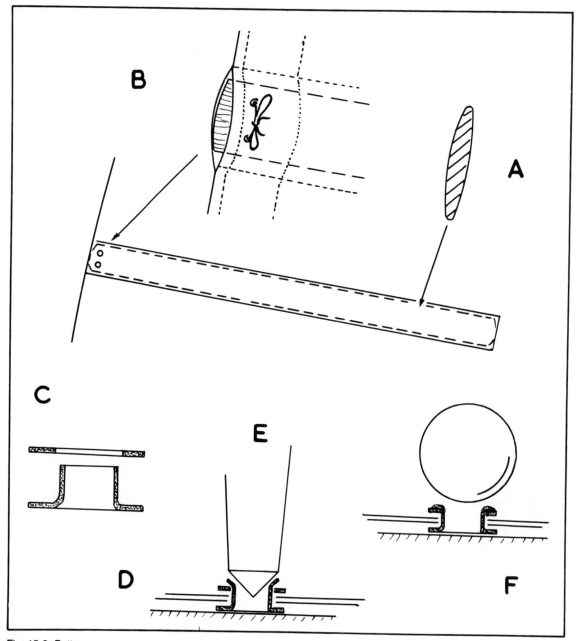

Fig. 15-9. Battens.

a sail of moderate size the wood should be not much more than ⅛-inch thick and of a width that will go easily into a pocket. An elliptical section is preferable to a flat one (Fig. 15-9A). Round the ends well so the wood cannot damage the canvas or cut stitching. There are several ways of retaining the batten in its pocket. It may enter and be sprung sideways, using rubber at the bottom of the pocket. The traditional way uses line through holes (Fig. 15-9B). Make the holes just big enough to pass the line and countersink each side. If new line has to be fitted, seal and compress its ends so it is easy to pass through. Sew its center to one side of the pocket. At the other side there are usually metal grommets. If they have to be replaced, you may have to use larger ones to hold the torn edges of the fabric. This type of grommet should be squeezed into place with punch and die or a plier-type tool with suitable dies.

If an eyelet or grommet has to be fitted when suitable tools are unavailable, it is possible to improvise, but difficult to finish with a truly round shape. If it is to be fitted in a new position, do not punch a round hole. It will be stronger if you cut a cross and let the tabs turn up inside the grommet. Sailmaking grommets consist of the grommet itself and a ring to go over it (Fig. 15-9C).

Support the grommet on a block of wood and press the canvas over it, followed by the ring (Fig. 15-9D). Hold the ring down and use a large center punch to start spreading the tubular part of the grommet over the ring (Fig. 15-9E). Follow with a steel ball (Fig. 15-9F) or the round ball-peen of a machinist's hammer. Finish with direct blows from the flat face of a hammer.

BOSUN'S CHAIR

More correctly spelled *boatswain's chair*, but pronounced "bosun," this is a seat for sending a man aloft. He can be hoisted up a mast by one of the halyards. There are canvas bosun's chairs, but the more usual type is a piece of wood. It is made of a suitable size to sit on, but not so big that the man can slide to one side. There are holes for ropes near the corners. A modern one is probably better made of stout marine-grade plywood than of solid wood.

Support is by a bridle arranged as continuous ropes that cross and are spliced underneath the seat. This means that the ropes are taking the weight without regard to the strength of the wood (Fig. 15-10A). At the top the eye is double rope held by a seizing (Fig. 15-10B). There is no need for a thimble and it would be unwise to provide any attachment similar to that used to hoist a sail with the halyard, as that might not take the weight of a man, although the rope is strong enough.

Attachment of the halyard to the loops may be with a *double sheet bend* (Fig. 15-10C). Hoisting the man aloft would normally be by men below, but if the purpose of going aloft is to varnish the mast or do some other work that necessitates lowering from time to time, there is a special knot that allows the man in the bosun's chair to make his own adjustments safely and conveniently, if both parts of the halyard are available. If part of the halyard is inside the mast, the knot cannot be used and adjustment would have to be from below.

The man on the seat brings the two parts of the line together above his head with one hand. With his other hand he brings a bight of the hanging part through the bridle of the seat. Enough of the bight is brought through to pass over the body (Fig. 15-10D), under his legs and up in front of the bridle. When the slack has been pulled through, it leaves the bight around the bridle with both parts projecting from the same side above it (Fig. 15-10E).

When tight, this will hold the weight of the man, but if he draws up some of the slack and lets the line run around the bridle, he can lower to a new position.

BOOM CRUTCH

When sail is lowered something has to be done with the boom. If it is small open boat, the boom will usually be taken off its gooseneck and stowed in the boat. Even then it may be kept in position and used as the ridge for a canvas cover. In larger craft the boom stays pivoted to the mast. Its weight may be taken temporarily with the topping lift, but that does not serve as a permanent support.

If there is a backstay, it may be possible to use a short line and hook to retain the boom (Fig. 15-

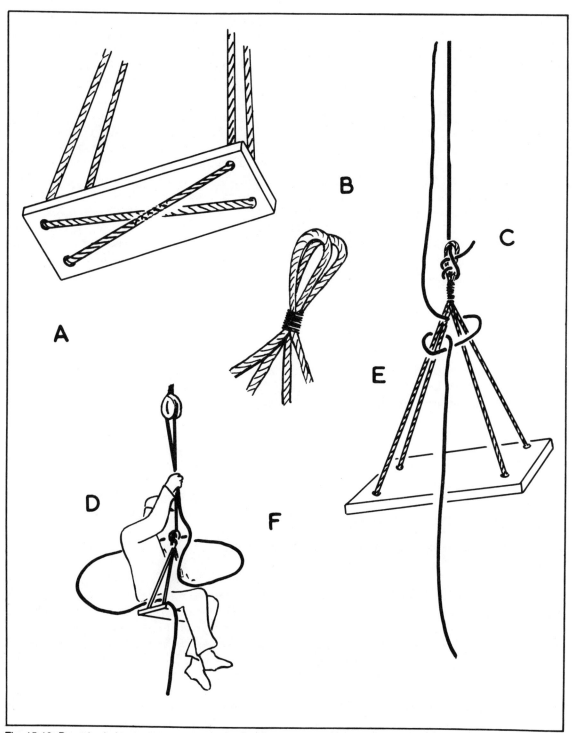

Fig. 15-10. Bosun's chair.

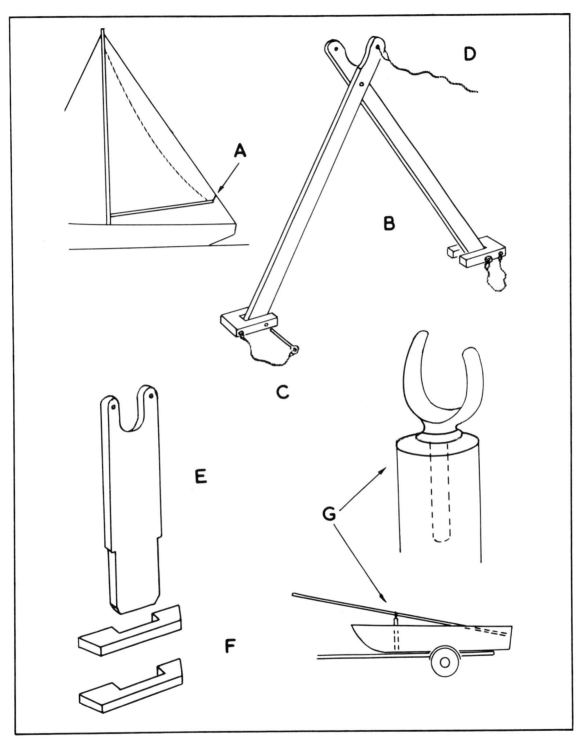

Fig. 15-11. Boom crutch.

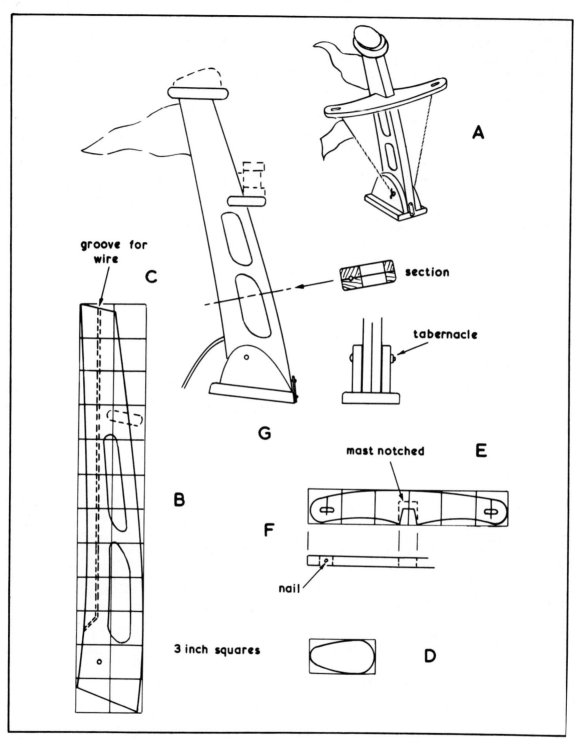

groove for
wire

C

A

section

tabernacle

G

mast notched

E

B

F

nail

3 inch squares

D

Fig. 15-12. The signal mast.

11A). The line should be short, or the boom may swing too much as the boat rolls.

The traditional type of support is a *boom crutch* that is a form of sheer legs with a scissor action. The two parts can be folded together for compact stowage (Fig. 15-11B). A weakness of some crutches is the absence of any security of the feet. When the boat is stationary the deadweight of the boom may keep the feet in place, but rolling will lift one foot and the whole thing comes away. It is better to arrange pegs on lanyards through the feet (Fig. 15-11C). Similarly, provide a lanyard to go around the boom and prevent it lifting from the crutch (Fig. 15-11D).

Another form of boom is a *mitch board*. Instead of a sheer leg arrangement this is a board notched to take the boom (Fig. 15-11E) and fitted into notched brackets on the transom or at the back of the cockpit (Fig. 15-11F). In some boats the support may go to a step in the bottom of the boat. One advantage of a mitch board is that it need not be central. In some boats it is more convenient, possibly for the sake of headroom, to let the boom rest over one corner of the transom.

A similar idea may be used where the boat trailed behind a car has a mast that is so long that when traveling it has to be carried sloping over the back of the car. A short section of wood the same size as the mast can go in the mast step and carry a support for the mast. It might be an oarlock in a hole in the wood (Fig. 15-11G).

SIGNAL MAST

A powerboat has no use for a mast except that on a cabin boat it improves appearance and will carry a navigation light, either on its front or top, and any flags the owner is entitled to. There may be a club or personal flag at the truck, then another club flag at the end of the crosstree. The starboard end (right) is considered superior to the port end (left), so the starboard end should be used for a second club or association flag, while the port end is kept for signal flags (Fig. 15-12A). The national flag does not go on this mast, but should be on an ensign staff at the stern.

If a mast has to be made, it could be a simple pole fitting into a socket, but it looks better if it is cut with a slope back (Fig. 15-12B) and is able to hinge down in a tabernacle. The main part of the mast is in two pieces, so it is possible to plow a groove for the electric cable to the navigation light (Fig. 15-12C). With the straight wood grooved it is advisable to make one side and use it as a pattern for the other. Glue the parts with the electric wires in place. True up the shape and round all edges. At the top the truck is egg-shaped (Fig. 15-12D) and may match a navigation light. The crosstree is shown swept back. It is glued and screwed into a notch in the mast (Fig. 15-12E).

There is no need for blocks or sheaves for the halyards. They can go over nails through slots in the crosstree (Fig. 15-12F). The masthead pendant can clip on or have its own halyard.

If the mast is to be mounted on a sloping cabin top, allow for that so that the truck and crosstree come parallel with the waterline.

Build up the tabernacle (Fig. 15-12G). Friction may hold the mast up if the pivot bolt is tight, but there can be a sheet metal clip on the forward side. Bolt the tabernacle through the cabin top, with a reinforcing piece inside if necessary. Bed it in jointing compound or fiberglass resin.

Glossary

ANYONE CONCERNED WITH THE RIGGING OF A sailing boat, whether making new equipment or repairing existing gear, needs to know the technical terms which apply. Much of the language of the sea is a carry-over from the days when sail was the only power other than oars and a large craft carried a multiplicity of sail and rigging, all of which had to be identifiable. Those days have gone, but some of the names live on. The meanings of some have been altered to suit modern rigs and this sometimes leads to confusion.

There is sometimes a tendency for sailing people to use terms that are obsolete and not strictly applicable to the circumstances being described. Reading an old dictionary of the sea may be interesting, but it can lead to sometimes adopting old terms that either have no meaning in a modern rig or now have different meanings. If there is any doubt about particular terms it is usually better to use plain language, so both parties know what is meant, even if this does not sound very nautical.

This list gives terms applicable to modern sailing craft. Although there are a few square-rigged craft about, it is unlikely that the reader will be concerned with their sails and rigging. The very large number of older terms still applicable to the few remaining square-riggers have been omitted as they might be confused with the same or other terms used now for fore and aft rigs. Some alternatives have been given, where it is possible that different names or spellings may be met.

The language of the sea is fairly uniform internationally, but there are just a few terms applicable to rigging that are different. For instance an American boom vang is an English kicking strap. Only such terms as apply to rigging and sails are included here, with only those sailing terms that are necessary for a rigger to appreciate the function of the gear with which he is dealing. For a more comprehensive coverage of sailing terms in general the reader should refer to book on sailboat handling.

aback—Having the wind on the wrong side of the sail.

about—Change direction from one tack to the other.

aerodynamics—Study of the effect of solid bodies moving through air, applicable to sails in the same way as to aircraft wings.

aft—In a direction towards or over the stern.

anodizing—Chemical treatment that puts a protective coating on aluminum, and which may change its color.

aspect ratio—The relations between the breadth and depth of plane in relation to the air it is passing through. The relation of luff to foot of a mainsail.

astern—Behind a boat.

athwart—Across a boat.

awning—A canvas cover to keep off sun or rain.

backstay—A supporting wire aft of a mast.

baggywrinkle—Antichafe padding, usually on standing rigging where a sail might rub.

balanced lug—A four-sided fore-and-aft sail with yard and boom both passing forward of the mast.

balloon jib—A very fully cut head sail. A reacher.

bare poles—A vessel driven by the wind when no sails are set.

battens—Stiffening strips of wood or other material put into pockets square to the edge of a sail, such as are used to extend the curved roach at the leach of some mainsails.

beam—The greatest width of a boat.

beating—Sailing to windward by tacking.

beeswax—Wax commonly used on thread for sailmaking and rope whipping to toughen and waterproof.

before the wind—Sailing with the wind aft.

belay—Secure or make fast a rope. Nautical alternative for "tie."

belaying pin—Peg through a board to provide a means of securing a rope, as alternative to a cleat.

bendy mast—A mast designed to have a control-led bend so as to affect the set and fullness of its sail.

Bermudan (Bermudian)—Jib-headed mainsail.

bight—Loop formed by doubling back a rope.

bitter end—Inboard end of an anchor cable.

block—Case containing one or more sheaves.

board—One leg sailed when tacking.

bobstay—Stay from the end of a bowsprit to a low point on the stem.

bollard—A substantial fitting used for securing a rope.

bolt rope—Rope around the edge of a sail or net.

boom—Spar along the foot of a sail. Pole used as strut.

boom vang—Tensioning cable diagonally from boom to a low point on the mast, to prevent the boom rising. A kicking strap.

bowsprit—A spar projecting forward over the bow.

boxed spar—Spar made with four pieces of wood having a rectangular shape in cross section.

brace—Rope used to swing a yard.

braided rope—Having an exterior woven with diagonal strands.

brail—Rope used to gather in a sail to the mast or a spar.

brummel eye—Form of eye splice with two ends, where the parts are passed through each other.

brummel hooks—Clips used in pairs, each with a slotted edge that can be engaged with the other only when they are crossed. Inglefield clips.

burgee—A small flag, which may be a swallow-tailed (double points) or a triangular pendant (pennant).

cam cleat—Device for temporarily holding a rope between two serrated sprung cams.

carbine hook—Hook with spring closing side.

carry away—Break a rope or spar.

cat boat—Single-masted, single-sailboat with its mast close to the bow.

chain plate—Attachment piece for shroud attached to the side of the boat at the gunwale.

chains—The location position of the shroud and chain plates.

clam cleat—Device for temporarily holding a rope in a tube between tapered teeth.

cleat—Device for temporarily belaying or making fast a rope. The basic form has two arms, but there are several special types. Alternative to a belaying pin.

clew—Lower aft corner of a sail, to which the sheet is attached.

close-hauled—Sailing at as close an angle towards the wind as possible.

clove hitch—A jamming form of two half hitches for joining a rope to a spar or ring.

coir—Natural fiber rope made from the husks of coconuts. It will float.

cold heading—Expanding an end of rod rigging to retain it in a terminal.

concave—A hollow curve.

convex—An outward curve.

cordage—Collective name for all the ropes and lines used on a boat.

cotton—Natural fiber used for making ropes and sails.

cringle—Rope loop usually worked into the edge of a sail.

crutch—Support for boom or gaff when lowered.

Cunningham control—Arrangement at tack of mainsail for gathering in cloth to adjust sail.

cut splice—Splice between two ropes arranged so they overlap and include an eye or loop.

cutter—A single-masted rig with a mainsail and more than one sail forward of the mast.

Dacron—Trade name for polyester material used for sails and ropes.

deadeye—Block of wood with holes through which ropes are rove to obtain purchase instead of over sheaves in a block.

dipping lug—Four-sided, fore-and-aft sail with the tack forward of the mast and the sail having to be moved to the other side of the mast when changing tack, by dipping the yard behind the mast.

downhaul—Line to assist in pulling down a sail or other part of the rigging.

earing—Rope attached to the cringle of a sail.

eyebolt—Bolt with an open eye instead of the usual head.

eyelet—Two-part metal ring for fitting through hole in canvas. A grommet.

eye plate—Plate with holes for fixing screws and a projecting lug with an eye to take a shackle or other attachment.

eye splice—Loop in the end of a rope with the strands tucked back into the rope.

fairlead—Device for guiding or changing the direction of a rope.

fall of rope—The free end or hanging part of a rope.

fathom—A length of six feet. The old common nautical measure.

fender, fend-off—Padding hung over the edge of a vessel to prevent it chafing against a dock or other boat.

fiber rope—Rope made from natural or synthetic fibers, but not wire.

fid—A wooden spike used for opening the strands of rope.

flow—The curve induced in a sail by its cut. The incoming tide.

flying jib—The upper jib when there are several sails forward of the mast.

foot—Bottom edge of a sail. *See also* groove, luff.

foresail—Sail forward of the mast. A headsail.

forestay—The forward stay supporting a mast.

forestay sail—The inner headsail of a cutter.

frapping turn—Extra turn put around a seizing or lashing across the other turns to tighten them.

fully battened sail—Sail with battens right across it.

furl—Stow a sail on its boom or other spar.

gaff—Spar to support a sail entirely aft of the mast. If it crosses the mast it is a yard.

gaff-headed—Four-sided sail with its head requiring support by a gaff.

gallows—Crutch to support boom when lowered.

gear—General name for all equipment needed for sailing. Cog wheel used with others to change the ratio of their shafts.

genoa—Large headsail overlapping mainsail.

gibe, gybe—Sudden change of sail from one side to the other with the wind aft.

go about—Change tack by turning into wind.

gooseneck—Universal joint between end of boom and the mast.

grass rope—Sailor's name for coir rope.

grommet—Metal or sewn edged hole in canvas. *See also* sewn eyelet.

groove—Groove in spar to take rope edge of sail. *See also* luff, foot.

gudgeon—Part of a set of rudder hangings with a hole to take a pintle.

gunter sail—A gaff-headed sail, with the gaff going vertically, or nearly so, above the mast.

guy—Controlling rope to restrict movement of a spar.

gypsy—Wheel on a windlass or other winding device, shaped to match the links of a chain.

halyard, halliard—Rope used for hoisting a sail or a flag.

handy billy—Light tackle with rope tails on the blocks, so it can be attached anywhere required for a temporary pull.

hank—Spring clip. Attachment of a sail to a stay.

harden—In sailing, to flatten the sail by tightening the sheets.

headboard, headstick—Wood or metal plate set in the head of a jib-headed sail.

head of sail—Top edge of sail.

headstay—Forward supporting stay for a mast. Less common name for a forestay.

heave to—Turn into a safe position head to wind in heavy weather, to make minimum progress ahead or astern.

heel—Tilt sideways. Bottom of mast or other spar.

helm up or down—Moving tiller towards or away from wind.

hemp—Natural fiber used for rope and canvas.

high aspect ratio—Sail or wing long or tall in relation to its width. Sail with a tall mast and short boom.

high-peaked sail—Sail with its gaff or yard at an acute angle to vertical.

horse—Arrangement across deck or transom to allow block on sheet to slide across. May be rope, a metal rod or a track.

Inglefield clip—Alternative name for a Brummel clip. Usual British name.

in irons—Turned directly into the wind so the sails are flapping.

insignia—Badge or emblem on a sail.

internal halyards—Sail halyards with their falls carried up the inside of a hollow mast.

jamming cleat—Any cleat that will grip a rope without the need for hitches.

jib—One of the headsails of a cutter. The only sail forward of the mast in a sloop.

jib-headed—Any sail with a pointed head, but particularly applied to a triangular Bermudan mainsail.

jib snaps—Hanks or clips attaching the luff or a jib to a forestay.

jib topsail—Highest of three headsails in a cutter. A flying jib.

jigger—An extra sail aft. Less common name for a mizzen sail.

junk rig—Fully battened sails, based on those of Chinese junks.

jute—Natural fiber used for coarse fabric.

ketch—Two-masted rig with the mizzen mast forward of the rudder head and mizzen sail smaller than the mainsail.

killick bend—Combination of a timber hitch and a half hitch for attaching rope to a rock as a temporary anchor.

larboard—Old term for the port side of a vessel. The left side when facing forward.

lateen sail—Triangular sail with a very long head supported by a spar on a short mast.

lay of rope—The direction of twist of the strands in three-stranded rope. It is right-hand lay (the common direction) if the strands curve away from you as you look along a rope.

lee—Side away from wind. Sheltered.

leech—Aft edge of sail.

leech line—Line through leech of sail, which can be used to adjust tension.

lee helm—Necessity to sail with the tiller towards the lee side of the boat to maintain a straight course. Opposite to weather helm.

lee-ho—Call made by helmsman to indicate that the tiller is to be put over so the boat goes about to the other tack. Also *ready about*.

leeward—Direction away from wind. Pronounced "loo-ard."

leeway—Movement sideways as well as forward through the water.

leg-o-mutton-sail—Obsolescent term, sometimes applied to a balanced lug or a jib-headed sail.

linen—Good quality flaxen cloth.

liner—Strengthening piece along the edge of a sail.

long splice—End-to-end splice between two ropes that joins them without increasing their thickness.

loose-footed—Sail without a boom, or one only attached to the boom at clew and tack.

luff—Forward or leading edge of a sail. *See also* groove, foot.

luff, to—To turn a boat towards the wind.

lugsail—Four-sided fore-and-aft sail.

mainsail—Largest sail. Normally the one aft of a single mast.

make sail—Set the sails.

Marconi sail—Bermudan sail. Jib-headed mainsail.

mare's tail—The end of a rope that has been allowed to unlay and fray.

marline—Light lashing line.

marline spike—Metal spike used to open rope strands.

mast hoops—Wood or metal hoops attached to the luff of a mainsail and sliding on the mast.

mast jack—A screw jack below the foot of a mast.

mast step—Support for the foot of a mast.

mechanical advantage—Moving a greater weight than that expended, usually by operating over a greater distance than the weight is moved.

mildew—Form of rot on natural fiber ropes or sails, leaving dark spots on the surface.

miss stays—Fail to go about when changing tacks and go into irons.

mizzen mast and sail—Aft smaller sail in a two-mast rig.

needle—Tool for sewing, usually triangular for canvas work.

neutral axis—When a rope or other thing is bent, the part in the thickness that does not stretch or compress.

norman—A rod through a samson post for twisting rope around.

nylon—Slightly elastic synthetic fiber, used for rope and sails.

off the wind—Reaching.

on the wind—Sailing close-hauled.

outhaul—Line for pulling sail along a spar.

palm—Leather fitting for hand, with metal pad for pushing a needle.

parachute spinnaker—A fully-cut spinnaker.

parrels—Balls, usually wood, threaded on a line and used around a mast to retain gaff jaws or the luff of a sail.

pay off—Let vessels go away from the wind.

peak—Highest point of a gaff-headed sail.

pendant, pennant—Small triangular flag.

pintle—Part of rudder hanging assembly with a pin to fit into a gudgeon.

piston hank—Hank for attaching luff of a headsail to a forestay, using a spring-operated piston to secure and release it.

plain sail—Sailing with all normal sails set.

plaited rope—Alternative name for braided rope.

polyester—Synthetic base for fibers of filaments used to make rope and sails.

pop rivet—Type of hollow rivet used for riveting from one side of the work.

port—The left side of a boat when facing forward. Opposite to starboard. Originally "larboard."

preventer—Rope to limit movement of a spar.

purchase—Gaining a mechanical advantage.

raffee—Triangular sail set above a square sail.

rake—Slope, particularly of mast.

reacher—Large headsail or jib. Genoa.

reaching—Sailing with wind on beam.

reef—Reduce the area of a sail by gathering up part of it.

reef band—Strip across sail to take reef pendants.

reefing, roller—Method of reefing by rolling sail around the boom.

reef knot—A square knot, used for joining reef pendants.

reef pendant—Light line attached to sail and used for gathering up surplus at foot when the sail is reefed.

rig—General arrangement of sails and spars on a sailing vessel. The action of setting up sailing gear.

rigging—All the lines needed to support masts and hoist and control sails.

rigging screw—A device with left- and right-hand threads used to tension rigging.

ring bolt—An eyebolt with a ring through the eye, used for attaching a rope.

roach—Edge of sail given a curve, usually a convex one held to shape by battens, as on a mainsail leech.

roping—Strengthening the edges of a sail with rope, either sewn on or enclosed in the sailcloth.

running—Sailing with the wind astern.

running backstay—One of a pair of backstays to support a mast, taken to the gunwales and arranged to release on the lee side.

running rigging—All of the rigging used to hoist and control sails.

samson post—Strong post through foredeck, used for mooring and towing.

schooner—Vessel with two or more masts. Unlike a ketch or yawl the largest sail is not necessarily on the forward mast.

serve—Bind light line around a rope as a protection.

set up—Tighten rigging, etc.

sewn eyelet (also, **grommet**)—Hole edged by a stitched ring, as distinct from a metal eyelet fixed with punch and die.

shackle—Looped metal with screw closure, used for joining blocks, spliced eyes, and similar items.

shake—A natural split in wood, due to drying out of sap.

sheave—A pulley wheel to take fiber or wire rope.

sheet—Rope used to control a sail, normally attached to the clew.

shorten sail—Reduce the amount of sail in use, either by reefing or using smaller or fewer sails.

shroud plate—Metal fitting attached to the gunwales for taking the end of a shroud. A chain plate.

shrouds—Mast stays brought down to the gunwales at the sides of the mast.

sleeved sail—Mainsail with a long pocket to fit over the mast.

slide, slug—Metal or plastic piece to attach to a sail and run along a track.

sloop—Single-mast rig, with a mainsail and one headsail.

snap shackle—Quick-action shackle.

snatch block—Block with one side that can open so it can be put on to a rope without the need for the rope to be fed through it.

snotter—Bottom support for a sprit against the mast.

snug down—Stow sails.

sny—Alternative name for a toggle, particularly a small one.

spike—Pointed tool for splicing or opening holes.

spinnaker—Large balloon-shaped headsail for use in light winds.

splice—Ropework involving tucking strands instead of knotting the complete rope.

spring stay—Top stay between masts. Triatic stay.

spritsail—Four-sided sail supported by a spar (sprit) diagonally across it.

square sail—Four-sided sail hung from a yard and set across the vessel.

stancheon, stanchion—Upright support for handrail.

standing lug—Four-sided sail with the head and its yard going forward of the mast and the boom and foot of the sail going to a gooseneck at the mast.

standing rigging—All of the rigging that provides support for the mast and other fixed spars.

starboard—Right side of vessel when facing forward.

stay—Support for mast.

stays, in—Going about.

staysail—Lower headsail, hanked to forestay.

sternboard—Sailing backwards. "Making sternway."

swaging—Method of compressing an end fitting on a wire rope.

synthetic fibers—Chemically-produced manmade fibers used for ropes and sails.

tabernacle—Support for the foot of a mast, so the mast can be lowered by swinging down on a pivot included in the tabernacle.

tack—Lower forward corner of a sail.

tacking—Sailing to windward close-hauled in alternate directions.

tackle—Rope through two or more blocks, used to provide a purchase. Pronounced "tayckle."

tack line—Line attached to the tack of a sail, as with a balanced lugsail to haul the sail and boom back to the mast.

tail—End of rope.

tapered rope—Rope unlaid and some fibers removed, then laid up again to make a reduced end.

Terylene—Trade name for polyester material used for ropes and sails.

thimble—Metal or plastic piece to fit into a rope eye.

throat—The angle between luff and head of a gaff-headed sail.

thumb cleat—A part cleat used to guide a rope.

toggle—Wood or plastic peg spliced across the end of a rope, usually to make a connection to an eye in another rope.

topping lift—Line used to take the weight of a spar, as from the end of a boom to the masthead to support the boom while the sail is hoisted or lowered.

topsail—Sail set above a gaff mainsail.

transom—The board across the stern of a boat.

traveler—Metal ring to slide on a spar. It may have a hook to engage with a sail and eye for a halyard.

triatic stay—Stay between two masts.

u bolt—U-shaped bar forming an eye, with both ends screwed for nuts.

una rig—Single-sail rig.

under way—Moving through the water.

under weight—With the anchor about to be disengaged from the bottom.

unhand—Cast off.

unrig—Dismantle the whole rig.

uphelm—Move the tiller towards the windward side.

upwind—Towards the wind.

vang (vane, whang)—Steadying rope from a spar.

vertical cut—Sail made up with the cloths parallel with its leech.

way—Movement of a boat through the water.

wear—Change direction of sailing so the boat turns a complete circle. Used when sailing off the wind to bring the boom to the other side as an alternative to a give. A boat "wears" flags and does not "fly" them.

weather helm—When the tiller has to be held to windward to maintain a straight course.

weather side—The side of a vessel towards the wind.

whipping—Binding the end of a rope to prevent it unlaying.

winch—A device for gaining a purchase by winding rope around a drum.

windlass—Alternative name for winch.

windward—Direction towards the wind.

wire luff—Wire enclosed in the luff of a sail to prevent stretch.

yankee—Large, light headsail.

yard—Spar to support the head of a sail, that crosses the mast, as distinct from a gaff, which serves the same purpose but is entirely aft of the mast.

yaw—Go from side to side instead of keeping on course.

yawl—Two-masted rig with the mizzen mast aft of the rudder head.

Index